China and the Twenty-First-Century Crisis

Johannes W Klink
March 2019

China and the
Twenty-First-Century Crisis

Minqi Li

PlutoPress
www.plutobooks.com

First published 2016
by Pluto Press
345 Archway Road, London N6 5AA

www.plutobooks.com

British Library Cataloguing in Publication Data
A catalogue record for this book is available from the British Library

ISBN 978 0 7453 3537 7 Hardback
ISBN 978 0 7453 3538 4 Paperback
ISBN 978 1 7837 1705 7 PDF eBook
ISBN 978 1 7837 1707 1 Kindle eBook
ISBN 978 1 7837 1706 4 EPUB eBook

This book is printed on paper suitable for recycling and made from
fully managed and sustained forest sources. Logging, pulping and
manufacturing processes are expected to conform to the environmental
standards of the country of origin.

Typeset by Swales & Willis
Text design by Melanie Patrick
Simultaneously printed by CPI Antony Rowe, Chippenham, UK
and
Edwards Bros in the United States of America

CONTENTS

I

CHINA AND THE
TWENTY-FIRST-CENTURY CRISIS

Before 2008, capitalism was celebrated as the best of all possible economic and social systems. It was "the End of History" – "There is no alternative!" The Great Recession of 2008–2009 nearly destroyed the global capitalist economy and brought the era of "the End of History" to an end.

Since then, mass protests and popular rebellions have transformed the political map throughout the world. In Western Europe and North America, growing poverty and mass unemployment led to young people's political awakening and popular desires for social change. In the Middle East, dictatorial regimes that had lasted for decades were overthrown by popular uprisings. In Latin America, several progressive governments were elected. Cuban socialism began to revive and a successful socialist transition in Venezuela became a possibility. In China, the Maoist New Left became a significant political and intellectual force. For several years, Bo Xilai (who was a member of the Chinese Communist Party's Politburo) led an economic and social experiment in the Municipality of Chongqing that seemed to provide a viable progressive alternative to the neoliberal capitalist model.

In 2012, Bo Xilai was purged from the Party and later sentenced to life imprisonment ostensibly on the indictment of corruption. In 2013, the new Chinese leadership led by Xi Jinping re-confirmed their commitment to "reform and openness". The Chinese govenrment has undertaken a new round of neoliberal "economic reforms" including privatization of the remaining state-owned enterprises and financial liberalization.

Despite growing popular opposition, European capitalist classes were determined to impose fiscal austerity programs on the working classes. In the Middle East, the initial promises of the "Arab Spring" have been replaced by political chaos and social miseries as the region plunged into a complex web of class conflicts, religious fundamentalism, and imperialist intervention.

The economic and social success of Latin American progressive governments has been partially based on the global commodity boom driven by China's demands for energy and raw materials. Ironically, as the Chinese capitalist economy slows down, global commodity prices have collapsed. Latin American progressive governments are now struggling for their political survival.

It appears that, for the moment, the global ruling elites have brought the system back to life and put the popular challenges against the system under control. However, underneath this apparent stability, a new crisis is approaching.

This book will argue that by the 2020s, economic, social, and ecological contradictions are likely to converge in China, leading to a major crisis for Chinese and global capitalism. Unlike the previous major crises, the coming crisis may not be resolved within the historical framework of capitalism.

Global Capitalism: Crisis and Restructuring

Capitalism is a unique historical system based on the endless accumulation of capital. The modern capitalist world system emerged in Western Europe in the sixteenth century and became the globally dominant system in the nineteenth century. The rise of global capitalism depended upon a set of historical conditions that provided cheap and abundant supply of labor force, energy, and material resources. However, by the early twenty-first century, the various conditions that historically have underpinned the operation of the capitalist world system are beginning to be undermined.

The capitalist world system operates as a "world-economy" with multiple political structures rather than as a "world-empire" with a single dominant political structure (Wallerstein 1979: 5–6). The competition between multiple states compels the "nation-states" to provide favorable political conditions for capital accumulation. But excessive inter-state competition undermines the system's long-term common interests and threatens the survival of the system. Thus, a state more powerful than all the other states or a hegemonic power is needed to regulate the inter-state competition and promote the "systemic interests" (Arrighi and Silver 1999: 26–31).

Historically, the United Provinces (the Dutch Republic), the United Kingdom, and the United States have been the successive hegemonic powers. US-led global capitalist restructuring in the mid-twentieth century helped to resolve the system-wide major crisis over the period 1914–1945 and paved the way for the unprecedented boom of the global capitalist economy from 1950 to 1973.

The US-led restructuring succeeded in part by accommodating the challenges of the "anti-systemic movements". These movements represented the interests of the social groups that were created during the previous stages of global capitalist expansion. These included the "social democratic movement" which represented the western working classes, the "national liberation movement" which represented the non-western indigenous elites (the "national bourgeoisies"), and the "communist movement" (Wallerstein 2003).

The modern communist movement originated from the left wing of the social democratic movement in the early twentieth century. But by the mid-twentieth century, it had evolved into a radical variant of the national liberation movement (Wallerstein 2000a). In several peripheral and semi-peripheral states (most importantly in Russia and China) where the old ruling elites were unable to establish the necessary social conditions required for effective capital accumulation, the communist movement succeeded by mobilizing the great majority of the population (the peasants and the proletarianized industrial workers) to create viable nation-states capable of effective competition within the capitalist world system (Chapter 4 of this book will discuss in detail the core, semi-periphery, and periphery as structural positions in the capitalist world system).

During the global economic boom from 1950 to 1973, historical anti-systemic movements were consolidated and new social forces were created. By the late 1960s, the collective demands of the working classes in the core and the semi-periphery started to exceed the capacity of the system to accommodate. The general decline of the profit rate led to a system-wide economic and political crisis.

In response to the crisis, the global capitalist classes organized a counter-offensive. China was one of the key battlegrounds in the global class struggle. By the late 1970s, China's internal class struggle ended with the decisive victory of the "capitalist roaders in authority within the Communist Party" (a political term used during China's Cultural Revolution from 1966 to 1976, referring to the faction of the Chinese Communist Party leadership who were in favor of greater economic and social inequality). China's reintegration into the global capitalist economy provided the system with the fresh supply of a large cheap labor force. This helped to turn the global balance of power in favor of the capitalist classes who went on to win the global class war in the late twentieth century.

The essence of "neoliberalism" was the dismantling of the global social contract established after 1945 (the "New Deal") in order to recreate favorable conditions for global capital accumulation. The neoliberal triumph in the 1990s led to the global redistribution of income from the workers to the capitalists. The drastic decline of living standards in many parts of the world reduced the global level of effective demand. Trillions of dollars of speculative capital flowed across national borders, generating financial bubbles followed by devastating crises. The neoliberal global economy was threatened by the tendency towards stagnation and amplified financial instability.

In the late 1990s and the early 2000s, the United States acted as the "consumer of last resort" for the global economy. The US current account deficits helped to absorb surpluses from the rest of the world, allowing China, Japan, and Germany to pursue export-led growth. Within the United States, economic growth was led by debt-financed household consumption. The global economic expansion in the early 2000s rested upon a set of financial imbalances that soon became unsustainable.

The Next Global Economic Crisis?

The Great Recession of 2008–2009 was the deepest economic crisis global capitalism has had since 1945. As the United States, Europe, and Japan struggle to recover from the crisis, global economic momentum shifts from the "developed countries" to the "emerging economies".

Figure 1.1 compares the relative contribution to global economic growth by the United States, the European Union, China, and India for the period 1990/2000–2003/2013. For the period 1990–2000, the United States contributed 24 percent of the total world economic growth, the European Union contributed 18 percent, China contributed 18 percent, and India contributed 7 percent. For the decade 2003–2013, China contributed 31 percent of the total world economic growth, India contributed 11 percent, the United States contributed 8 percent, and the European Union contributed only 6 percent.

Before 2008, China's economic growth was driven by investment and net exports. Since then, China's economic growth has been dominated by investment. Figure 1.2 compares the relative contribution to China's economic growth by the four components of gross domestic product (GDP): household consumption, government consumption, capital formation (investment), and net exports (exports less imports) for the period 2000–2012.

For the period 2005–2007, investment contributed about 40 percent of China's economic growth and net exports contributed about 20 percent. In 2009 (at the

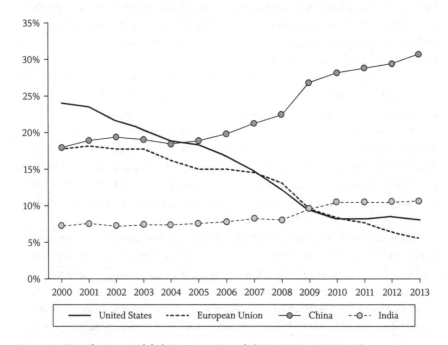

Figure 1.1 Contribution to Global Economic Growth (1990/2000–2003/2013)

Source: Gross Domestic Product (GDP) in constant 2011 international dollars for the world and individual countries from 1990 to 2013 is from the World Bank (2014). An economy's contribution to global economic growth is calculated as the ratio of the economy's cumulative growth of GDP over the cumulative growth of world GDP over a ten-year period.

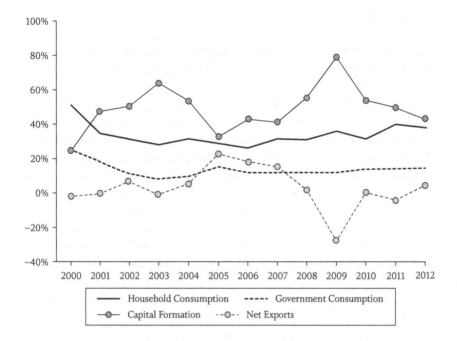

Figure 1.2 Contribution to China's Economic Growth (2000–2012)

Source: National Bureau of Statistics of China (2013 and earlier years). A macroeconomic component's contribution to economic growth is calculated as the ratio of the component's annual change over the nominal GDP's annual change.

depth of the global economic crisis), China's net exports growth turned negative, subtracting 28 percent from China's economic growth. Fueled by massive fiscal stimulus programs, investment contributed 80 percent of China's economic growth in 2009.

Since then, western capitalist economies have struggled with debt crises and economic stagnation. China's exports growth has slowed and net exports have made only an insignificant contribution to the overall economic growth. Investment, on the other hand, has been the largest source of China's economic growth.

The excessively high level of investment is driving down China's capital productivity, leading to falling profit rates for the capitalists. As a capitalist economy is driven by the pursuit of profit, declining profit rates threaten to undermine capital accumulation. If many capitalists fail to pay back debts as their returns on capital fall below expectations, an accumulation crisis will turn into a financial crisis.

Before 2008, the United States functioned as the main stabilizing force for the global capitalist economy. Since then, China has become the driving engine of global economic growth. If both the United States and China are trapped in economic crisis, what else can prevent the global capitalist economy from falling into a vicious downward spiral?

Class Struggle

In *The Communist Manifesto*, Karl Marx predicted that the modern proletariat – or the social class of wage workers – would one day become the "grave diggers" of the capitalist system.

Marx's argument was based on the following reasoning. The growth of capitalist industry tended to destroy handicrafts and small farms, turning peasants and small producers into "proletarians" who did not own the means of production and had to sell their labor power to make a living. As individuals, proletarians were vulnerable to capitalist exploitation. However, modern capitalist production was based on collective labor processes. The workers worked together in capitalist factories and lived together in towns and cities. Their concentration made it relatively easy for the workers to get organized. Capitalist economic development provided improved means of transportation and communication, making it possible for the workers to get organized in entire regions and countries. The growth of workers' organizations made the working class stronger. Eventually, the entire working class would be organized as a revolutionary political party, overthrowing the capitalist system (Marx and Engels, 1978[1848]).

By the beginning of the twentieth century, there were working class political parties in most European countries. Many of them adopted Marxism as their official political program. Although a European workers' revolution did not materialize after the First World War, the "specter of communism" was a constant threat to the European capitalist classes throughout the first half of the twentieth century. The threat forced the global capitalist classes to make major concessions after 1945.

The post-1945 "New Deal" included a "capital-labor accord", a welfare state, and Keynesian macroeconomic policy. The "capital-labor accord" promised that the Western working classes could expect steadily rising real wages in proportion with the growth of labor productivity. In return, the working class would refrain from challenging the capitalist ownership of the means of production (Gordon, Weisskopf, and Bowles 1987). The welfare state provided that the government would guarantee a minimum lifetime income (in the form of pensions and unemployment benefits) and cover a substantial portion of the cost of labor power reproduction (in the form of socialized education and health care). In addition, the government was expected to use Keynesian macroeconomic policy to ensure a reasonably high level of employment.

In effect, the post-1945 "New Deal" allowed the western working classes to receive a portion of the world surplus value in exchange for their political cooperation with the capitalist system. The global capitalist concessions were made possible by the transfer of surplus value from the periphery to the core and the massive consumption of cheap fossil fuels, especially oil.

By the 1960s, strengthened by the long economic boom and welfare state institutions, the western working classes demanded an even bigger share of the world surplus value. The semi-peripheral working classes (in the former Soviet Union, Eastern Europe, and Latin America) also demanded a share of the world surplus value. Squeezed by higher wages, higher taxes (to pay for the welfare state expenditures), and rising energy costs, global capitalism was in deep crisis. The global capitalist classes responded with a counter-offensive. But in the 1970s, the outcome of the global class war was by no means certain.

China's counter-revolution changed the global balance of power. The "opening-up" of China made it possible for the western industrial capital to be relocated to China, exploiting China's massive cheap labor force. By the beginning of the twenty-first century, China became the center of global manufacturing exports.

What happened in Europe in the nineteenth century is now taking place in China. Capitalist industrialization and urbanization have brought about fundamental changes to China's social structure. Proletarianized working class is becoming the majority of the Chinese population. A new generation of Chinese workers is demanding economic, social, and political rights. The Chinese workers' struggles have grown in size and in militancy. Despite government repression, the workers have been able to win concessions from the capitalists. In recent years, wages have grown more rapidly than labor productivity. Both the capitalist profit share (the share of profit in economic output) and the profit rate (the rate of return on invested capital) begin to fall.

Under the current trend, in a few years, a militant Chinese working class movement will emerge. The "specter" of a working class revolution, which haunted the European capitalist classes for almost a century after 1848, is resurfacing in China in the twenty-first century.

Peak Oil

In the natural world, all physical and chemical transformations require the consumption of energy (or strictly speaking, transformation from one form of energy into another). All human societies depend on the production and consumption of material goods to function and develop. Production and consumption of material goods consists of many different forms of physical and chemical transformation, which in turn depend on energy consumption. Thus, in terms of material production and consumption, a society's level of development largely depends on the level and composition of the society's energy consumption.

Pre-capitalist societies relied upon traditional forms of renewable energy (such as wood and animal power). As a result, the level of energy consumption (and therefore the overall level of material production and consumption) was limited by the natural rates of regeneration of the renewable resources.

Fossil fuels (coal, oil, and natural gas) were formed from fossilized ancient organisms. The world's coal resources were mostly formed during three geological eras: between 360 million years and 290 million years ago, between 200 million years and 65 million years ago, and between 65 million years and 2 million years ago (Heinberg 2009: 18). The oil and natural gas resources were mostly formed during two geological eras: the Jurassic period of 169–144 million years ago and the Cretaceous period of 119–89 million years ago (Aleklett 2012: 25).

Fossil fuels contain gigantic amounts of energy that originated from solar energy, which was transformed and stored as chemical energy over hundreds of millions of years. The consumption of fossil fuels has made possible the exponential growth of global capitalist economy over the past two centuries.

Without coal, there would not have been an industrial revolution and the expansion of the capitalist world system might have come to an end by the eighteenth century. Without oil, the successive technological revolutions during the twentieth century would not have materialized and US-led global capitalism would probably have insufficient resources to accommodate the economic and social demands of the western working classes.

The long boom of the global capitalist economy from the 1950s to the early 1970s rested upon cheap and abundant supply of oil. Figure 1.3 shows the relationship between world oil spending and world economic growth from 1960 to 2013. During

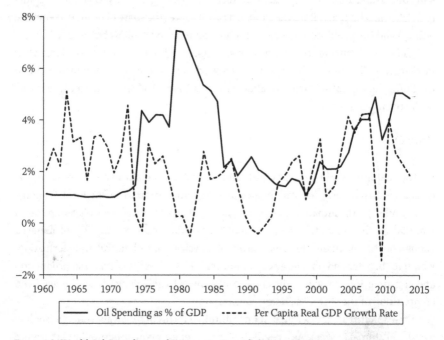

Figure 1.3 World Oil Spending and Economic Growth (1960–2013)

Source: Oil spending as % of world GDP is calculated as the ratio of estimated world total spending on oil consumption over world GDP in current US dollars. World total spending on oil consumption is world oil consumption multiplied by oil price. World oil consumption from 1965 to 2013 and oil price from 1960 to 2012 are from BP (2014). Oil consumption from 1960 to 1964 is estimated using data from Rutledge (2007). World GDP in current dollars from 1960 to 2013 and world per capita real GDP from 1990 to 2013 are from the World Bank (2014). World per capita real GDP from 1960 to 1990 is from Maddison (2010).

the 1960s, the world's total spending on oil consumption was only about 1 percent of world GDP (that is, gross world economic product). Cheap oil helped to sustain rapid growth of world per capita real GDP by 2–4 percent a year.

US oil production reached its first peak in 1970, allowing the OPEC (the Organization of the Petroleum Exporting Countries) to control the world oil market. In October 1973, Arab oil exporters proclaimed an embargo against the United States and several other western capitalist countries. World oil spending surged from 1.5 percent of world GDP in 1973 to 4.4 percent of world GDP in 1974. In 1979, because of the Iranian Revolution, world oil spending surged again to 7.4 percent of world GDP.

The surge of oil spending increased the costs of capitalist businesses and reduced the real purchasing power of consumers in oil-importing countries. The global capitalist economy suffered two deep recessions in 1974–1975 and in 1980–1982 (the International Monetary Fund defines "global recession" as an annual decline in world per capita real GDP, see IMF 2009: 11–14).

In the early 1980s, world oil consumption fell sharply as the global economy stagnated and the western capitalist economies improved energy efficiency. Despite falling oil demand, oil supply outside OPEC surged as new oil fields (Alaska and the North Sea) were brought on line. Oil price collapsed. By the late 1980s, world oil spending fell back to about 2 percent of world GDP.

In the early 2000s, oil consumption in China, India, and other "emerging economies" grew rapidly. But world oil production was unable to catch up with the demand and began to stagnate after 2005. World oil spending rose from 2.2 percent of world GDP in 2003 to 4.9 percent of world GDP in 2008, and reached 5.1 percent of world GDP in 2011.

Figure 1.4 shows the historical evolution of real oil price (in constant 2013 US dollars) in relation to world oil production. "Real oil price" is the oil price adjusted for inflation. A "constant 2013 US dollar" has the same purchasing power of an average US dollar in the year of 2013.

From 1950 to 1970, world real oil price declined from 17 dollars per barrel to 11 dollars per barrel as world oil production more than quadrupled from 11 million barrels per day to 48 million barrels per day. After the two oil shocks in the 1970s, real oil price peaked in 1980 at 104 dollars per barrel. From 1986 to 2003, real oil price fluctuated around 30 dollars per barrel and world oil production expanded from 60 million barrels per day to 78 million barrels per day.

From 2004 to 2008, real oil price surged from 47 dollars per barrel to 105 dollars per barrel. Despite the skyrocketing oil price, world oil production only grew from 81 million barrels per day to 83 million barrels per day. In the economics term, the world oil supply became highly "inelastic", that is, world oil supply was no longer responsive to rising oil price.

Although the real oil price fell sharply during the Great Recession, it rose again as the global economy recovered and reached the record high level of 115 dollars per

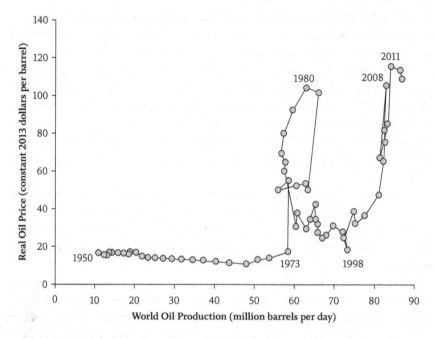

Figure 1.4 World Oil Production and Real Oil Price (1950–2013)

Source: World oil production from 1965 to 2013 and real oil price from 1950 to 2013 are from BP (2014). BP's definition of oil production includes conventional crude oil, shale oil, oil sands, and natural gas liquids. World oil production from 1950 to 1964 is from Rutledge (2007).

barrel in 2011. Since then, US oil production has surged, helping to lower the oil price.

In the *Annual Energy Outlook 2014*, the US Energy Information Administration projected that US oil production would peak in 2019 (EIA 2014a). In an independent study, David Hughes, a geoscientist and a research fellow of Post Carbon Institute, studied the shale oil "plays" using detailed production data (an oil "play" refers to a group of oil fields in a geographical region sharing the same geological circumstances). Hughes finds that US shale oil production from the major plays will peak before 2020 and shale oil's future production rates after 2020 are likely to be substantially below what were forecasted by EIA (Hughes 2014).

The US oil production peak is likely to coincide with the world oil production peak. When world oil production begins to lag behind the rising demand, oil price is likely to surge again, precipitating the global economy into the next recession.

Beyond 2020, if world oil production enters into permanent decline, the global capitalist economy will have to struggle with falling economic growth rates. Being a system based on the endless accumulation of capital, the capitalist system needs a certain level of economic growth rate to maintain economic and social stability. If economic growth rate falls below the threshold required for the system's stability and fails to recover, the system will be confronted by a structural crisis.

The Twenty-First-Century Crisis

All social systems depend on a certain set of historical conditions to function and develop. As the underlying historical conditions evolve and change, sooner or later a point will be reached when the underlying historical conditions become incompatible with the normal operation of the system. Beyond that point, the system can no longer function according to its own basic laws of motion and will have to be replaced by one or several other systems.

Capitalism is based on the pursuit of endless accumulation of capital. Capitalist accumulation is motivated by the pursuit of profit. High and stable profit rates are required for the normal operation of the capitalist economic system. Historically, high profit rates were made possible by the cheap and abundant supply of labor, energy, material resources, and low taxes.

However, the development of capitalism has transformed social structures. Over the course of capitalist development, there has been a tendency for a growing proportion of the labor force to become preletarianized wage workers. Compared to other sections of the working population, the proletarianized working class has a greater capacity to organize. As the majority of the labor force becomes proletarianized and demands a growing range of economic and social rights, there is a tendency for labor and taxation costs to rise relative to the value of economic output, depressing the capitalist profit rate.

Historically, capitalists have responded to the rising labor and taxation costs by relocating capital to new areas where labor force is relatively cheap and abundant. China may turn out to be the last large geographic area that can provide a large cheap labor force in combination with other necessary conditions required for effective capital accumulation. As the Chinese working class starts to demand economic and social rights, both the Chinese and the global labor cost will tend to rise and there is not another large geographic area to which global capital can relocate.

The pursuit of infinite economic growth is the defining feature of modern capitalism. But the exponential growth of material production and consumption has depleted natural resources and degraded the environment. Much of the global environmental space was used up by the global capitalist expansion during the second half of the twentieth century. In the early twenty-first century, various global ecological systems are on the verge of collapse. In particular, impending climate catastrophes threaten to undermine the foundation of human civilization.

These developments suggest that the various conditions, which historically have underpinned the normal operation of the capitalist world system, are being fundamentally transformed and the basic laws of motion of capitalism can no longer be sustained.

China is set to overtake the United States to become the world's largest economy. The Chinese working class is the world's largest. In a few years, a militant working class movement is likely to emerge in China. China is also the world's largest energy consumer and greenhouse gas emitter. Therefore, China is at the center of the contemporary global economic, social, and ecological contradictions.

In the 1970s, China was one of the key battlegrounds in the global class struggle. The defeat of the Maoist revolutionaries paved the way for China's transition to capitalism and was probably a decisive factor in deciding the outcome of the global class war in the late twentieth century. In the coming years, China will again be a key battleground in the global class struggle. Victory or defeat by the Chinese working class may largely decide how the global crisis of the twenty-first century will be resolved.

The next chapter discusses China's evolving class structure and class struggle. In the 1990s, the Chinese Communist Party leadership responded to the post-1989 crisis by accelerating the transition to capitalism. Politically isolated and disoriented, the state sector working class was defeated and the post-1949 socialist social contract was dismantled.

After years of rapid economic growth, China's social structure has been transformed. A new generation of working class begins to demand a growing range of economic and social rights. Radicalized intellectuals, college students, worker-activists, and veteran revolutionaries have joined forces to form China's "New Left". Historical experiences from several semi-peripheral countries suggest that Chinese capitalism will be unable to accommodate the growing demands from the Chinese working class and the urban middle class. China is likely to face an accumulation crisis and a political crisis by the 2020s.

Chapter 3 discusses the theoretical concepts and the historical evidence of capitalist economic crises. Karl Marx hypothesized that capitalist technological progress would result in rising "organic composition of capital" (rising ratios of capital stock to economic output), leading to a "tendency for the rate of profit to fall". Immanuel Wallerstein argues that capitalist development tends to drive up wage, material, and taxation costs, eventually leading to the structural crisis of the capitalist system.

The historical evidence so far has been mixed. In the leading capitalist countries, the output–capital ratios fell in the eighteenth century and the nineteenth century, but stabilized in the twentieth century. In Britain, the profit share tended to fall from the eighteenth century to the twentieth century, under the pressure of rising wage, taxation, and capital costs. In the United States, the profit share fell from the early twentieth century to the mid-twentieth century. But in the neoliberal era, labor income has been depressed and the profit share has recovered strongly in both Britain and the United States.

Historically, geographical expansion has played a crucial role in helping global capitalism to contain rising costs and restore favorable conditions of capital accumulation. David Harvey refers to this historical strategy of capitalism as "spatial fix". Chapter 4 discusses successive "spatial fixes" in the history of global capitalism from the sixteenth century to the twentieth century.

Historically, the periphery has functioned as the strategic reserve of the capitalist world system, providing a cheap labor force and resources when these were demanded. However, by the late twentieth century, to contain the rising costs in the core and the semi-periphery, it became necessary to mobilize China – a large geographic area in the periphery – to restore favorable conditions of global capital accumulation. As China enters into the semi-periphery, both the global labor and resources costs will tend to rise. The capitalist world system is approaching the limit of "spatial fix".

Chapter 5 argues that the inherent contradictions of Chinese capitalism will lead to a major economic crisis in the coming years. Being a large peripheral economy specializing in manufacturing exports, it is necessary for China to maintain heavy investment in industrial equipment and infrastructure. The excessively high level of investment has driven down China's profit rate. As wage, taxation, and capital costs rise, Chinese capitalism has entered into the era of profit squeeze leading to further declines of the profit rate.

Historical experience from British and American capitalism suggests that a major crisis is likely to happen when the economy-wide profit rate falls below 10 percent. The combination of excessively high investment and profit squeeze implies that China's economy-wide profit rate is likely to fall towards 10 percent by the 2020s, leading to a major economic crisis. But with the rapid escalation of China's debt–GDP ratios, a major financial and economic crisis before 2020 is a distinct possibility. Given China's current economic weight, a major crisis of the Chinese economy will almost certainly drag the global economy into the next recession, which may turn out to be far more damaging than the Great Recession of 2008–2009.

In the past, global capitalism has managed to recover from major crises by undertaking restructuring without changing the basic institutional framework of capitalism. However, in the twenty-first century, global capitalism will have to confront not only the traditional economic and social contradictions, but also the rapidly escalating ecological contradictions. Chapter 6 argues that for all practical purposes, it is no longer possible to limit global warming to no more than two degrees Celsius from the pre-industrial time. Some forms of dangerous climate change are already unavoidable. The question is whether humanity can manage to prevent the worst climate catastrophes that threaten to destroy the material foundation of human civilization.

World production of oil, natural gas, and coal is likely to peak before the mid-twenty-first century. Growth of nuclear and renewable energies will be insufficient to offset the decline of fossil fuels. World energy consumption will begin to decline after the 2030s, leading to a prolonged (and possibly a permanent) major crisis of global capitalism. Despite the decline of carbon dioxide emissions after the late 2020s, the cumulative emissions over the twenty-first century may be large enough to lead to climate catastrophes beyond the twenty-first century.

Chapter 7 discusses the ecological constraints on China's capitalist accumulation. In the short- and the medium-term, the Chinese capitalist economy needs an economic growth rate of more than 5 percent to maintain economic stability. However, if the Chinese economy grows by more than 5 percent a year, China's demand for oil, natural gas, and coal is likely to impose unbearable burden on the world energy markets in the coming years. China's water demand will stay above the ecologically sustainable amount of fresh water supply. Only a few indicators of air pollution (such as sulfur dioxide emissions) may improve in the coming years.

Assuming that China is entitled to 20 percent of the global carbon dioxide emissions budget, for all practical purposes, it is no longer possible for China to meet the climate stabilization requirements consistent with global warming of less than two degrees Celsius. To avoid the worst climate catastrophes, China's carbon dioxide emissions need to peak by 2030 and decline rapidly between 2030 and 2050. The required emissions reduction implies drastic reduction of China's economic growth rate by the 2020s and possibly negative economic growth by the 2040s. In other words, the basic requirements of climate stabilization are fundamentally incompatible with the normal operation of the Chinese capitalist economy.

Chapter 8 argues that the global capitalist system has entered into a structural crisis that can no longer be resolved through another round of "spatial fix". The coming crisis will create opportunities for socialist transformation in China and the rest of the world.

After 1989, a consensus was established among mainstream economists that the socialist economic system was fundamentally flawed and the capitalist market provided the best of all possible economic systems. However, the reality of the global capitalist system provides ample evidence that the capitalist market not only fails to meet the basic needs of the great majority of the population but also threatens to undermine the foundation of human civilization. Rather than producing socially optimal results, capitalism may be an economic system that strongly motivates every individual to pursue socially adverse outcomes.

The chapter concludes by wondering whether there is any alternative to socialism for humanity in the twenty-first century.

2

CHINA: CLASSES AND CLASS STRUGGLE

On March 14, 2012, Wen Jiabao, then China's Prime Minister, publicly reprimanded Bo Xilai at the press conference held after the concluding session of the Eleventh National People's Congress. Bo Xilai had gained national reputation through his successful campaign against organized crime and the experiment of the "Chongqing Model," which promoted a strategy of economic development based on the growth of state-owned enterprises and egalitarian income distribution. The "Chongqing Model" represented a significant deviation from the neoliberal strategy of privatization and liberalization promoted by China's national leadership. At the press conference, Wen Jiabao reminded people of "the Party's fundamental line" established at the Third Plenum of the Eleventh Central Committee of the Chinese Communist Party held in December 1978, which set China on the path of "reform and openness." Wen Jiabao maintained that the ills of the Cultural Revolution had not yet been fully eliminated (Feng Huang Wang 2012). China's right-wing liberal commentators interpreted Wen's statement as an indictment against the "Chongqing Model," accusing Bo Xilai of trying to revive the Cultural Revolution and challenge the Party line of "reform and openness" (Zhao, X. 2012).

The next day, Bo Xilai was dismissed as the Party Secretary of the Municipality of Chongqing. On September 28, 2012, the Chinese Communist Party's Politburo adopted a decision to expel Bo Xilai from the Party, accusing Bo of accepting bribery, corruption, and abuse of power. In August 2013, Bo's trial was held in Jinan (the capital city of Shandong Province). Bo Xilai denied all charges and waged a vigorous defense (*Economist* 2013). A month later, Bo Xilai was sentenced to life imprisonment.

After the Bo Xilai incident, the neoliberal faction took over the Chinese Communist Party's leadership. In November 2013, the Party's Third Plenum of the Eighteenth Central Committee adopted the decision to "comprehensively deepen" economic reform. The decision confirmed that "we must deepen the economic system reform by centering on the decisive role of the market in allocating resources" and promised to "vigorously develop the mixed ownership economy" (Xin Hua Wang 2013). The term "mixed ownership" is generally regarded as a euphemism for privatization.

The Bo Xilai incident was the outcome of intense struggles between competing factions of the Communist Party leadership, ending with the victory of the neoliberal faction and the defeat of those who were in favor of a state-directed, more egalitarian model of development. It reflected China's broad economic and social contradictions. After three decades of capitalist transition, these contradictions have grown to such levels that China's apparent political stability can no longer be taken for granted.

To understand the economic and social contradictions in contemporary China and to evaluate their future trajectories, it is necessary to consider how these contradictions have evolved over the course of modern Chinese history.

The Chinese Revolution

Modern China (China as a part of the capitalist world system) began with the Opium War, when British imperialism used force to open up the Chinese market to opium and other western commodities. By the late nineteenth century, China was reduced to a semi-colonial peripheral member of the capitalist world system.

China's traditional ruling elites responded to the major crisis by undertaking a limited program of military modernization, which was known as the "Westernization Movement." The "Westernization Movement" failed miserably as the Qing Empire suffered a humiliating defeat in the 1894–1895 war against Japan.

A nationalist movement that was based on the modern intellectuals influenced by western ideas and China's indigenous capitalists (the national bourgeoisie) emerged at the beginning of the twentieth century. The Chinese national bourgeoisie was small, weak, and dependent on foreign capital. After the 1911 revolution, Sun Zhongshan and his Nationalist Party comrades were unable to establish a viable national government. China fell into the hands of a dozen warlords, backed by competing foreign imperialist powers.

In the 1920s, the Soviet Union decided to support the Chinese national liberation movement and a Nationalist Party–Communist Party alliance was formed. However, when the workers in Shanghai took over the city and welcomed the Nationalist army, Jiang Jieshi (the new Nationalist leader) decided that it was time to massacre the workers and the communists. The counter-revolution of 1927 demonstrated that the Nationalist Party was unable to challenge either the traditional landlord class in the rural areas or the dominance of foreign capital in China's modern economic sectors.

By 1928, the Nationalist army had defeated most of the warlords in Northern China. Jiang Jieshi became the internationally recognized leader of China. But the Nationalist government was unable to establish effective political control beyond the Yangzi valley. In the first few years of the Sino-Japanese War, which started in 1937, the Nationalist army suffered numerous catastrophic defeats. Before the Pacific War started, China's industrial and commercial centers were all under Japanese occupation.

From 1840 to 1949, successive Chinese ruling regimes had failed to mobilize a sufficient amount of economic surplus to undertake industrialization and military modernization. Without strong military capabilities, China was unable to function as a viable nation-state in the capitalist world system.

Until the victory of the Communist Party in 1949, China had seen virtually no modern economic growth for the entire century following the Opium War. According to the statistics compiled by Angus Maddison, the average annual growth rate of China's per capita GDP was −0.6 percent from 1850 to 1870, 0.1 percent from 1870 to 1913, and −0.6 percent from 1913 to 1950. China's per capita GDP was estimated to be 600 dollars in 1850. By 1950, it declined to 448 dollars (measured in 1990 international dollars, Maddison 2010).

To mobilize the economic surplus required for modern economic growth, the agricultural surplus product (the part of the agricultural production that was above what was needed to provide the rural population with basic necessities) had to be concentrated in the hands of the state. Moreover, the relationship between China and the capitalist world economy had to be redefined so that the Chinese state could have a monopoly over the domestic market, providing the initial space of expansion for China's indigenous industries.

This could only be achieved through a massive social revolution that would mobilize the peasants and the workers, eliminate the traditional ruling classes (the rural landlord class and the urban oligarchies), and expel foreign capital from China's domestic market. It took the Communist revolution (or, using the historical terminology of the Chinese Communist Party, a New Democratic Revolution that was anti-imperialist and anti-feudal) to establish in China the necessary social conditions required for effective capital accumulation and modern economic growth.

The Socialist Social Contract

The primary task of the new People's Republic was to achieve rapid industrialization and "catch up" with the western capitalist countries in industrial and military capacity. But this task had to be accomplished under the post-revolutionary historical conditions. The new Chinese state was a "socialist state," that is to say, it was the historical product of a great popular revolution based on the mobilization of the peasants and the workers. As a result, the socialist state was defined by an implicit social contract between itself and the great majority of the population (the peasants and the workers).

Under the post-1949 social contract, the socialist state would mobilize economic surplus to achieve rapid industrialization and economic growth. In the short run, workers and peasants would make a contribution to "socialist economic construction" by generating economic surplus and accepting low levels of material consumption. In return, the socialist state would provide the workers and the peasants with basic social security, health care, and education. The Communist Party cadres would give up their material privileges and share the material hardship with the masses. In the long run, the socialist state would not only provide high material living standards to everyone but also eliminate all forms of inequality, preparing the material and social conditions for the classless communist society.

The socialist social contract began to be undermined when the material privileges of the Communist Party cadres and intellectual "experts" were expanded and institutionalized during the implementation of the Soviet-style First Five-Year-Plan (1953–1957). The gross mismanagement of the bureaucratic elites led to the failure of the "Great Leap Forward" campaign (a campaign with the intention to accelerate industrialization). This was followed by natural disasters and a major economic crisis from 1960 to 1962.

The crisis of the early 1960s led to a major split of the Communist Party leadership. The Maoists, led by Mao Zedong (the great leader of the Chinese Revolution), argued that the crisis could only be resolved through "continuing revolution under the dictatorship of the proletariat." The post-1949 social contract had to be honored and the Communist Party would have to uphold its stated objective of "transition to communism" by constantly reducing and eventually eliminating various forms of economic and social inequality.

Against the Maoists, Liu Shaoqi (who was then the President of the People's Republic) and Deng Xiaoping (who was then in charge of the Party Central Committee's daily affairs) argued that economic growth and industrialization could only be achieved by providing the Communist Party cadres and the intellectual experts with greater managerial power (unchecked by the workers and the peasants). Moreover, the cadres and the experts would have to be rewarded with more material privileges in accordance with their greater managerial power. For the Maoists, the economic development strategy advocated by Liu Shaoqi and Deng Xiaoping would sooner or later lead to "capitalist restoration" in China.

The battle between the Maoists and the Liu-Deng faction led to the massive political upheaval of the Cultural Revolution (1966–1976). Unable to win the support from the majority of the Party and state bureaucrats, Mao Zedong made one last attempt to save the revolution by directly calling upon the workers and the young students to rebel against the bureaucracy. But the workers and the student rebels were politically inexperienced and divided. The Party and state bureaucrats survived the initial panic and organized counter-attacks. In many cities, the army intervened to support the established bureaucrats. Radical workers and student rebels were brutally repressed. By 1969, the radical phase of the Cultural Revolution came to an end (on the bureaucrats' counter-attacks and the army's repression of Maoist rebels, see Lao Tian 2008).

Internationally, China found itself in hostility against both the United States and the Soviet Union, a situation that could not be sustained. To break the geopolitical isolation and have access to western technology, it became necessary for China to improve relations with western capitalist countries. In 1971, the People's Republic of China was admitted into the United Nations as "the only lawful representative of China." Richard Nixon visited China the following year, paving the way for the eventual normalization of diplomatic relations between the United States and China. In 1973, China decided to import 4.3 billion dollars of industrial equipment from the western countries and Japan. China began to depend on imports of western technology to accelerate economic growth (Zhang, H. 2008).

In September 1976, Mao Zedong died. Within a month of Mao's death, Hua Guofeng (the new Party leader) staged a counter-revolutionary coup, arresting Jiang Qing (Mao's wife) and other Maoist leaders. By 1978, Deng Xiaoping came back to power and China entered into the era of "reform and openness."

Transition to Capitalism

Deng Xiaoping's economic reform began with agricultural privatization. In 1982, People's Communes (the Chinese form of collective agriculture) were officially dismantled. On paper, the rural land remained under collective ownership by village communities. In fact, land was distributed to individual households, who had full control over the use of land.

Initially, individual households were not allowed to buy or sell land contracted to them and village communities were supposed to adjust land assignments every few years to reflect changes in population. In 2002, China's National People's Congress approved the Law on the Contracting of Rural Land, extending the duration of rural land contract to 30 years (National People's Congress 2002). In practice, village communities in most areas have stopped making land adjustments and many peasant households have sold their land contracts to rural capitalists.

In the 1980s, the urban working class continued to enjoy the socialist economic rights known as the "iron rice bowl" (a comprehensive package of social security including job security, pensions, housing, health care, and education). The security provided by the "iron rice bowl" gave the state sector workers strong bargaining power. Attempts by Chinese state-owned enterprises to introduce capitalist-style "scientific management" (the labor management system designed to increase the intensity of labor and reduce the workers' control over the production processes) were met with strong resistance by the workers. From the capitalist point of view, the state-owned enterprises were inherently "inefficient" and could not compete effectively in the capitalist world market.

To accelerate economic growth, China needed to increase the imports of foreign capital goods and technologies. The Party and state bureaucrats, the emerging capitalist class, and the urban middle class also desired to have imported consumer goods. Chinese imports grew rapidly in the 1980s but exports failed to catch up, resulting in large trade deficits by the second half of the 1980s. To finance the trade deficits, China borrowed foreign debt, which surged from 16 billion dollars in 1985 to 53 billion dollars in 1990. If the trade imbalances were not reversed, the escalation of foreign debt could lead to a debt crisis by the 1990s (the various Chinese economic statistics cited in this section are from National Bureau of Statistics of China 2013 and earlier years, unless otherwise stated).

In 1988, Milton Friedman (one of the world's leading neoliberal economists) visited China and met with Zhao Ziyang, who was then the general secretary of the Chinese Communist Party. Zhao and Friedman had a very lively and friendly discussion. The conversation was scheduled to be half an hour but Zhao decided to extend it to two hours. After the conversation, Zhao was so excited that he accompanied Friedman all the way to the car Friedman was riding (Li, Z. 2006).

Zhao Ziyang decided to implement a radical program of neoliberal "economic reform," liberalizing all prices within a short period of time. Zhao's reform plan further destabilized the Chinese economy. Consumer price inflation rate surged to 21 percent in 1988. Surging inflation and growing corruption hurt not only the urban working class, but also intellectuals and college students. The rapid escalation of social discontent led to the political crisis in 1989.

The 1989 political crisis temporarily shifted the balance of power in favor of the "left wing" within the Communist Party leadership. The "left wing" was led by Chen Yun who was in favor of a state-led economic model with limited roles for the private capitalist sector. But the "left wing" had no connection with the working class and had only limited support from the Party and state bureaucrats. On the other hand, Deng Xiaoping could count on the loyalty of the army.

In January and February 1992, Deng Xiaoping made the famous "Southern Tour," visiting Guangzhou, Shenzhen, Zhuhai, and Shanghai. Guangzhou is the capital city of Guangdong province where China's export-oriented manufacturing industries are concentrated. In 1978 and 1980, Shenzhen and Zhuhai became "special economic zones" designed to attract foreign investment. Before the 1949 revolution, Shanghai symbolized foreign imperialist domination in China. According to Deng's plan, Shanghai would be the leading city in a new round of market-oriented economic reform. Deng's "Southern Tour" demonstrated his determination to complete the capitalist transition in China.

Sensing the changing political climate, Jiang Zemin (who became the general secretary of the Communist Party after 1989 and was originally a protégé of Chen Yun) swiftly shifted his political allegiance and became a follower of Deng Xiaoping.

In October 1992, the Fourteenth National Congress of the Chinese Communist Party was held. The Fourteenth Congress promoted Deng Xiaoping's "Theory on Socialism with Chinese Characteristics" as the guiding principle of the Chinese Communist Party and decided that the goal of reform was to build a "socialist market economy." In effect, the Fourteenth Congress officially approved China's transition to capitalism.

By the end of the 1990s, most state-owned enterprises were privatized. The remaining large-scale state-owned enterprises were transformed into capitalist-style corporations. State sector employment peaked in 1995 at 113 million. It fell to 81 million by 2000 and 64 million by 2007. Between 1995 and 2007, about 50 million state sector workers were laid off. As the state sector employment contracted, the rural non-agricultural labor force was greatly expanded.

After the dismantling of the People's Communes, the rural labor force was no longer mobilized for the building of local public infrastructure (such as water-conservancy and irrigation works). Tens of millions from the rural labor force began to seek new employment opportunities in industry and services. In the 1980s, China's non-agricultural labor force on average grew by 12 million a year. Initially, most of the rural surplus labor force was absorbed by collectively owned "town and village enterprises."

By the 1990s, most town and village enterprises were privatized. After privatization, employment by the town and village enterprises stagnated. Many rural workers had to seek employment outside their home areas and became migrant workers. The potential supply of a massive surplus labor force reduced the migrant workers' bargaining power, forcing them to accept low wages and harsh working conditions.

In 1990, there were 93 million "local rural workers" who were employed by local town and village enterprises and 22 million "migrant rural workers" who were employed in the cities or the rural areas outside their official residence. By 2000, local rural workers increased to 97 million and the migrant rural workers surged to 106 million (Yang C. and Yang L. 2010). The massive increase of migrant workers provided the domestic and foreign capitalist enterprises with a large cheap labor force. Sweatshop exploitation became the standard practice in China's export-oriented manufacturing industries.

The transformation of the Chinese labor force in the 1990s solved the "competitiveness" problem for Chinese capitalism. The intense exploitation of a large cheap labor force allowed Chinese capitalists to earn high profit rates and capture a growing share of the world market.

China's merchandise exports surged from 62 billion dollars in 1990, 249 billion dollars in 2000, to 2.05 trillion dollars in 2012. China's share of the world total merchandise exports was 1.8 percent in 1990, 3.8 percent in 2000, and 11.1 percent in 2012. Since 2010, China has been the world's largest exporter of goods (data are from World Bank 2014).

A Class War the Chinese Working Class Lost

It took a broad and massive social revolution to create the necessary social conditions for effective capital accumulation to take place in China. The post-revolutionary state recognized the historical contribution of the peasants and the workers through the provision of basic social needs and the promise of achieving economic and social equality in the long run. The provision of basic social needs and the long-term promises together constituted a socialist social contract.

However, socialist China remained a part of the capitalist world system and had to follow the basic laws of motion of the system. Within the capitalist world system, states are compelled to compete against one another in economic and military terms.

Those who failed the competition would become vulnerable, risking either internal instability or external intervention.

In the 1950s, Soviet technological assistance helped China to lay down the foundation of industrialization. By the 1970s, it became necessary for China to import western technology in order to sustain economic growth. But to import western technology, China had to increase exports and capture a larger share of the world market. China was not able to compete with the western core capitalist countries in term of technology. Nor was China able to compete with some semi-peripheral countries (such as the Middle East oil exporters) in term of natural resources. China had to compete with many peripheral countries with the only significant "comparative advantage" China had – a large supply of cheap labor force. To take full advantage of this "comparative advantage," the Chinese ruling class decided to renege on the historically established socialist social contract through privatization and the destruction of the "iron rice bowl" in the state sector.

An alternative path of development, advocated by Mao Zedong in the 1960s, was to "continue the revolution under the dictatorship of the proletariat." Under the Maoist alternative strategy, China would pursue a greater degree of economic and social equality. In return, the workers and the peasants would accept a longer period of material hardship. Socialist China would refuse to play by the rules of game of the capitalist world system with the anticipation that the global rules of game would be fundamentally transformed by the coming world revolution.

By the 1970s, both the Chinese revolution and the world revolution were in retreat. The Chinese Communist Party officially abandoned the Cultural Revolution almost immediately after Mao's death. The urban working class was politically confused and disoriented. Although the urban working class had strong economic bargaining power in the 1980s, they did not have political leadership and were unable to advance their own interests as a class. It was a class war the Chinese working class could not win.

Despite divisions between different factions of the Chinese Communist Party leadership, a consensus emerged by the early 1990s that China had to embrace capitalism and turn itself into the manufacturing exports platform for the global capitalism. Such a development would help to resolve China's immediate economic and political crisis. Most importantly, it would provide the ruling elites with not only political power but also enormous economic wealth.

The transition to capitalism was welcomed and even enthusiastically supported by China's urban middle class. The urban middle class mainly included the professional and technical workers, such as managers, engineers, university professors, lawyers, and doctors. In the 1980s, they were generally referred to as "intellectuals" in China. Chinese intellectuals hoped that the transition to capitalism would provide them with the opportunity to study and work abroad and to be employed by transnational corporations. Because of the enormous wage gap that existed between China and western core capitalist countries, participation in the globalized professional and technical labor market promised to bring about a dramatic improvement of material living standards for the Chinese professional and technical workers.

Initially, many Chinese intellectuals hoped that in the transition to capitalism, the urban middle class could be provided with some access to political power. That hope was smashed by the Tiananmen massacre in 1989. After 1989, most Chinese intellectuals became politically disillusioned and focused on the improvement of material living standards. A *de facto* pro-capitalist alliance was formed between the Communist Party elites and the urban middle class.

Agriculture was the weakest link of the traditional socialist system. Agricultural privatization in the early 1980s was met with little resistance from the peasants (though the official propaganda that the peasants enthusiastically supported privatization was mostly unfounded). After agricultural privatization, a large cheap labor force was made available for capitalist exploitation. Domestic and foreign capitalist enterprises prospered. The capitalist economic sector overtook the state sector in terms of employment and output value by the early 1990s.

When the Communist Party elites decided to undertake massive privatization in the 1990s, the urban working class found itself politically isolated. Because of the presence of a large and rapidly growing capitalist economic sector, the state sector working class was left with little economic bargaining power. The class war of the 1990s ended with the victory of the new Chinese capitalist class.

China's Changing Class Structure

The capitalist economy is based on the exploitation of the working class (extraction of surplus value produced by the workers). The level of capitalist exploitation varies depending on the relative bargaining power of the workers under different forms of labor organization. Depending on how their labor is organized, the workers in a capitalist society may be divided into several sectors: highly skilled professional and technical workers, fully proletarianized wage workers, the semi-proletarian migrant workers, and agricultural petty-commodity producers (Wallerstein 1979: 102–103).

The highly skilled professional and technical workers perform economic and social functions that are of strategic importance to the capitalist system, such as political administration, business management, research and development, and engineering. They tend to have high costs of labor power reproduction (high expenses of consumption and education) and comparatively strong control over their own labor processes. The capitalists have to pay the professional and technical workers a "loyalty rent" to secure their economic and political cooperation. These workers constitute the "middle class" between the capitalist class and other workers (Wright 1997: 19–26).

The fully proletarianized wage workers are the skilled and semi-skilled workers in the urban sector. They usually have full-time jobs in the "formal sectors" (the economic sectors that are subject to effective government regulation and legal protection) and derive their money income entirely or mostly from wage labor.

Semi-proletarian unskilled workers have part-time or insecure jobs. They are frequently unemployed. Their wage incomes are not sufficient to meet their essential needs and they have to engage in economic activities in the "informal sectors" (economic sectors that are illegal or not subject to effective government regulation) to supplement their money incomes. In the periphery and the semi-periphery of the capitalist world system, many semi-proletarian workers are "migrant workers" who spend part of their lifetime in urban areas and the rest in rural areas. A substantial part of their income derives from rural family production.

Agricultural petty-commodity producers are often known as "peasants," who own some means of production and derive most of their incomes from rural family production. In the periphery and the semi-periphery, peasants and semi-proletarian wage workers often belong to the same household. Many semi-proletarian workers live as peasants during part of their lifetime.

In the capitalist world system, the core countries tend to have a relatively large urban middle class (the professional and technical workers) and fully proletarianized working class. All types of wage workers often account for more than 90 percent of the total labor force of a core capitalist country. This reflects the fact that the world surplus value is concentrated in the core countries, allowing the capitalists to pay a large amount of "loyalty rent" to co-opt the internal middle class and working class.

By comparison, the peripheral countries tend to have a large number of agricultural petty commodity producers and semi-proletarian workers. The combined bargaining power of the agricultural producers and the semi-proletarian workers tends to be weak, consistent with the fact that the peripheral countries tend to specialize in low value-added activities and receive a relatively small share of the world surplus value.

Under certain historical conditions, some peripheral countries may be able to move upwards in the hierarchy of the capitalist world system. If a peripheral country is transformed into a semi-peripheral country, a large proportion of the labor force would become proletarianized. The proletarianized working class has the capacity to demand more economic and political rights. If a semi-peripheral country fails to meet the working class demands under conditions consistent with effective capital accumulation, the country is likely to suffer from both an accumulation crisis and a political crisis.

Table 2.1 shows China's changing structure of labor force from 1990 to 2012. Agricultural producers are rural residents whose incomes derive mainly from agricultural production. In China, agricultural producers are usually "self-employed" small farmers who own their family plots of land (technically a "family plot" is a part of the land collectively owned by the village community). The total number of agricultural producers declined from 381 million in 1990, 355 million in 2000, to 254

Table 2.1 China's Labor Force, 1990–2012 (million persons)

	1990	1995	2000	2005	2010	2012
Agricultural Producers	381	349	355	330	276	254
Rural Local and Migrant Workers	104	173	192	207	242	263
Urban Formal Wage Workers	130	113	116	126	125	109
Professional and Technical Workers	17	19	22	32	41	47
Party and State Bureaucrats	9	10	11	12	14	15
Urban Self-Employed	7	16	21	28	45	56
Private Enterprise Investors	0	1	4	11	18	22
Unemployed	6	8	19	15	23	22
Total Economically Active	653	689	740	761	784	789

Sources: National Bureau of Statistics of China (2013 and earlier years). Data for rural local and migrant workers are from Yang C. and Yang L. (2010) and National Bureau of Statistics of China (2014a). Data for professional and technical workers are from Ministry of Science and Technology (1998–2005) and Ministry of Human Resources and Social Security (2009–2013).

million in 2012. From 2000 to 2012, the number of agricultural producers on average fell by more than 8 million a year. At this rate, by 2020, China will have less than 200 million agricultural producers.

Rural local workers are rural residents who work in non-agricultural activities for six months or more within a year within the township of their official residence. Migrant workers are rural residents who work in non-agricultural activities for six months or more within a year in the cities or the rural areas outside the township of their official residence. The total number of rural local and migrant workers increased from 104 million in 1990, 192 million in 2000, to 263 million in 2012. Rural workers have already become the single largest employment group in China. From 2000 to 2012, the number of rural local and migrant workers on average grew by 6 million a year. At this rate, by 2020, there will be more than 300 million rural workers employed in non-agricultural activities.

Urban formal wage workers are workers with official urban residence, excluding Communist Party and state bureaucrats, professional and technical workers, and the self-employed. Urban formal wage workers derive most of their incomes from wage employment. They work in domestic or foreign enterprises that are subject to relatively effective government regulation. In 1990, China had 130 million urban formal wage workers. The number of formal wage workers declined to 113 million in 1995 and 116 million in 2000, reflecting the massive privatization in the 1990s. The number of formal wage workers recovered to 126 million in 2005 but fell to 109 million by 2012.

Professional and technical workers include engineers, technicians, research and development personnel, doctors and nurses, teachers, airplane and ship operators, accountants and statisticians, writers and translators, journalists, lawyers, artists, sports men and women, and managers with professional and technical titles (using the definition of "professional and technical workers" in *China Statistical Yearbook*). In 2012, China had 47 million professional and technical workers.

Party and state bureaucrats include all employees of the government, the Chinese Communist Party, and other "social organizations" (such as official trade unions). In 2012, China had 15 million Party and state bureaucrats. These include the ruling elites as well as the rank-and-file public sector employees.

The urban self-employed grew rapidly from 7 million in 1990, 21 million in 2000, to 56 million in 2012.

In China, many big capitalists have connections with the Party and state bureaucrats. The category "private enterprise investors" refers to capitalists with investments in what are officially classified as private enterprises. These are often very small enterprises. In 2012, there were 22 million private enterprise investors out of a total employment in private enterprises of 76 million. On average, there were only 2.5 employees for each private enterprise investor.

China's total economically active population (total labor force) increased from 653 million in 1990, 740 million in 2000, to 789 million in 2012. From 1990 to 2010, China's labor force on average grew by 9 million a year. From 2000 to 2010, China's labor force on average grew by more than 4 million a year. From 2010 to 2012, China's labor force on average grew by only 2.5 million a year. The slow-down of China's labor force growth could undermine China's capitalist accumulation in the future.

Figure 2.1 shows China's changing class structure from 1990 to 2012. From 1990 to 2012, the share of "self-employed" agricultural producers in the total labor force declined from 58 percent in 1990 to 32 percent in 2012, with a total decline of 26 percentage points.

A large portion of the labor force has been transferred out of agriculture to become wage workers in industry and services. The total semi-proletarian working class (including migrant workers, rural local workers, and the unemployed) grew from 17 percent of the labor force in 1990 to 36 percent of the labor force in 2012, with a total increase by 19 percentage points.

In 1990, the urban proletariat and middle class (including the urban formal wage workers and the professional and technical workers) accounted for 22 percent of the total labor force. By 2000, it declined to less than 19 percent. During the economic boom in the early 2000s, the formal sector employment expanded. By 2008, urban formal sector wage employment reached 22 percent of the total labor force. But in 2012, the share of urban formal sector wage employment fell to about 20 percent.

Despite privatization and other neoliberal "economic reforms," the normal operation of a modern capitalist economy depends on the employment of a large number of skilled and highly skilled workers to perform important technical, managerial, and ideological functions. As a result, even in the neoliberal era, capitalism

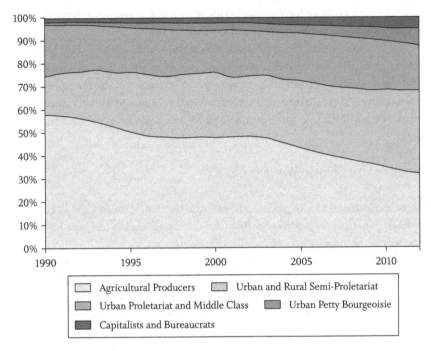

Figure 2.1 China's Class Structure (% of Labor Force, 1990–2012)

Sources: See Table 2.1.

has had great difficulty in significantly reducing the size of the urban formal sector employment. In China, urban formal sector wage employment has stayed at around one-fifth of the total labor force.

In 2012, the urban petty bourgeoisie (the self-employed) accounted for 7 percent and capitalists and bureaucrats accounted for 5 percent of the total labor force. The category "capitalists and bureaucrats" includes all private enterprise investors and public sector employees. Some investors in very small private enterprises may be better defined as members of urban petty bourgeoisie. Low-rank public sector employees should be included in the urban middle class rather than as a part of the ruling elites. Thus, the category "capitalists and bureaucrats" overstates the current size of the Chinese capitalist class (including the Communist Party ruling elites). The true size of the Chinese capitalist class is probably 2–3 percent of the total population. After making the correction for small private investors and low-rank public sector employees, urban formal sector wage employment may account for 21 percent of the total labor force and urban petty bourgeoisie may account for 8–9 percent.

Over the past two decades, China's social structure has been fundamentally transformed. The total wage-earning labor force (including rural wage workers, urban wage workers, professional and technical workers, and public sector employees, excluding the unemployed) grew from 39 percent of the total labor force in 1990 to 55 percent of the total labor force in 2012. This growth can be entirely accounted for by the growth of the semi-proletarian rural workers.

The intense exploitation of semi-proletarian rural workers has been the foundation of Chinese capitalist prosperity. But experience from other capitalist countries suggests that within one or two generations, many of the semi-proletarian rural workers will evolve into fully proletarianized urban wage workers. During this process, they will learn to get organized and become a powerful political and social force.

The Rise of the Chinese Working Class

Intense exploitation of a large cheap labor force has underpinned China's capitalist accumulation. Chapter 5 will show that Chinese capitalism has had very high profit rates in comparison with other capitalist economies.

A recent study of Chinese wages finds that on average, workers employed by Chinese domestic private enterprises are paid 30–32 percent less than the "living wage," defined as the wage income required to support a four-person household based on the lowest living standard in Chinese cities. If Chinese private enterprises pay workers just the "living wages," their total profits would be reduced by about a quarter (Xu, Chen, and Li 2014).

According to a survey conducted in the Pearl River Delta in the Guangdong province in 2003, about two-thirds of the workers worked more than eight hours a day and never took weekends off. Some workers had to work continuously for up to 16 hours. The capitalist managers routinely used corporal punishment to discipline the workers (Wen 2005). About 200 million Chinese workers work in hazardous conditions. There are about 700,000 serious work-related injuries in China every year, claiming more than 100,000 lives (Hart-Landsberg 2011).

In The Communist Manifesto, Marx and Engels argued that the working-class struggle against capitalists followed several stages of development. At first, the struggle was carried on by individual workers against the capitalists who directly exploited them. With the development of capitalist industry, the proletariat increased in number and became concentrated in greater masses. The workers' strength grew and they began to form unions to fight capitalists as a collective force.

The same law of motion is operating in China today. As many rural workers settle in the cities and increasingly regard themselves as proletarianized wage workers rather than peasants, a new generation of workers with growing class consciousness and organizational capacity has emerged. The Chinese government documents now recognize the rise of the "Xinshengdai Nongmingong (new-generation rural workers)."

According to China's "National Rural Workers Monitoring and Survey Report," there are 125 million "new-generation rural workers" defined as rural workers who were born in 1980 or after. New-generation rural workers account for 47 percent of total rural workers.

Compared to traditional rural workers, new-generation rural workers are better educated, concentrated in big cities and coastal provinces, more likely to search for employment outside of their home areas, mainly employed in manufacturing, and have higher consumption expectations (National Bureau of Statistics of China 2014a).

In 2007, crane drivers at the Shenzhen port terminals went on strike. The strikers not only won pay raises but also forced their employers to compensate them for unpaid overtime pay and housing subsidies. The total increases in wages and housing funds amounted to 90 million Yuan (about 15 million US dollars). This was a significant victory for Chinese workers in their struggle against sweatshop exploitation in the export-oriented capitalist sectors.

In 2010, strike waves swept through China's automobile, textile, and electronics industries. Millions of workers participated in the strikes. Following the 2010 strikes, local governments began to raise minimum wages. From 2010 to 2014, Shenzhen's local minimum wage surged from 900 Yuan (about 150 dollars) per month to 1808 Yuan (about 301 dollars) per month; Shanghai's local minimum wage rose from 960 Yuan (about 160 dollars) per month to 1820 Yuan (about 303 dollars) per month.

From 2011 to 2013, Chinese workers continued to win strike victories. In December 2011, workers of the Japanese-owned Hailiang storage-products company in Shenzhen went on strike for nearly a month and won a pay raise of 30 percent. In October and November 2013, workers of the Taiwanese-owned Xianjin microelectronics company in Shenzhen went on strike for three weeks and won a pay raise of 20 percent (Gong Ping She 2014).

At a time when large parts of the world are suffering under the tyranny of neoliberal austerity, China may be the only large country where the working class is making significant gains in their struggle against capitalist exploitation.

Figure 2.2 shows the share of total wages in China's non-agricultural GDP (gross domestic product). China's wage share declined sharply from 31 percent in 1990 to less than 23 percent in 1997, suggesting that Chinese workers' bargaining power was greatly weakened by massive privatization in the 1990s. The wage share recovered slowly from 1997 to 2008. After 2008, the wage share growth accelerated. By 2012, the wage share reached near 30 percent.

In the future, as China's rural surplus labor force continues to be depleted and China's total labor force begins to decline, Chinese workers' bargaining power is likely to be further strengthened. As a growing proportion of the Chinese labor force becomes proletarianized, the working class consciousness and organizational capacity will continue to grow. At some point, Chinese workers will begin to make not only economic demands but also political demands.

This raises the question whether the economic and political demands of Chinese workers can be accommodated by China's current capitalist system. If not, can the contradiction between the working class and the capitalist class be contained

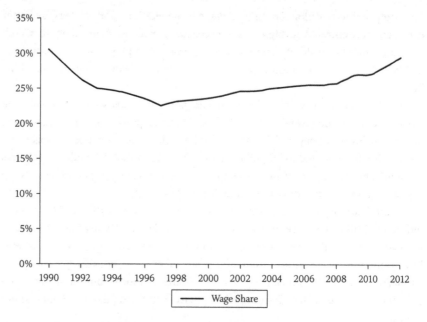

Figure 2.2 China's Wage Share (Total Wages as % of Non-Agricultural GDP, 1990–2012)

Sources: Total wages are the sum of the total wages of the urban non-private units employees, the urban private units employees, the urban unregistered workers, and the rural local non-agricultural workers. Data are from the National Bureau of Statistics of China (2013 and earlier years, 2014a). It is assumed that urban unregistered workers and rural local non-agricultural workers are paid the same wages as the migrant workers. It is assumed that before 2008, urban private units employees were paid 90 percent of the urban collective units' wages; urban unregistered workers and rural local non-agricultural workers were paid 70 percent of the urban collective units' wages.

within a reformed capitalist framework? Or, will the Chinese working class struggle bring about a fundamental social transformation that goes beyond the historical framework of capitalism?

The Socialist Legacy

The Chinese Revolution was based on the broad mobilization of the peasants and the workers. The post-revolutionary socialist state reflected this basic historical reality and was constructed on the basis of an implicit social contract that provided the peasants and the workers with a range of economic and social rights. State sector workers were provided with a comprehensive package of social security, known as the "iron rice bowl." In the early years of the Cultural Revolution, large sections of the population enjoyed *de facto* freedom of speech and association. Mass organizations took over power in many cities. Many were inspired by the aspiration for a truly democratic and egalitarian socialist society.

After the Cultural Revolution, state sector workers were politically disoriented. They were unprepared for the capitalist offensive in the 1990s and suffered a catastrophic defeat. But the memories of socialism did not die. Instead, the historical experience of socialism has helped to define the political and social expectations of the contemporary Chinese working class.

Since the 1990s, large sections of state sector workers have participated in anti-privatization struggles. In the anti-privatization struggles, some worker leaders have developed not only basic working class consciousness but also a certain level of socialist consciousness. These worker leaders consider themselves as participants in a broader political movement with the objective of replacing the current capitalist system with a socialist economic and social system.

According to a leading Chinese worker activist, compared to workers in many other countries, Chinese worker leaders have developed a "relatively complete class consciousness." They have had personal experiences under both the socialist and the capitalist system. They understand that the capitalist transition has destroyed the socialist social and economic rights that the working class once enjoyed (Zhang, Y. 2010).

In the words of "Master Wu" or Wu Jingtang, a worker leader of national reputation, "Chairman Mao led us to fight for the rivers and mountains [*da jiang shan*, that is, to fight for revolution or political power] and to build socialism. Chairman Mao gave the poor kids, like me, a certain standing in society. We were called the working class. We were masters of businesses, masters of the state. But now we workers have no say. Only the new capitalists count. Restore public ownership! This is our hope and this is our determination!" (Wu 2010).

Master Wu was a leader of the Tonghua Steel anti-privatization struggle in 2009. Tonghua Steel was a state-owned steel factory in Tonghua, Jilin Province. In 2005, Tonghua Steel was privatized. State-owned assets, worth 10 billion Yuan (about 1.5 billion US dollars), were appraised to be only 2 billion Yuan (about 300 million US dollars). Jianlong, a powerful private company having connections with high-ranking officials in Beijing, actually paid only 800 million Yuan (about 130 million dollars) and took over the factory.

Tonghua Steel had 36,000 workers before privatization. After privatization, 24,000 were laid off. Workers performing "dangerous tasks" (tasks with high rates of work-related injuries) used to be paid relatively high wages. After privatization, their wages were cut by two-thirds. The capitalist manager imposed various arbitrary penalties and punishments on the workers.

In 2007, the Tonghua Steel workers started to protest. During the protests, Master Wu emerged as one of the leaders. He made it clear to the workers that the real issue was not about individual grievances, but about "the political line of privatization."

In July 2009, the Tonghua workers went on general strike. The Jianlong general manager threatened to fire all workers. The furious workers beat the manger to death. The provincial governor came and thousands of armed police surrounded the workers. But no one dared to intervene. Shocked by the workers' mobilization, the provincial government was forced to reverse the privatization scheme (Wu 2013).

The Tonghua workers' struggle was a significant victory for the Chinese working class. It forced the Communist Party leadership to suspend large-scale privatization for several years and signaled a turning point in the relative balance of power between the workers and the capitalists.

In the 1990s, the state sector working class was isolated and disoriented, the migrant working class had little economic power (under the competitive pressure of a large rural surplus labor force), and the urban middle class embraced the capitalist transition. After the ruling elites solved their internal divisions, the state sector working class was left defenseless in a class war in which all measures of relations of forces were against them.

Since then, state sector workers have undertaken many anti-privatization struggles. In these struggles, a new generation of worker activists has emerged. They have gained political experience and consciousness in their struggles against the capitalists and the government. Many worker activists identify themselves as "Maoists" and have become politically active.

In the meantime, migrant workers have become the largest section of the Chinese working class. After years of struggle against capitalist exploitation, many migrant workers have developed a certain level of class consciousness and organizational capacity. Migrant workers' struggles have already pushed up the wage share and imposed pressures on the capitalist profit rate. In a few years, the growing economic and political demands of the migrant working class will be in conflict with the limited capacity of the Chinese capitalism to accommodate these demands.

In the 1980s and the 1990s, the urban middle class provided an important social base for the pro-capitalist "reform and openness." But since the early 2000s, many among the urban middle class have become victims of rising health care and education costs, surging housing prices, growing crimes, and environmental degradation. Many college graduates were unemployed and had to compete with migrant workers in the labor market. In this context, many intellectuals and college students have been attracted by anti-capitalist ideas and become leftist activists.

The Chinese New Left

In the 1980s, college students were considered a relatively privileged social group. College education provided a seemingly fair passageway for the young people from the workers' and the peasants' families in pursuit of upward social mobility.

In the 1990s, China undertook market-oriented "education reform." Many for-profit private colleges were established. The publicly owned colleges and universities were restructured as market-oriented institutions that became dependent on student tuitions and business donations rather than government funding as their main source of revenue. To increase revenue, universities and colleges competed with each other to expand student enrollment. College student enrollment (including both regular undergraduate programs and associate degree programs) grew from 280,000 in 1980, 610,000 in 1990, 2.2 million in 2000, to 6.9 million in 2012. College graduates grew from 150,000 in 1980, 610,000 in 1990, 950,000 in 2000, to 6.2 million in 2012 (data are from National Bureau of Statistics of China 2013 and earlier years).

The dramatic increase in college graduates has led to sharp devaluation of their bargaining power in the job market. In 2010, about a quarter of Chinese college students who graduated in the year were unemployed. Many college graduates live in slum-like conditions on the outskirts of China's major cities and are known as "ant tribes" (Hambides 2010).

Those college graduates who are "employed" often have to accept a wage that is no higher than that of an unskilled migrant worker. According to a survey by Beijing University, the national average monthly starting pay for college graduates in 2014 was expected to be 2,443 Yuan (about 400 US dollars). By comparison, in 2013, the national average monthly pay of migrant workers was 2,609 Yuan (about 430 US dollars). About 30 percent of college graduates depend on *ken lao* (originally a Cantonese word, meaning "eating" their parents or being dependent on their parents) to survive. Nearly 40 percent of college graduates have no savings at all (Xin Hua Wang 2014).

An anonymous college graduate posted his thoughts on the Internet about his "miserable life." After years of work, he found that he could not afford to buy a flat and it was beyond his financial capacity to marry his girlfriend and raise a child.

The young man asked himself: "Why do I need to have a girlfriend? Why do I need to have a child? Why do I need to care about my parents? Let us change our philosophy. If we do not care about our parents, do not marry, do not have children, do not need to buy flats, do not need to take buses, do not ever get sick, do not have any entertainment, do not ever buy lunch, we will have found the truth of a happy life! Society is driving us crazy. We cannot meet some simple basic needs. Are we wrong? We just want to survive" (Anonymous College Graduate 2008).

Compared to other Chinese college graduates, the anonymous college graduate complaining about his "miserable life" was actually lucky. He had a white-collar job paying 4,000 Yuan a month in 2008, about twice as high as the national average wage rate in China's urban formal sector.

Since the 1990s, many of China's college graduates have seen their "middle class dreams" smashed and have undergone a process of proletarianization. To these young people, the promise of a "free" and prosperous capitalism is no more than empty words.

In the 1980s, many Chinese intellectuals and college students were attracted by neoliberal ideas, taking the promise of free market capitalism seriously. By the second half of the 1990s, observing the rapid increase in economic and social inequality, some leading Chinese intellectuals began to question the neoliberal model of economic development. They became known as the "New Left" intellectuals.

By the early 2000s, leftist ideas were no longer limited to university campuses. Progressive intellectuals, radicalized students, worker activists with experience in anti-privatization struggles, old Communist Party cadres who kept their commitment to socialism, and old rebels in the Cultural Revolution, merged into a broadly based leftist social movement. Most of the new Chinese leftists accept Mao Zedong's theory on "the continuing revolution under the dictatorship of the proletariat" and consider China's "reform and openness" as "capitalist restoration." In this sense, most of the new Chinese leftists consider themselves as "Maoists."

The global capitalist crisis of 2008–2009 undermined many people's faith in the neoliberal capitalism. After 2009, the influence of the Maoist left grew rapidly. By 2011, three Maoist websites, *Wuyou Zhi Xiang* (the Utopia), *Mao Zedong Qizhi* (Mao Zedong Flag), and *Hongse Zhongguo* (Red China), had gained national reputation. In 2010 and 2011, workers and students in hundreds of cities organized spontaneous mass meetings to commemorate Mao Zedong, often in the face of local government opposition and harassment. Many of these mass meetings turned into anti-capitalist mass protests (Wuyou Wangkan 2011).

By 2011, a popular anti-capitalist alliance that included leftist intellectuals, radical students, state sector workers, migrant workers, old Communist Party cadres, and old Cultural Revolution rebels began to take shape. This took place when Chinese capitalism was rapidly losing its political legitimacy.

The Illegitimacy of Chinese Capitalism

A large portion of Chinese capitalist wealth derived from the plunder of the state and collective assets accumulated in the socialist era. Because of this historical origin, much of this wealth is considered illegitimate by the general population.

According to one estimate, during the process of privatization and market liberalization, about 30 trillion Yuan (5 trillion US dollars) of state and collective assets were transferred to capitalists with strong government connections (Qi 2006). In 2006, China had about 3,200 people with personal property worth greater than 100 million Yuan (about 15 million US dollars). Of the 3,200 people, about 2,900 or 90 percent were children of senior Party and state officials. Their combined assets were estimated to be 20 trillion Yuan (about 3 trillion US dollars), about the size of China's GDP in 2006 (Zhang and Jiang 2010).

According to a report published in 2013, China's "grey income" amounted to 6.2 trillion Yuan (about 1 trillion US dollars) or 12 percent of China's GDP in 2011. The author of the report believed that most of the grey income derived from corruption and theft of public assets (Wang, X. 2013).

In October 2012, the *New York Times* published a detailed report that was highly embarrassing for the Chinese government. The *New York Times*, by studying China's corporate and regulatory records, revealed that Wen Jiabao's family had accumulated assets worth at least 2.7 billion US dollars (Barboza 2012). The *New York Times* report makes it clear that corruption and theft of state assets are taking place at the very top of the Chinese ruling class.

Pervasive corruption undermines not only the legitimacy of Chinese capitalism but also the ability of the ruling class to safeguard its own class interest. In 2011, Sun Liping (one of China's leading sociologists) commented that "Chinese society is decaying at an accelerating rate." According to Sun, members of the Chinese ruling elites are completely driven by their personal and short-term interests so that no one cares about the long-term interests of Chinese capitalism. Corruption has "run out of control" and has become "ungovernable" (Sun 2011).

The Chongqing Model

In the late 1980s, Communist Party ruling elites were confronted with a major political and economic crisis. The underlying contradiction had to do with the incompatibility between the remaining elements of the socialist social contract established after the 1949 Revolution and the necessity for emerging Chinese capitalism to compete effectively in the global capitalist market.

In the historical era of neoliberalism and global counter-revolution, China had to compete effectively in order to consolidate and improve its relative position in the capitalist world system. Even with the industrial foundation built in the Maoist era, China was in no position to compete with the western core capitalist countries on the technology front. China was not able to benefit from any significant monopolistic rent based on high-value natural resources (unlike the Middle East oil exporters, large Latin American economies, or the Russian Federation). The only realistic "comparative advantage" China could rely upon was to combine the Maoist industrial foundation and a large cheap labor force and turn itself into the center of manufacturing exports in the global capitalist economy. China's pursuit of manufacturing exports coincided with the global capital relocation that took place in the late twentieth century and played a crucial role in changing the global balance of power in favor of the global capitalist classes, helping global capitalism to overcome the system-wide crisis of the 1970s.

The only conceivable alternative would require the Chinese Party and state elites to give up a substantial portion of their material privileges. By sharing material hardships with the working class and continuing to provide workers and peasants with basic social security, the Communist Party leadership might be able to convince the great majority of the population to live within a relatively closed socialist system for a prolonged period of time. If China were to follow this alternative path, it might create a relatively favorable political environment for a new wave of global revolution when neoliberal capitalism enters its own major crisis.

The Cuban experience after 1990 has demonstrated that it is possible for a socialist state surrounded by neoliberal capitalism to maintain the basic socialist framework for several decades, provided that the Communist Party leadership was willing to sacrifice its own material interests. But in the absence of a major socialist revolution in a big country, even Cuba has been under growing pressure to undertake neoliberal-style "economic reform".

In China, with the end of the Cultural Revolution, the majority of the Party and state bureaucrats had abandoned their original revolutionary ideals. Any development strategy that demanded the sacrifices of the ruling elites became politically unfeasible. After the "Tiananmen Massacre" of 1989, the Communist Party ruling elites had secured the political subservience of the urban middle class. By 1992, the ruling elites reached the consensus to respond to the post-1989 domestic and international crisis by accelerating the transition to capitalism.

From 2000 to 2008, China enjoyed rapid economic growth with an average annual economic growth rate of 10.6 percent. The Chinese economy was more than doubled and became the world's second largest economy. China's rapid economic growth was based on the intense exploitation of a large cheap labor force and the rapid expansion of exports to western markets. It was underpinned by the massive increase in coal consumption and the acceleration of environmental degradation.

The global economic crisis of 2008–2009 brought the double-digit growth of the Chinese capitalist economy to an end. By 2011, it was clear that the western capitalist economy would struggle with economic stagnation for a long time and might never return to the "normal" conditions before the Great Recession. The state sector workers' anti-privatization struggles and the workers' strikes in the export-oriented manufacturing sectors suggested that working class militancy was growing and the regime of cheap labor exploitation was not sustainable in the long run. There was also growing concern about China's various ecological systems, which were rapidly approaching total collapse.

A serious debate took place within the Communist Party leadership regarding the best strategy to respond to the rapidly intensifying economic, social, and ecological contradictions. One faction, led by Bo Xilai, advocated greater state control of the economy and some redistribution of wealth from the capitalist class to the working class under the political slogan of "*Gongtong Fuyu* (common prosperity)."

Bo Xilai is one of the sons of Bo Yibo, one of the "first-generation" Chinese revolutionary leaders. In 2007, Bo Xilai was appointed as the Party Secretary of the Municipality of Chongqing and a member of the Politburo of the Chinese Communist Party. Chongqing was Nationalist China's wartime capital from 1937 to 1945. In the Maoist era, Chongqing was an industrial center with a high concentration of industrial working class. In 1997, Chongqing became China's fourth "directly administered municipality" with a provincial status.

Because of growing corruption and the neoliberal "economic reform" that weakened the state, China's internal political and social conditions have evolved to resemble what are often observed in many peripheral countries in the capitalist world system. State power at the local level has been greatly weakened. In many parts of China, local governments no longer perform the function of securing public safety. The power vacuum was filled by traditional clans, underground religions, sects (such as Falun Gong), and mafias. Before Bo Xilai came to Chongqing, a criminal network that included corrupt government officials, local capitalists, and mafia bosses controlled local politics.

Bo Xilai launched a massive anti-corruption and anti-crime campaign, known as the *Da Hei* (Striking the Black) movement. Many other Chinese provinces had launched anti-corruption and anti-crime campaigns. But those campaigns were little more than political showcases. None of them had achieved the effectiveness of Bo Xilai's *Da Hei* movement. When Bo Xilai came to Chongqing, he brought with him some loyal police officers. In the *Da Hei* movement, the Chongqing police actively sought support from the general public. This was associated with the Maoist strategy of "mass line" (relying upon and mobilizing the "masses" in order to achieve the Party's political objectives), which had been abandoned by the Communist Party leadership for many years. Most importantly, Bo Xilai was willing to confront the mafia-connected local capitalist class. The *Da Hei* movement was very successful. Public safety in Chongqing was evidently improved and Bo Xilai himself became immensely popular among the Chongqing residents.

Chang Hong (Singing the Red) was another important component of Bo Xilai's "Chongqing Model." *Chang Hong* referred to the Chongqing government's official campaign to promote socialist-oriented "red songs" and "red culture." Singing the red songs directly appealed to the working class masses which had been victims in the capitalist transition. *Chang Hong* took place when nostalgia for Maoist socialism was growing rapidly among various disenfranchised social groups. The *Chang Hong* movement may be seen as an implicit critique of the official Party line of "reform and openness."

In economic policy, Bo Xilai promoted a state-led model of development. The Chongqing government created eight state-led investment corporations, supervising about 1,000 local state-owned enterprises. These were used as the government's strategic instruments to achieve various economic and social objectives. About three million rural residents were provided with *Chengzhen Hukou* (urban residence) along with access to urban employment, pensions, public rental housing, education, and health care (Zhao, Y. 2012). Under Bo Xilai's leadership, Chongqing achieved one of the highest economic growth rates among all provincial-level regions and income inequality declined (Chongqing Ribao 2012).

By 2011, Bo Xilai emerged as the leader of the Communist Party faction arguing for an alternative to the neoliberal capitalist model. According to the neoliberal ideology, the government should let the capitalists "make the cake first" and wealth would trickle down to the general population later. Bo Xilai criticized the neoliberal doctrine, arguing that without a fair distribution of the cake first, the growth of the "cake" would be undermined (Zhao, Y. 2012).

From the beginning, Bo Xilai's experiment was met with strong opposition by the neoliberal faction in the Communist Party. Anglo-American news outlets, Chinese overseas websites (including right-wing websites funded by the US National Endowment for Democracy and Falun Gong media), and the so-called "liberal" media within China joined forces to portray Bo Xilai and the Chongqing Model as an attempt to revive the Cultural Revolution. Some right-wing "liberal" media portrayed Bo Xilai's *Da Hei* movement as fascist lawlessness (Zhao, Y. 2012).

On February 6, 2012, Wang Lijun, Chongqing's police chief, suddenly went into the US consulate at Chengdu (the capital city of Sichuan Province) and demanded political asylum. On April 10, Bo Xilai was stripped of his membership in the Central Committee and the Politburo of the Communist Party. The official announcement also revealed that Gu Kailai, Bo Xilai's wife, was involved in the murder of Neil Heywood. Heywood was a British businessman who had provided information to the British intelligence agency (BBC 2012).

What actually happened behind all of the drama remains unclear. But many Chinese would not be too surprised if future historians find out that before the Wang Lijun incident, the neoliberal faction within the Communist Party leadership had conspired for months to find a politically convenient way to eliminate Bo Xilai as an opponent. The Wang Lijun incident certainly served their political purpose.

The neoliberal faction within the Party had won a decisive victory. But the future development of Chinese politics may reveal that, by purging Bo Xilai from the Party, Communist Party leadership may have foregone their last and best opportunity to resolve China's rapidly escalating economic and social contradictions in a relatively peaceful manner.

China: How Far Away from Crisis?

As a country undergoes industrialization and urbanization, a growing proportion of the labor force tends to be proletarianized (becoming urbanized wage workers). The proletarianized working class has the capacity to demand higher incomes and more political and social rights. If a country is unable to meet these demands while maintaining sufficient economic resources for capital accumulation, the country is likely to suffer from both an accumulation crisis and a socio-political crisis. This happened to Brazil, South Korea, Poland, and many other semi-peripheral countries from the 1980s to the 1990s.

Like China, Brazil is a large "emerging economy." From 1964 to 1985, Brazil was ruled by military dictatorship. In the 1970s, the Brazilian economy grew rapidly and was considered one of the "economic miracles." By 1982, Brazil was hit by the Latin American debt crisis. Brazil entered into an era of economic and political instability.

In 1975, Luiz Inácio da Silva (Lula) was elected the president of the Brazilian Steel Workers' Union. Lula helped to organize several major strikes. In 1980, the Brazilian Workers' Party (*Partido dos Trabalhadores*, or PT) was founded. In 1989, Lula ran for the President of Brazil on a program of immediate land reform and default of foreign debt and won 47 percent of the vote in the second round.

In the 1970s, South Korea became a leading "newly industrializing country," one of the "Asian tigers." Korean economic success was based on export-led manufacturing. In 1979, South Korean dictator Park Chung-hee was assassinated. In 1980, popular uprisings erupted in the city of Gwangju, which were brutally repressed. In 1987, South Korea began democratic transition under the pressure of workers' strikes and student demonstrations. By the late 1990s, South Korean capitalism was shaken by the Asian financial crisis and massive workers' strikes.

In the 1960s, the Polish socialist economy was relatively successful. However, in 1970, the Polish government attempted to raise food prices to overcome its fiscal crisis. Mass demonstrations forced the government to cancel the food price increase and Władysław Gomulka, the First Secretary of the Polish United Workers' Party, resigned. The new Communist leadership under Gierek attempted to accommodate the working class demands by raising the workers' wages and importing consumer goods. Poland borrowed capital from western banks, hoping to pay back the foreign debt by increasing exports. But western demands for Polish exports declined during the global economic recession and Polish foreign debt rose rapidly.

By July 1980, under the pressure of western banks, the Polish government was forced to raise the price of consumer goods. Within a month, Poland was overwhelmed by waves of strikes and factory occupations. Political instability continued through the rest of the 1980s. By 1990, Lech Wałęsa (the leader of the Solidarity movement) became the Polish president. In the following years, Poland went through economic and social disasters under the neoliberal economic restructuring known as "shock therapy."

Figure 2.3 compares the share of non-agricultural employment in the total employment in Brazil, China, South Korea, and Poland from 1980 to 2012. Non-agricultural employment is used as an approximate indicator of the degree of proletarianization of a country's labor force.

In the 1980s, non-agricultural employment reached 70–80 percent of the total employment in Brazil, South Korea, and Poland. From 1980 to 2012, China's non-agricultural employment rose from 31 percent to 66 percent of total employment, with an average growth rate of about 1 percentage point a year. At this rate, China's non-agricultural employment will approach 75 percent of total employment by 2020 and may exceed 80 percent by 2025. By 2020, China will have a level of proletarianization comparable to that in Brazil, South Korea, and Poland in the 1980s.

Based on the historical experience of Brazil, South Korea, and Poland, when China's non-agricultural employment reaches the range of 70–80 percent of total

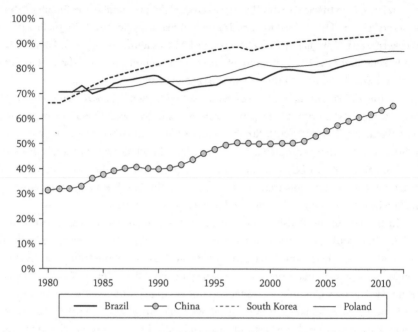

Figure 2.3 Non-Agricultural Employment (% of Total Employment, 1980–2012)
Source: World Bank (2014).

employment, the political and economic demands of the Chinese working class and the urban middle class may begin to exceed the capacity of the Chinese regime of capital accumulation to accommodate. This incompatibility will lead to an accumulation crisis and a socio-political crisis.

In the case of Brazil, South Korea, and Poland, their crises happened when global revolution was in retreat and neoliberalism was advancing in every geographic area in the world. The crises were all resolved within the capitalist framework by reestablishing favorable economic and political conditions required for capital accumulation.

Brazilian economic and political conditions remained unstable until the early 2000s. By then, the global commodity boom (driven by China's rapid economic growth) provided Brazilian capitalism (under the progressive Lula government) with the economic resources to achieve both acceleration of economic growth and expansion of progressive social programs.

After the 1997 financial crisis, South Korean capitalism underwent a restructuring. Low-end manufacturing production was relocated to China, allowing South Korean capitalists to specialize in higher value-added activities. After the economic disasters in the 1990s, the Polish economy recovered. By the early 2000s, Poland was integrated into the European capitalist market, becoming a supplier of cheap labor force to the core European countries.

Unlike Brazil, South Korea, and Poland in the 1980s, the coming economic and political crisis of Chinese capitalism will take place as the structural crisis of the global capitalist system is approaching.

The following chapters will argue that the coming crisis for both Chinese capitalism and global capitalism is unlikely to be resolved within the historical framework of capitalism.

3

ECONOMIC CRISIS
Cyclical and Structural

An often-heard argument in favor of capitalism is that capitalism is supposed to be a uniquely flexible and resilient system. From time to time, the capitalist economy would fall into crisis. But capitalism has always found a way to recover from a crisis and rebuild conditions for capital accumulation on increasingly larger scales. In this sense, crisis may be seen as an indispensable mechanism regulating capitalist life processes, eliminating the inefficient and wasteful elements while making the system stronger and healthier.

However, according to Immanuel Wallerstein, the world system theorist, there is nothing unique about capitalist "flexibility" or "resilience." Every economic, social, or physical system relies upon "cyclical rhythms" to restore "equilibrium." But in addition to "cyclical rhythms," there are "secular trends" that over time change the parameters of operation of the system. At some point, the underlying parameters diverge from the equilibrium so much that the equilibrium can no longer be restored. The system starts to undergo wider and more violent fluctuations, forcing the system into "bifurcation" (Wallerstein 2000b: 437).

The "cyclical rhythms" that capitalism has relied upon to keep itself not too far away from equilibrium have included short-term business cycles, "long waves," and "hegemonic cycles."

Business Cycles

The profit rate is a crucial economic indicator of how well a capitalist economy is performing. High and rising profit rates encourage capitalists to increase investment and hiring, leading to rapid economic growth and high levels of employment. Low and falling profit rates discourage capitalist investment, leading to sluggish economic growth and rising unemployment.

If the profit rate falls below a certain critical level, capitalist investment may collapse, causing a general contraction of economic activities, known to economists as "recession." The alternating pattern between expansion and recession is known as a "business cycle," with each cycle lasting several years.

Profit rate is defined as the ratio of profit over the capital stock invested by the capitalists:

Profit Rate = Profit / Capital Stock

Profit rate can be analyzed as the product of the profit share and the output–capital ratio:

$$\text{Profit Rate} = (\text{Profit} / \text{Economic Output}) * (\text{Economic Output} / \text{Capital Stock})$$
$$= \text{Profit Share} * \text{Output–Capital Ratio}$$

Capitalist economic expansion is usually motivated by rising and high profit rates. But in the process of capitalist accumulation, it tends to generate one or several tendencies that would undermine the conditions of accumulation by lowering the profit rate.

One of such tendencies is known as "profit squeeze." As capitalist economic expansion proceeds, it tends to increase the demand for labor. If a capitalist economy grows sufficiently rapidly, the demand for labor would outpace the supply; reducing the pool of unemployed and underemployed workers (what Marx called "the industrial reserve army of labor," see Marx 1967[1867]: 574–606). The depletion of the "reserve army of labor" gives the workers stronger bargaining power, pushing up wages and making it more difficult for capitalists to control the labor process. Both higher wages and weakened capitalist control tend to reduce the profit share. If the output–capital ratio is held constant, lower profit share would translate into lower profit rate.

Another tendency is known as "under-consumption" which works in the opposite direction. If capitalist power is too strong and capitalists exploit workers intensively, the workers' wages would decline or grow more slowly than the overall economic output. In this case, the workers' demand for mass consumer goods would fall behind the overall economic growth, leading to the problem of "under-consumption." At some point, demand for capital goods would also decline as capitalists in the consumer goods sector reduce investment in response to over-production. When both consumption and investment decline, the overall output–capital ratio would fall (because the economic output contracts in response to lower "effective demand" but the capital stock stays unchanged in the short run), leading to a falling profit rate and economic crisis (for a summary of Marxist theory on capitalist crisis tendencies, see Devine 1987).

Thus, capitalist economic crisis could happen if the capitalist class is either too "weak" or too "strong" relative to the working class. However, in terms of short-term business cycles, economic crises are to some extent self-correcting. If the crisis is caused by strong working class bargaining power and falling profit share, crisis would lead to rising unemployment, undermining the workers' bargaining power. As wages fall and the workers who are lucky to get jobs are forced to work harder, the profit rate would recover, leading to the next phase of economic expansion.

In the nineteenth century, many economic crises were caused by under-consumption. Many Marxist theorists at the time thought that under-consumption economic crisis would eventually lead to the breakdown of capitalism. However, since the mid-twentieth century, institutional changes have made capitalism less vulnerable to traditional forms of under-consumption crisis. Unemployment subsidies and welfare state institutions help to stabilize working class purchasing power during recessions. A big government sector and Keynesian macroeconomic policy help to sustain the overall effective demand. However, with the rise of neoliberalism, the conditions that had historically contributed to under-consumption economic crises (such as falling real wages and rising inequality) have again become prominent features of contemporary capitalism.

Long Waves and Hegemonic Cycles

Global capitalist economy has experienced longer-term alternations between rapid economic growth and sluggish economic growth, with the full cycle lasting approximately 50 years. The 50-year long cycle is often known as "Kondratiev long waves," named after the Soviet economist Nikolai Kondratiev who first proposed the concept.

Marxist economists have related the long waves to institutional changes and stages of capitalist development. During the A-phase of a long wave (the phase of rapid growth), a certain set of economic, political, and social institutions provided favorable conditions for capital accumulation. However, due to changing historical conditions and the internal contradictions of the prevailing institutions, the various economic, political, and social institutions were eroded. During the B-phase (the phase of sluggish growth and major economic crisis), the exiting institutions disintegrated. Intense conflicts between social classes and states broke out. The outcome of these conflicts would determine the next set of institutions that would recreate favorable conditions for capital accumulation (Gordon, Weisskopf, and Bowles 1987; Bowles, Edwards, Roosevelt 2005: 158–164).

Giovanni Arrighi argued that the evolution of global capitalism had involved even longer cyclical movements, with each cycle lasting between 150 and 250 years. According to Arrighi, the expansion and reproduction of the capitalist world system has required the successive recreation of increasingly more powerful hegemonic powers. The rise and fall of a hegemonic power constituted what Arrighi called a "systemic cycle of accumulation" (Arrighi 1994).

Each hegemonic cycle consisted of a "material expansion" phase and a "financial expansion" phase. In the material expansion phase, the rising hegemonic power led the creation of a new set of geopolitical and organizational conditions, leading to rising profit rates and rapid expansion of material production. With rising costs and growing competition, capital became over-accumulated and the profit rate declined. The incumbent hegemonic power entered into what Arrighi called the "signal crisis."

In response to the "signal crisis," the incumbent hegemonic power would transfer capital from material production to financial accumulation. The phase of financial expansion allowed the incumbent hegemonic power to re-inflate its power and wealth, but only temporarily. In the long run, financial expansion tended to deepen the accumulation crisis and intensify the inter-state conflicts, culminating in the "terminal crisis" which brought a hegemonic cycle to its end.

Figure 3.1 and 3.2 shows the long-term movement of the profit rate for the United Kingdom and the United States, the hegemonic powers in the nineteenth century and the twentieth century respectively.

In the nineteenth century, the United Kingdom led the "material expansion" of the global capitalist economy. The industrial revolution in the nineteenth century was based on the massive consumption of coal and the intense exploitation of the western working classes. The British monopoly over world industry and the British colonial empire in India ensured high profit rates for the British capitalists.

By the 1870s, British hegemonic power was challenged by newly industrialized powers, especially the United States and Germany. Heavy investment in capital-intensive industries led to widespread over-capacity, depressing prices and profits. In response, the leading capitalist powers undertook a new wave of colonization, in search for new markets, cheap raw materials, and a cheap labor force. From 1875 to 1914, European imperialist powers added 24 million square kilometers (9 million

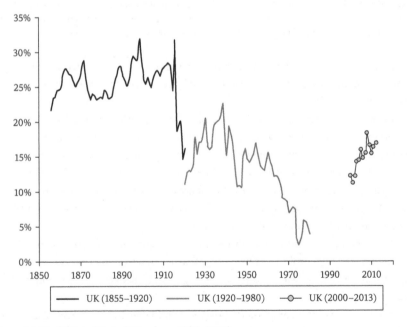

Figure 3.1 Profit Rate (United Kingdom, 1855–2013)

Source: See Appendix of Chapter 3. The profit rate series from 1855 to 1920; from 1920 to 1980; and from 2000 to 2013 are constructed from different sources and are not completely comparable. The profit rate is defined as the ratio of total capitalist profit over the estimated business sector net stock of fixed capital (including private non-residential fixed capital and public corporate sector fixed capital). For 1855 to 1920, the total capitalist profit includes net property income from abroad.

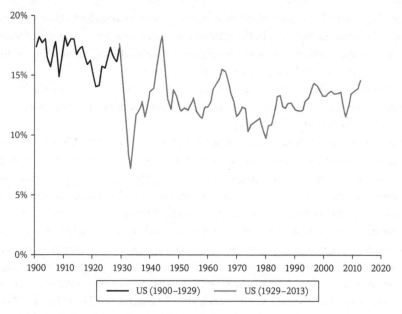

Figure 3.2 Profit Rate (United States, 1900–2013)

Source: See Appendix of Chapter 3. The profit rate series from 1900 to 1929 and from 1929 to 2013 are constructed from different sources and are not completely comparable. The profit rate is defined as the ratio of the total capitalist profit over the net stock of private non-residential fixed assets.

square miles) to their colonial territories. The entire Asian and African continents were turned into colonies of western imperialist powers or their spheres of influence (Stavrianos 1981: 264).

In this period, the focus of British capital accumulation shifted from "material expansion" towards "financial expansion." Profits from overseas financial investments became a major source of income for the British capitalist class. British net property income from abroad surged from 35 million pounds in 1870, 104 million pounds in 1900, to 200 million pounds in 1913. As a share of British gross national product, net property income from abroad rose from 3.7 percent in 1870, 5.8 percent in 1900, to 8.6 percent in 1913 (Mitchell 1988: 828–830).

The re-inflation of British wealth and power in the early twentieth century was reflected by the high profit rates British capitalists enjoyed in this period. From 1886 to 1915, the economy-wide profit rate was generally between 25 percent and 32 percent.

The rivalry between imperialist powers culminated in the "Great War," with massive calamities humanity had never seen before. Towards the end of World War I, the British economy was bankrupt and the profit rate collapsed. By the 1920s, the United States had already become the world's largest industrialized economy as well as the largest creditor. But the United States was not yet ready to replace Britain as the regulator of the global capitalist economy.

The American economic boom in the 1920s was fueled by financial speculation which ended with the stock market crash in 1929. Under the gold standard, the prevailing international monetary system at the time, central banks were forced to raise interest rates in order to maintain convertibility between gold and national currencies. The contractionary monetary policy deepened the Great Depression.

In September 1931, the Bank of England ceased exchanging gold for British pounds, allowing British pounds to depreciate and interest rates to fall. By leaving the gold standard, the British economy was able to recover earlier and more strongly than other advanced capitalist economies. In 1938, the British profit rate reached another peak at 23 percent.

By the end of World War II, the United States had established unquestionable industrial and military supremacy over the capitalist world system. On the other hand, World War II destroyed what remained of British industrial superiority.

The United States led a successful restructuring of the capitalist world system. Based on cheap and abundant oil, global capitalist economy entered a period of unprecedented rapid expansion, which became known as the "golden age." In the first half of the 1960s, the United States enjoyed high and rising profit rates (the US profit rate peaked at about 15 percent in 1965). On the other hand, the British profit rate declined sharply in the 1960s.

By the 1970s, British capitalism was in deep crisis. The economy struggled between deep recessions and high inflation. There was widespread working class militancy. The Labour government increased tax rates to pay for rising social spending. The economy-wide profit rate plummeted to less than 5 percent.

The Labour Party, which was traditionally in favor of social reform within the capitalist system, was unable to solve the crisis. The Thatcher government took over power in 1979 and implemented a full package of neoliberal economic policy, including monetarist macroeconomic policy (designed to undermine workers' power by generating high unemployment), privatization, deregulation, and a "flexible" labor market (weakening the trade unions). In 1985, the Thatcher government defeated the coal miners' strike which had lasted for a year. The British labor movement was decisively weakened.

By 2000, Britain's economy-wide profit rate recovered to 12 percent. By 2008, Britain's profit rate surged to 18 percent, exceeding the previous peak reached in 1954 (when the profit rate was 17 percent).

Like British capitalism a century ago, American capitalism responded to the 1970s crisis by shifting its capital from material production to financial accumulation. In the early 1980s, both the United States and Britain practiced monetarist macroeconomic policies. Interest rates were raised to unprecedented levels. High interest rates allowed financial capital to accumulate more rapidly than industrial capital.

However, unlike British capitalism in the late nineteenth century, net profits from overseas investments were not a major part of American capitalist profits in the late twentieth century. By the 1990s, the United States had become the world's largest net debtor and began to run large current account deficits to absorb the excess production from the rest of the world.

Since the Great Recession of 2009, the US profit rate has recovered strongly. But the US economy has ceased to be the leading engine of the global capitalist economy. Instead, China has been driving the global economic growth. Will China be able to lead a successful restructuring of the capitalist world system as the United States did after 1945?

In addition to China's internal class struggle, the answer to this question will depend on how the various "parameters" of the capitalist world system have been transformed over the past several centuries.

Tendency for the Rate of Profit to Fall?

Historically, short-term and long-term cyclical movements have provided the mechanisms through which global capitalism has continually reproduced its own basic laws of motion. But as global capitalism expands through short-term and long-term cycles, various economic, political, social, and ecological parameters have been transformed. It is by studying how these parameters have been transformed that one can begin to grasp the historical limit of capitalism.

In *Capital*, volume 3, Marx famously proposed the "law of the tendency for the rate of profit to fall," a "law" that may be more appropriately called a theoretical hypothesis. According to Marx, capitalist technological progress had a strong tendency towards mechanization (substitution of fixed capital for labor). As capitalist production became more and more capital intensive, the "organic composition of capital" would tend to rise, driving down the profit rate (Marx 1967[1894]: 211–266).

Using today's statistical concept, what Marx called the "organic composition of capital" (the value of capital invested in the means of production relative to the value of capital invested on labor power) can be represented by the ratio of capital stock over economic output. That is, it is the inverse of the output–capital ratio (the ratio of economic output over capital stock). The hypothetical tendency towards rising "organic composition of capital" is equivalent to a tendency towards falling output–capital ratio. From the formula of the profit rate (see the section on "Business Cycles"), it is easy to see that if the output–capital ratio tends to fall and if the profit share is held constant (or moving within a limited range), the profit rate would tend to fall.

What does the available statistical evidence say about Marx's hypothesis? Figure 3.3 shows the long-term movement of the output–capital ratio (measured by the ratio of gross national product over the net stock of non-residential fixed assets) of five advanced capitalist economies from the mid-eighteenth century to the late twentieth century.

From 1760 to 1850, Britain's output–capital ratio declined by 68 percent. But from 1850 to 1937, Britain's output–capital ratio rose strongly, with a cumulative

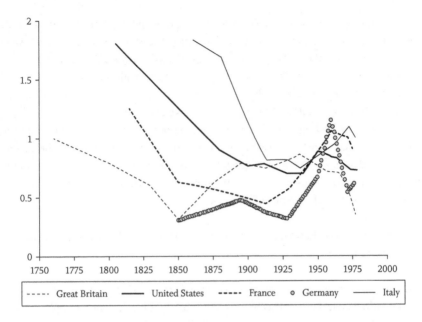

Figure 3.3 Output–Capital Ratio (Leading Capitalist Economies, 1760–1978)

Source: Goldsmith (1985: 195–304). The output–capital ratio presented in this graph is defined as the ratio of gross national product over the net stock of non-residential fixed assets, including private and public non-residential structures and equipment.

increase by 174 percent. Since then it had tended to fall again. By 1977, Britain's output–capital ratio declined by 60 percent from the 1937 level and returned to the level of the mid-nineteenth century.

The US output–capital ratio declined from a very high ratio of 1.81 in 1805 to 0.77 in 1900, with a cumulative decline of 58 percent. It declined further to 0.7 in 1929. By 1950, the US output–capital ratio rose to 0.89. By 1978, it fell to 0.73. Overall, the US output–capital ratio stabilized between the early twentieth century and the late twentieth century.

Italy's output–capital ratio declined by 56 percent from 1862 to 1914. It stabilized during the early twentieth century and rose strongly between 1938 and 1973. France's output–capital ratio declined by 64 percent from 1815 to 1913. From 1913 to 1960, France's output–capital ratio rose strongly from 0.44 to 1.06, before falling back to 0.91 by 1976.

The historical trajectory of Germany's output–capital ratio had been somewhat erratic. It started at the very low ratio of 0.3 in 1850. It rose to 0.48 by 1895 and fell back to 0.31 by 1929. Since then, it had risen strongly and jumped to 1.15 by 1960, before falling sharply to 0.54 by 1972.

Overall, there is evidence suggesting that for the advanced capitalist economies (with the exception of Germany), the output–capital ratio did tend to fall in the early phase of industrialization. From the mid-eighteenth century to the mid-nineteenth century, the leading capitalist economies' output–capital ratios started at levels between 1 and 1.8. By the early twentieth century, the ratios fell to a range between 0.4 and 0.8. Since then, the US output–capital ratios had stabilized and Britain's output–capital had declined. The French, German, and Italian output–capital ratios rose strongly from the 1930s to the 1960s. By the 1970s, the leading capitalist economies' output–capital ratios were in the range of 0.4 to 1.

Why did the leading capitalist economies' output–capital ratios stabilize during the twentieth century? To answer this question, we need to consider the factors that would determine the output–capital ratio in the long run. The rise or fall of the output–capital ratio depends on the difference between the growth rate of economic output and the growth rate of capital stock:

> Output–Capital Ratio Growth Rate = Economic Growth Rate – Capital Stock's Growth Rate

If the economic growth rate is greater than the capital stock's growth rate, the output–capital ratio would rise. If the economic growth rate is lower than the capital stock's growth rate, the output–capital ratio would fall.

The capital stock's growth rate is the ratio of the net increase in capital stock over the level of capital stock. The net increase in capital stock is the same as the net investment in new capital goods. Net investment is gross investment less depreciation of fixed capital. Thus:

> Capital Stock's Growth Rate = Net Investment / Capital Stock = (Net Investment / Economic Output) * (Economic Output / Capital Stock) = (Net Investment / Economic Output) * Output–Capital Ratio

Therefore, the capital stock's growth rate is positively related to the output–capital ratio. If the economic growth rate is greater than the capital stock's growth rate, the output–capital ratio would rise. However, as the output–capital ratio rises, the capital stock's growth will gradually accelerate. At some point, the capital stock's growth rate will rise to a level that is equal to the economic growth rate. When the capital stock's growth rate equals the economic growth rate, the output–capital ratio stabilizes, reaching "equilibrium."

If the economic growth rate is smaller than the capital stock's growth rate, the output–capital ratio would fall. However, as the output–capital ratio falls, the capital stock's growth will gradually decelerate. At some point, the capital stock's growth rate will fall to a level that is equal to the economic growth rate. At that point, the output–capital ratio would stabilize and be in "equilibrium."

Thus, either way, in the long run, there is a tendency for the output–capital ratio to converge towards an equilibrium level where the economic growth rate equals the capital stock's growth rate:

Economic Growth Rate = Capital Stock's Growth Rate

Substitute the formula for the capital stock's growth rate into the above equation:

Economic Growth Rate = (Net Investment / Economic Output) * Output–Capital Ratio

Re-arrange terms and the equilibrium output–capital ratio can be solved as follows:

Equilibrium Output–Capital Ratio = Economic Growth Rate / (Net Investment/Economic Output)

Thus, in the long run, the output–capital ratio is positively related to the long-term average economic growth rate but negatively related to the net investment–economic output ratio. In the early phase of capitalist development, net investment tended to rise as a share of economic output, driving down the output–capital ratio. In the 1950s and the 1960s, global capitalism enjoyed unprecedented rapid economic growth. The rapid economic growth rates pushed up the output–capital ratios.

Modern advanced capitalist economies on average invest about 20 percent of their gross domestic product (GDP) on the purchase of new capital goods. Suppose that total productive and unproductive capital stock (including residential and government buildings) is about three times a country's GDP. If the depreciation rate is 4 percent, depreciation of fixed capital would subtract 12 percent of GDP. Thus, net investment would be about 8 percent of GDP. Out of the total net investment, about one-half is investment made by capitalist businesses. The rest is investment made by the government and households.

Thus, productive net investment is about 4 percent of economic output. If economic growth rate is 3 percent, then the output–capital ratio can stabilize at 0.75. But can the current economic growth rate be sustained indefinitely?

The End of Economic Growth? The Neoclassical Perspective

Traditional neoclassical economics assumes that economic growth can continue indefinitely. According to the neoclassical economic theory, economic growth is generated by inputs of "factors of production" (capital and labor) and technological progress (which raises the "total factor productivity").

In neoclassical theory, capital accumulation can raise economic growth in the short run. But in the long run, the pace of economic growth (especially the growth of per capita real income) is determined by the pace of technological progress. So long as technological progress continues, there is no reason to think that economic growth will come to an end.

However, in a recent research paper, Robert Gordon, a prestigious neoclassical economist specializing in economic growth, questioned this neoclassical assumption with some powerful historical evidence (Gordon 2012). Gordon argues that the rapid economic progress made over the past two and a half centuries may turn out to be "a unique episode in human history."

Gordon observes that there have been three industrial revolutions since 1750. The first industrial revolution, which invented steam engines and railroads, lasted from 1750 to 1830. The second industrial revolution, which invented electricity and internal combustion engines, lasted from 1870 to 1900 and had many spin-off inventions (such as airplanes, air conditioning, and interstate highways) that drove economic growth for much of the twentieth century. The third industrial revolution, which invented computers, the web, and mobile phones, lasted from 1960 to the present.

Gordon argues that the second industrial revolution was far more important than either the first or the third. The third industrial revolution has nearly run its course but has produced only a short-lived growth revival from 1996 to 2004. Many of the important inventions that took place in the second and third industrial revolution could only happen once in history.

In the future, we will have to face a world with fewer and less important innovations. Improvement in living standards will be further hampered by "six headwinds": the declining share of labor force in the population, the stagnation of educational attainment, rising inequality, competition from foreign workers (depressing wages of American workers), energy and environmental constraints, and heavily indebted households and government. Economic growth will slow down and eventually approach zero.

Gordon's argument can be illustrated by the historical growth performance of the United States, the hegemonic capitalist economy in the twentieth century. Figure 3.4 shows the historical and projected growth rates of the US per capita real GDP from 1800 to 2100. The growth rates are shown as 50-year moving average annual growth rates to smooth out the short-term business cycles as well as "long waves."

Before the nineteenth century, there was little economic growth. The average annual growth rate of the British per capita real GDP from 1700 to 1800 was only 0.3 percent. For the first half of the nineteenth century, the US per capita real GDP grew at an average annual rate of 0.7 percent. The US per capita real GDP growth rate accelerated from the mid-nineteenth century to the early twentieth century, reaching 1.9 percent for the half-century ending in 1926. After large fluctuations during the Great Depression and World War II, the US per capita real GDP growth rate continued to accelerate, peaking at 2.8 percent for the half-century ending in 1983.

Since 1983, the long-term tendency towards accelerating economic growth has been reversed and the US long-term average economic growth rates have trended downwards. Based on the current trend, the US long-term average economic growth rate will decline to 0.3 percent by the second half of the twenty-first century, returning to the growth rates in the eighteenth century. For all practical purposes, this would be the end of modern economic growth.

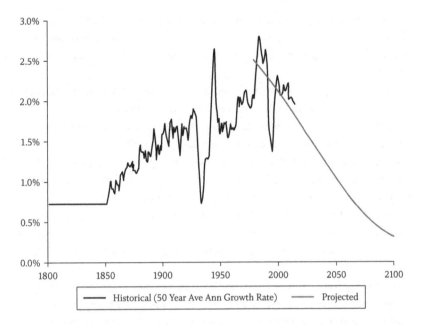

Figure 3.4 Long-Term Growth of Per Capita Real GDP (United States, 1800–2100)

Source: US per capita real GDP in constant 1990 international dollars from 1800 to 1990 is from Bold and Zanden (2013). This is linked to US per capita real GDP in constant 2011 international dollars from 1990 to 2013 (World Bank 2014). Growth rates in per capita real GDP are shown as 50-year moving average annual growth rates. Projections of future per capita real GDP are based on the historical trend of per capita real GDP from 1950 to 2013.

Capitalism is an economic system based on accumulation of capital on increasingly larger scales. If the economic growth rate approaches zero but the capitalists continue to invest in new capital, then the output–capital ratio would collapse. For example, if productive net investment is 4 percent of economic output but economic growth rate is only 0.5 percent, then the output–capital ratio would fall to 0.125. If output–capital ratio collapses, the profit rate would also collapse. If capitalists stop making investments in response to the collapse of the profit rate, the capitalist economy would cease to operate as a viable economic system (Chapter 5 will further discuss how the capitalist economy tends to fall into major crisis when the profit rate falls below a certain threshold).

Will Marx's hypothesis on the "tendency for the rate of profit to fall" made in the nineteenth century be verified by the structural crisis of capitalism in the twenty-first century?

The Structural Crisis of Capitalism?

Like Marx, Immanuel Wallerstein sees capitalism as a historically specific system that can operate only under a certain set of historical conditions. Being a system based on the endless accumulation of capital, the effective functioning of the capitalist system requires high profit rates, which in turn depend on the availability of a cheap labor force, cheap material inputs, and effective state with low taxes.

Wallerstein argues that as capitalism develops, there has been a tendency for the wage cost, the material cost, and the taxation cost to rise relative to the value of economic output. As the population moves from rural areas to the cities and as a growing proportion of the labor force becomes proletarianized working class, the workers demand higher living standards and more extensive political and social rights. The expansion of the global capitalist economy has depleted natural resources and degraded the environment, raising the costs of material inputs. Both workers and capitalists demand state interventions that would help to improve their conditions relative to the workers and the capitalists in other states. The state is also under pressure to cover some of the rising wage cost and material cost through government spending.

As the rising wage, material, and taxation costs reach their respective asymptotes, capitalist profits will be squeezed and capital accumulation becomes increasingly unfeasible. The system will enter into a structural crisis that can no longer be resolved within its own institutional framework (Wallerstein 1998: 35–64).

Tendency for the Profit Share to Fall? Evidence from British Capitalism

Wallerstein's arguments can be evaluated by reviewing the long-term evolution of national income distribution of leading capitalist economies. National income is usually measured by gross domestic product (GDP) or gross national product (GNP), which includes incomes for workers (wages and other forms of labor compensation), incomes for the government (taxes), and incomes for capitalists (profits).

Conventional measures of GDP or GNP do not take into account environmental costs. Moreover, most of the resources consumption is subtracted as "intermediate inputs" and not included in GDP or GNP. However, GDP or GNP does include depreciation of fixed capital, which reflects a part of the material cost generated by capitalist accumulation.

Table 3.1 shows the long-term distribution of the British economic output between capital cost, wage cost, taxation cost, and profits. Capital cost is the depreciation of fixed capital. Wage cost includes the wages and salaries of the employed workers and the estimated labor income of the self-employed workers. Taxation cost is defined as taxes on the capitalist businesses, including indirect business taxes (such as sales tax, value added tax, customs, and property tax) and taxes on corporate profits. The taxation cost does not include personal income taxes on the capitalists due to the lack of appropriate data.

Table 3.1 Distribution of National Economic Output (United Kingdom, 1688–2013)

	Wage Cost	Taxation Cost	Capital Cost	Profits
% of GNP:				
1688	49.7	4.6	3.1	42.7
1759	43.9	9.5	3.9	42.7
1801	47.5	12.1	3.2	37.2
1860	60.7	8.8	4.3	26.2
1880	59.8	7.0	5.3	27.9
1900	59.4	6.7	5.0	28.8
1920	66.4	6.4	6.9	20.3
% of GDP:				
1920	70.5	6.6	7.7	15.2
1930	63.4	9.9	6.3	20.3
1940	66.5	12.6	6.7	14.2
1950	66.0	12.3	8.4	13.3
1960	65.5	9.3	9.1	16.1
1970	66.1	15.6	9.8	8.5
1980	66.6	13.7	13.6	6.1
2000	56.7	15.8	13.2	14.3
2010	56.8	13.8	13.3	16.1
2013	55.3	14.6	13.3	16.7

Sources: See Appendix of Chapter 3.

Before 1920, data are presented as shares of gross national product. After 1920, shares of gross domestic product are shown. For the year 1920, two different sets of data are shown. The first set shows costs and profits as share of gross national product and the second set shows costs and profits as shares of gross domestic product. The first set results in a considerably higher profit share but lower cost shares. This is because gross national product includes (and gross domestic product excludes) net property income from abroad. In 1920, net property income was about 4 percent of British gross national product or 5 percent of gross domestic product.

The estimates of British national income distribution for 1688, 1759, and 1801 are based on a modern reworking of England's "social tables" from 1688 to 1801. The original data are not considered reliable but provide some quantitative evidence for national income distribution before the nineteenth century.

From the late seventeenth century to the beginning of the nineteenth century, labor income (wage cost) was about 44–50 percent of British GNP. Capitalist income (profits) was about 37–43 percent of British GNP. The taxation cost was low in the late seventeenth century, about 5 percent of GNP; but surged to 10–12 percent of GNP by the second half of the eighteenth century.

During the second half of the eighteenth century, inter-state conflicts intensified. Britain fought multiple wars with France (the Seven-Years War, the War of American

Independence, and the Napoleonic Wars) that would determine which of the two powers would replace the Dutch Republic to become the next hegemonic power of the capitalist world system. High taxation costs during this period reflected surges in military expenditures.

For the years after 1855, reasonably consistent and reliable British national accounts data became available. From 1855 to 1914, the labor income share of British GNP had been around 60 percent. The British national accounts data for the period after 1855 are not comparable with the "social tables" data for 1801 and earlier. However, other available data suggest that despite the miserable conditions of the British working class in the first half of the nineteenth century, the labor income share might have increased during the period.

The British per capita real GDP increased by 35 percent from 1800 to 1860 (Bolt and Zanden 2013). The best available wage index for the period finds that the English worker's average real wage increased by 124 percent from 1797 to 1851 or by 134 percent from 1805 to 1851. Another index finds that the British worker's real wage increased by 3–5 percent between 1850 and 1860 (Mitchell 1988: 149–152). Overall, from 1800 to 1860, the per capita real GDP increased by about a third and the real wage probably more than doubled. This is consistent with a sizable increase in the wage share.

From the 1920s to the 1970s, British labor income share fluctuated around 65 percent. In the mid-1970s, militant working class struggles pushed the labor income share above 70 percent.

During the heyday of British hegemony, taxation cost stayed around 6–7 percent of GNP. The taxation cost increased through the 1920s and the 1930s, and surged to 15–17 percent of GDP during World War II. The taxation cost was lowered to less than 10 percent of GDP in the early 1960s but rose above 15 percent of GDP by 1970.

There appears to be a long-term tendency for the capital cost share to rise. Capital cost was about 3 percent of GNP in the eighteenth century. It rose to 4–5 percent of GNP by the second half of the nineteenth century. From the 1920s to the 1940s, it was about 6–7 percent of GDP. It rose to about 9 percent of GDP in the 1950s and the 1960s and to about 13 percent of GDP by the late 1970s.

As far as British capitalism is concerned, there was a long-term tendency for the profit share of national income to fall from the late eighteenth century to the mid-twentieth century. In the late eighteenth century, the profit share was probably about 40 percent. By the 1970s, it declined to less than 10 percent.

By implementing neoliberal economic policies, the Thatcher government and Blair's "New Labour Party" succeeded in defeating and weakening trade unions. By the early 2000s, the labor share of GDP fell sharply to about 57 percent. In 2013, Britain's labor income share fell to 55 percent, lower than British labor income share in the nineteenth century. On the other hand, British capitalism has not been able to lower the capital cost share and the taxation cost share.

From 1980 to 2000, British profit share more than doubled from 6 percent to near 14 percent. By 2011–2013, the profit share rose to near 17 percent, the highest since 1939.

Tendency for the Profit Share to Fall? Evidence from American Capitalism

Table 3.2 shows the long-term distribution of the US economic output between capital cost, wage cost, taxation cost, and profits.

In the early twentieth century, US labor income (wage cost) stayed below 60 percent of GNP. The labor income share increased in the 1930s and the 1940s, reaching the all-time high of 66 percent in 1945. In the postwar years, the labor income share fluctuated between 60 and 63 percent. By the 1980s, the American labor movement was in retreat. From 1980 to 2008, the labor income share fluctuated around 60 percent. Since the Great Recession, American workers' conditions have further deteriorated. By 2013, the labor income share fell to 58 percent, returning to early twentieth-century levels.

The US taxation cost was between 5 and 7 percent of GNP in the early twentieth century. By the 1920s, taxation cost rose to 7–8 percent of GNP. During World War II, taxation cost surged and peaked at 14 percent of GDP in 1941. In the 1950s and the 1960s, taxation cost fluctuated around 11–12 percent of GDP. In the neoliberal era,

Table 3.2 Distribution of National Economic Output (United States, 1900–2013)

	Wage Cost	Taxation Cost	Capital Cost	Profits
% of GNP:				
1900	57.5	6.7	9.7	26.4
1910	58.2	5.6	9.2	27.0
1920	61.4	6.3	11.1	21.4
1929	58.5	8.7	10.1	22.7
% of GDP:				
1929	59.0	7.9	10.0	23.1
1940	60.2	11.6	10.4	17.8
1950	61.8	13.4	11.2	13.7
1960	62.0	12.2	12.5	13.3
1970	63.5	11.2	12.8	12.5
1980	62.0	9.7	15.1	13.3
1990	61.0	9.3	15.1	14.6
2000	61.6	9.0	14.6	14.8
2010	58.3	9.0	16.0	16.7
2013	58.0	8.7	15.6	17.8

Sources: See Appendix of Chapter 3.

taxation cost has tended to fall. In 2013, the total taxes on capitalist businesses were less than 9 percent of GDP.

Overall, American capitalism has been relatively successful in containing the rise of wage and taxation costs. Both tended to rise from the early to the mid-twentieth century but have tended to fall since then. But American capitalism has been less successful in containing the rise of capital cost, which rose from 9–10 percent of GNP in the early twentieth century to 15–16 percent of GDP over the period 2010–2013. The high capital cost in recent years partly reflected heavy investment on research and development, which is now classified as investment of fixed capital by the Bureau of Economic Analysis (the US official statistical office).

US profit share fell from 26–27 percent of GNP in the early twentieth century to 12–13 of percent of GDP in the 1970s. But by 2013, US profit share recovered to near 18 percent of GDP (the highest level since 1940).

Spatial Fix?

Marx hypothesized that capitalist accumulation would lead to rising "organic composition of capital" (falling output–capital ratio), driving down the profit rate. The output–capital ratio fell in most leading capitalist economies in the eighteenth and the nineteenth centuries, but stabilized in the twentieth century.

Wallerstein argues that capitalist development tends to drive up wage, material, and taxation costs, leading to the system's structural crisis. In Britain, long-term historical data show that capitalist profit as a share of economic output tended to fall from the eighteenth century to the twentieth century. In the United States, the profit share fell from the early twentieth century to the mid-twentieth century. But during the neoliberal period (from the 1980s onwards), the leading capitalist economies have achieved a partial recovery of the profit share by lowering the wage cost. American capitalism has been successful in containing the taxation cost, though at the cost of large government deficits and rising government debt.

Thus, before the early twenty-first century, global capitalism had managed to survive several major crises by containing rising costs and stabilizing the output–capital ratios. However, if Robert Gordon's argument is correct and the most important technological innovations have already taken place, economic growth may slow down in the future and gradually approach zero. As economic growth rate approaches zero, both the output–capital ratio and the profit rate will tend to fall, making it impossible for a system based on endless accumulation of capital to function.

In the past, global capitalism has been able to contain rising costs through successive waves of geographical expansion. David Harvey, a leading Marxist geographer, refers to this historical strategy of capitalism as "spatial fix" (Harvey 2001). But in the twenty-first century, global capitalism may have exhausted the geographical space for further "spatial fix."

4

THE CAPITALIST WORLD SYSTEM

The Limit to Spatial Fix

In the fourteenth century, European feudalism was in a deep system-wide crisis. As soil degradation, forest depletion, and the exhaustion of frontiers brought late medieval economic expansion to an end, the feudalist system reached its socio-ecological limits. Great famines, epidemic diseases, wars, and peasant revolts led to severe reduction of the European population. The decline of the labor–land ratio shifted the balance of power to favor direct producers while reducing revenues available for the ruling classes. The crisis could no longer be resolved within the feudalist historical framework (Wallerstein 1974; Moore 2002).

The Western European ruling classes responded to the crisis by pursuing a strategy of geographic expansion. The conquest of the Americas greatly increased the land–population ratio for the European-centered "world-economy," which roughly doubled in geographic size between the early sixteenth century and the late seventeenth century (Wallerstein 1974: 68). New crops from the Americas substantially alleviated the European chronic food shortage and contributed to the population boom in the following centuries. The American silver and gold mines provided the Europeans with a massive supply of precious metals, leading to a century-long "price revolution" that redistributed wealth from workers to capitalists (Alva and Wilsey 1993).

The geographic expansion (what David Harvey called the "spatial fix") in the sixteenth century laid down the foundation of the modern capitalist world system. By the seventeenth century, three structural positions had emerged within the early capitalist world system. Northwest Europe emerged as the core regions, specializing in mass-producing manufacturing industries. The core regions were characterized by strong indigenous bourgeoisies controlling local and international commerce, relatively advanced and complex forms of agriculture, and strong states. The periphery specialized in mono-cultural cash crops produced by coerced labor. The peripheral regions (Eastern Europe and Latin America) were characterized by either weak states or the absence of indigenous states. Former core regions that were in the process of deindustrialization (such as Italy, Spain, and Portugal) had declined into the semi-periphery (Wallerstein 1979: 37–48).

Tables 4.1 and 4.2 show the population, gross domestic product (GDP), and per capita GDP of various regions of the capitalist world system and the rest of the world

Table 4.1 The Capitalist World System and External Areas, 1600

	Per Capita GDP (1990 Int. $)	Per Capita GDP (% of World Average)	Population (% of World Total)	GDP (% of World Total)
Core	**1381**	**232%**	**0.3%**	**0.6%**
Netherlands	1381	232%	0.3%	0.6%
Semi-Periphery	**890**	**149%**	**12.5%**	**18.7%**
Italy	1100	185%	2.4%	4.3%
United Kingdom	974	163%	1.1%	1.8%
Spain	853	143%	1.5%	2.1%
France	841	141%	3.3%	4.5%
Austria	837	141%	0.4%	0.6%
Germany	791	133%	2.9%	3.8%
Portugal	740	124%	0.2%	0.2%
Periphery	**519**	**87%**	**4.9%**	**4.3%**
Ireland	615	103%	0.2%	0.2%
Eastern Europe	548	92%	3.0%	2.8%
Latin America	438	73%	1.5%	1.1%
External Areas	**553**	**93%**	**82.3%**	**76.4%**
China	600	101%	28.8%	29.0%
West Asia	591	99%	3.8%	3.8%
India	550	92%	24.3%	22.4%
Japan	520	87%	3.3%	2.9%
Africa	422	71%	9.9%	7.0%

Source: Maddison (2010).

from 1600 to 1700. The historical economic statistics are from Angus Maddison's "Statistics on World Population, GDP, and Per Capita GDP, 1-2008 AD" (Maddison 2010).

Core, Periphery, and Semi-Periphery

By the late nineteenth century, the capitalist world system had expanded to include the entire globe. The three structural positions (core, periphery, and semi-periphery) within the capitalist world system, which first emerged in the sixteenth century, were consolidated by the nineteenth century and would remain relatively stable through the twentieth century.

Up to the late twentieth century, the core had functioned as the center of global capitalist accumulation. To undertake capital accumulation, especially investment in long-term and high-risk projects, capitalists need to be motivated by high-profit rates. Within the capitalist world system, the core countries have monopolies over the

Table 4.2 The Capitalist World System and External Areas, 1700

	Per Capita GDP (1990 Int. $)	Per Capita GDP (% of World Average)	Population (% of World Total)	GDP (% of World Total)
Core	**1410**	**229%**	**1.7%**	**4.0%**
Netherlands	2130	346%	0.3%	1.1%
United Kingdom	1250	203%	1.4%	2.9%
Semi-Periphery	**945**	**154%**	**11.3%**	**17.4%**
Italy	1100	179%	2.2%	3.9%
Austria	993	162%	0.4%	0.7%
France	910	148%	3.6%	5.3%
Germany	910	148%	2.5%	3.7%
Spain	853	139%	1.5%	2.0%
Portugal	819	133%	0.3%	0.4%
Periphery	**584**	**95%**	**7.9%**	**7.5%**
Ireland	715	116%	0.3%	0.4%
Eastern Europe	606	99%	3.1%	3.1%
Indonesia	580	94%	2.2%	2.0%
Latin America	527	86%	2.0%	1.7%
North America	511	83%	0.2%	0.2%
External Areas	**553**	**90%**	**79.0%**	**71.1%**
China	600	98%	22.9%	22.3%
West Asia	591	96%	3.4%	3.3%
Japan	570	93%	4.5%	4.1%
India	550	89%	27.3%	24.5%
Africa	421	68%	10.1%	6.9%

Source: Maddison (2010).

most profitable segments of the global commodity chains, ensuring high-profit rates for the core capitalists.

The core regions are where the world system's skilled labor force (including the skilled workers and the professionals), managerial staff, and military capacities are concentrated. The political stability of the core states is essential for the normal operation of the capitalist world system. To ensure the political loyalty of skilled workers, professionals, managers, and military personnel, the core states reward the working classes and the middle classes within the core regions with wage levels substantially higher than the wage levels in the rest of the world. In effect, the core regions' working classes and middle classes share a portion of the world surplus value and become what Lenin called "the labor aristocracy" within the capitalist world system.

For the core regions to function as the center of global capital accumulation and co-opt the domestic working classes and middle classes, world surplus value needs to be concentrated in the core. Throughout the twentieth century, the core regions (with about one-sixth of the world population) had controlled about 50–60 percent of the global economy.

In the sixteenth and the seventeenth century, the periphery mainly consisted of geographic areas with relatively low population density and abundant natural resources. Natural resources (precious metals and raw materials) were extracted from the periphery to supply the core. Since the nineteenth century, the periphery has included the great majority of the world population. The periphery specializes in highly competitive, low value-added economic activities. Economic surplus is extracted from the periphery and transferred to the core through "unequal exchange" (commodities exported by the periphery embodying greater amount of labor are exchanged for commodities imported from the core embodying smaller amount of labor) (Wallerstein 1979: 71).

The periphery has functioned as the strategic reserve for the capitalist world system. The great majority of the peripheral population lives in rural areas, providing a potentially large cheap labor force that can be drawn into the dynamics of global capital accumulation when it is called upon. Historically, effective capital accumulation (rapid economic growth at exponential rates) was largely limited to the core and the semi-periphery. The absence of effective capital accumulation in the periphery meant that the peripheral regions (with between two-thirds and three-quarters of the world population) had comparatively low levels of resource consumption and environmental impact. As a result, up to the mid-twentieth century, global capitalism had been able to expand without much concern over resources and environmental constraints.

The semi-periphery plays an indispensable role for the operation of the capitalist world system. Politically, the semi-periphery acts as the "middle stratum" that helps to prevent unified resistance by the oppressed great majority against the system's privileged few (Wallerstein 1979: 21–23). Economically, the semi-periphery is equally important for the stability of the capitalist world system.

From time to time, capitalist accumulation in the core regions tends to drive up the labor and resources costs and depress the profit rate. To restore the profit rate, the core regions need to transfer capital out of the old industries (with low and declining profit rates) and into new "leading" industries (with high and rising profit rates). For the capital transfer to take place, the old industries need to be relocated to geographic areas with comparatively low labor and resources costs. Historically, the semi-peripheral regions were the primary locations to receive the old industries relocated out of the core (Wallerstein 1979: 70–71).

In the nineteenth and the twentieth century, capital relocation or "spatial fix" had on several occasions helped the capitalist world system restore the profit rate and overcome the system-wide crisis.

Appendix A of this chapter gives a detailed description of the geographic distribution of the three structural positions of the capitalist world system as well as the "external areas" from 1600 to 2013.

Spatial Fix: The Nineteenth Century

Since Roman times, Asia had been a main supplier of exotic luxury goods to the European elites. The structural trade imbalance led to chronic outflows of precious metals from Europe to Asia. Up to the eighteenth century, those who controlled the Asian trade would have control over the most profitable segments of the European-centered "world economy" (Arrighi, Ahmad, and Shih 1999: 221).

In the seventeenth century, the colonization of the Indonesian archipelago and the monopoly over the Asian spices trade provided the geographical foundation for the Dutch commercial supremacy (Arrighi, Barr, and Hisaeda 1999: 99–109). In the eighteenth century, the British conquest of India was crucial for Britain to win the hegemonic struggle against France. Over the period 1770–1820, the transfer of wealth from India to Britain was estimated to be between 100 million and 1 billion sterling. Indian wealth allowed Britain to buy back nearly all the national debts from the Dutch and helped to finance the massive increase of British military expenditures during the Napoleonic Wars (Arrighi, Hui, Ray, and Refer 1999: 55).

By 1820, the British hegemonic power was consolidated. But about a half of the world population remained outside the capitalist world system. China was the world's largest economy, accounting for one-third of the global economy. Table 4.3 shows the population, GDP, and per capita GDP of various regions of the capitalist world system and the external areas in 1820.

In the eighteenth century, British imports of Chinese tea led to chronic trade deficits for Britain. Moreover, the revenue collected from India could not be easily transferred to Britain without heavy exchange losses (the British India Company had to exchange gold for silver at depreciated exchange rates to pay for the trade deficits with China). Starting with the late eighteenth century, the British East India Company increasingly relied upon opium exports to cover the trade deficits with China and to facilitate the so-called "revenue operations" (the transfer of tributes) between India and Britain (Arrighi, Ahmad, and Shih 1999: 227–233).

To stop the growing drain of silver caused by the imports of opium, the Chinese emperor banned the opium trade. In response, the British government sent an expeditionary force, ostensibly to enforce "the law of God and man" and to punish the Chinese for their "grievous sin" and "wicked offence" (Arrighi, Ahmad, and Shih 1999: 232). China's defeat in the Opium War (1839–1842) led to the Treaty of Nanjing, which marked the beginning of China's incorporation into the capitalist world system as a peripheral member.

After the defeat of the working class rebellions in 1848 (the European Revolution), the capitalist world economy enjoyed two and a half decades of peaceful expansion. By 1870, the capitalist world system had expanded to include the entire globe. Table 4.4 shows the population, GDP, and per capita GDP of various regions of the capitalist world system in 1870.

Table 4.3 The Capitalist World System and External Areas, 1820

	Per Capita GDP (1990 Int. $)	Per Capita GDP (% of World Average)	Population (% of World Total)	GDP (% of World Total)
Core	**1719**	**258%**	**2.3%**	**5.8%**
Netherlands	1838	276%	0.2%	0.6%
United Kingdom	1706	256%	2.0%	5.2%
Semi-Periphery	**968**	**145%**	**17.3%**	**25.1%**
United States	1257	189%	1.0%	1.8%
Austria	1218	183%	0.3%	0.6%
France	1135	170%	3.0%	5.1%
Italy	1117	168%	1.9%	3.2%
Germany	1077	162%	2.4%	3.9%
Spain	1008	151%	1.2%	1.8%
Portugal	923	139%	0.3%	0.4%
Russian Empire*	688	103%	5.3%	5.4%
Periphery	**565**	**85%**	**29.8%**	**25.3%**
Latin America	691	104%	2.1%	2.2%
Eastern Europe	683	103%	3.5%	3.6%
Indonesia	612	92%	1.7%	1.6%
West Asia	607	91%	2.4%	2.2%
India	533	80%	20.1%	16.1%
Egypt	475	71%	0.4%	0.3%
External Areas	**575**	**86%**	**50.7%**	**43.7%**
Japan	669	100%	3.0%	3.0%
China	600	90%	36.6%	33.0%
External Africa**	415	62%	6.0%	3.7%

Source: Maddison (2010).

* Russian Empire refers to the historical territory of the former Soviet Union.
** External Africa is all of Africa except Egypt, Tunisia, Algeria, Morocco, and South Africa.

The economic expansion during the second half of the nineteenth century created new social forces. The industrial working classes grew rapidly and were concentrated in strategic locations (key sectors of industrial capitalism, such as coal mines, railways, and sea ports). From 1873 to 1896, the global capitalist economy suffered from a prolonged depression. The capitalists undertook various restructurings in labor processes and business organizations to shift the burden of depression to the workers.

The workers responded by organizing economically and politically to defend their wages and working conditions. By the early twentieth century, one-quarter of the British labor force had joined trade unions. In continental Europe, working classes were organized into mass political parties. Militant working class struggles frequently erupted throughout Western Europe and North America.

Table 4.4 The Capitalist World System, 1870

	Per Capita GDP (1990 Int. $)	Per Capita GDP (% of World Average)	Population (% of World Total)	GDP (% of World Total)
Core	**2311**	**266%**	**13.3%**	**35.2%**
Australia	3273	376%	0.1%	0.5%
United Kingdom	3190	367%	2.5%	9.0%
United States	2445	281%	3.2%	8.9%
France	1876	216%	3.0%	6.5%
Austria	1863	214%	0.4%	0.8%
Germany	1839	211%	3.1%	6.5%
Semi-Periphery	**1141**	**131%**	**13.4%**	**17.5%**
Italy	1499	172%	2.2%	3.8%
Spain	1207	139%	1.3%	1.8%
Hungary	1092	125%	0.5%	0.6%
Portugal	975	112%	0.3%	0.4%
Russian Empire*	943	108%	7.0%	7.5%
Periphery	**560**	**64%**	**73.4%**	**47.3%**
West Asia	742	85%	2.4%	2.0%
Japan	737	85%	2.7%	2.3%
Latin America	676	78%	3.2%	2.5%
Indonesia	578	66%	2.6%	1.7%
India	533	61%	19.8%	12.2%
China	530	61%	28.1%	17.1%
Africa	500	57%	7.1%	4.1%

Source: Maddison (2010).

* Russian Empire refers to the historical territory of the former Soviet Union.

As British capitalism lost its monopoly of the world industry, the focus of British capital accumulation shifted from material production to financial expansion. The financialization of capitalism helped to restore the profit rate but led to further social polarization and conflicts. The leading capitalist countries saw overseas expansion as a strategic solution that would help to alleviate both social unrest and economic depression. The interweaving of social conflicts and interstate conflicts led to a vicious cycle, culminating in the major crisis of global capitalism from 1914 to 1945 (Silver and Slater 1999: 181–202).

Spatial Fix: The Twentieth Century

On the eve of World War I, world wealth was highly concentrated in a few core capitalist countries. The core countries (with 16 percent of the world population) accounted for 48 percent of the gross world economic product. The broadly defined western world (the core and the semi-periphery together, with about one-third of the world population) accounted for nearly 70 percent of the gross world economic product (see Table 4.5).

On the other hand, about two-thirds of the world population was excluded from effective capital accumulation. In the periphery, the great majority of the population were in rural areas and agriculture was dominated by pre-modern relations of production (highly uneven distribution of land ownership and share cropping). Much of the economic surplus produced by the periphery was transferred to the core. The greater part of the economic surplus kept at home was concentrated in the hands of pre-capitalist landlords who had little interest in capital accumulation.

The global capitalist expansion during the nineteenth century generated new social forces that could no longer be contained by the capitalist world system in

Table 4.5 The Capitalist World System, 1913

	Per Capita GDP (1990 Int. $)	Per Capita GDP (% of World Average)	Population (% of World Total)	GDP (% of World Total)
Core	**4461**	**293%**	**16.2%**	**47.5%**
United States	5301	348%	5.4%	18.9%
Australia	5157	338%	0.3%	0.9%
United Kingdom	4921	323%	2.5%	8.2%
Germany	3648	239%	3.6%	8.7%
France	3485	229%	2.3%	5.3%
Austria	3465	227%	0.4%	0.9%
Semi-Periphery	**1815**	**119%**	**17.5%**	**20.9%**
Argentina	3797	249%	0.4%	1.1%
Italy	2564	168%	2.1%	3.5%
Hungary	2098	138%	0.4%	0.6%
Spain	2056	135%	1.1%	1.5%
Russian Empire*	1488	98%	8.7%	8.5%
Japan	1387	91%	2.9%	2.6%
Periphery	**728**	**48%**	**66.2%**	**31.6%**
Mexico	1732	114%	0.8%	0.9%
Portugal	1250	82%	0.3%	0.3%
West Asia	1042	68%	0.8%	0.7%
Indonesia	874	57%	2.9%	1.7%
Brazil	811	53%	1.3%	0.7%
India	673	44%	16.9%	7.5%
Africa	637	42%	7.0%	2.9%
China	552	36%	24.4%	8.8%

Source: Maddison (2010).

* Russian Empire refers to the historical territory of the former Soviet Union.

the early twentieth century. Both the western working classes and the non-western national liberation movements demanded a share of the world surplus value. To accommodate these demands, the scope of global capital accumulation had to be expanded to allow for effective capital accumulation not only in the western world but also in the non-western world.

In Russia, the ruling class was unable to mobilize resources for rapid industrialization and military modernization. On the eve of World War I, the Russian empire struggled to survive as a viable state and was in danger of slipping into the periphery. The Bolshevik Revolution, by mobilizing the peasants and the workers, undertook fundamental transformation of the state structure. The new Soviet state, by eliminating the entire old ruling class, was able to concentrate all available economic resources on capital accumulation and industrialization.

The Russian Revolution led to the radicalization of the non-western national liberation movements. The national liberation movements were no longer political projects of the non-western elites or the "national bourgeoisies" but were transformed into mass-based movements with broad mobilization of the peasants and the workers. In China, the national liberation movement evolved into a general social revolution led by the Communist Party (Silver and Slater 1999: 194–202).

From 1914 to 1945, the capitalist world system survived the Great Depression and two world wars. At the end of World War II, the United States emerged as the undisputed hegemonic power. Table 4.6 shows the population, GDP, and per capita GDP of various regions of the capitalist world system in 1950.

The new global capitalist order had to accommodate the interests of the western working classes and the non-western national liberation movements. Through the Yalta Agreement, the United States recognized Eastern Europe and part of East Asia as the Soviet sphere of influence. This provided the geopolitical space for socialist industrialization for about one-third of the world population. The United States pressured Britain and France to abandon their colonies. The newly independent Asian and African countries were officially accepted as members of the capitalist inter-state system. They were promised to achieve "economic development" through the assistance of western core countries (Silver and Slater 1999: 208–210).

The global economic boom in the 1950s and the 1960s strengthened the bargaining power of the working classes in the core and the semi-periphery. The spread of American multinational corporations and mass production technologies contributed to the formation of large industrial working classes in Western Europe, Eastern Europe, and Latin America (Silver and Slater 1999: 215). Moreover, the massive expansion of global capitalist economy accelerated resources depletion and reduced the global environmental space.

In the 1970s, US oil production reached its first peak. The US became the world's largest oil importer. For the first time since the industrial revolution, the hegemonic capitalist power and the core zone as a whole lost self-sufficiency in energy supply.

Table 4.6 The Capitalist World System, 1950

	Per Capita GDP (1990 Int. $)	Per Capita GDP (% of World Average)	Population (% of World Total)	GDP (% of World Total)
Core	**7135**	**338%**	**15.3%**	**51.7%**
United States	9561	453%	6.0%	27.3%
Australia	7412	351%	0.3%	1.1%
United Kingdom	6939	329%	2.0%	6.5%
France	5186	246%	1.7%	4.1%
Germany	3881	184%	2.7%	5.0%
Austria	3706	176%	0.3%	0.5%
Semi-Periphery	**2788**	**132%**	**19.5%**	**25.7%**
Argentina	4987	236%	0.7%	1.6%
Italy	3502	166%	1.9%	3.1%
USSR	2841	135%	7.1%	9.6%
South Africa	2535	120%	0.5%	0.6%
Hungary	2480	117%	0.4%	0.4%
Mexico	2365	112%	1.1%	1.3%
Saudi Arabia	2231	106%	0.2%	0.2%
Spain	2189	104%	1.1%	1.2%
Portugal	2086	99%	0.3%	0.3%
Japan	1921	91%	2.9%	2.6%
Periphery	**732**	**35%**	**65.3%**	**22.6%**
Iran	1720	81%	0.6%	0.5%
Brazil	1672	79%	2.1%	1.7%
Turkey	1623	77%	0.8%	0.6%
Indonesia	803	38%	3.3%	1.2%
Africa*	785	37%	8.5%	3.2%
India	619	29%	14.2%	4.2%
China	448	21%	21.6%	4.6%

Source: Maddison (2010).

* Africa does not include South Africa.

Squeezed by rising labor cost, resources depletion, and growing competition between the core countries, capitalist profit rates declined. Global capitalism entered another major crisis by the late 1960s.

The Crisis of the Semi-Periphery

The Soviet Union and the larger Latin American countries were the main beneficiaries of the global capitalist restructuring during the first half of the twentieth century.

As the core countries suffered from massive over-production, the Soviet Union and Latin American countries were able to import capital goods at discounted prices. In the Soviet Union, socialist industrialization meant state monopoly of the domestic market. In Latin America, the withdrawal of western capital during the Great Depression and World War II left domestic markets to the indigenous industrial capitalists.

In 1905, the Russian Empire suffered a humiliating defeat against Japan. Its per capita GDP declined from 108 percent of the world average in 1870 to 98 percent in 1913. In 1945, the Soviet Union emerged victoriously from World War II as the strongest military power in Europe. By 1950, the Soviet per capita GDP stood at 135 percent of the world average, consolidating its position as a strong semi-peripheral state (see Table 4.5 and 4.6).

From 1913 to 1950, the average per capita GDP of the eight large Latin American countries (Argentina, Brazil, Chile, Colombia, Mexico, Peru, Uruguay, and Venezuela) rose from 106 percent of the world average to 128 percent of the world average (data are from Maddison 2010).

During the global economic boom in the 1950s and the 1960s, the Eastern European and Latin American economies grew rapidly. By 1975, most Eastern European countries and the large Latin American countries became a part of the semi-periphery. In 1975, the semi-periphery also included Spain, Greece, Portugal, most West Asian countries, and South Africa (see Table 4.7).

The postwar economic expansion had transformed the social structures of semi-peripheral countries. The proletarianized labor force and urbanized population demanded not only higher material living standards but also political and social rights. Figure 4.1 shows the share of urban population in the total population for several semi-peripheral countries from 1960 to 2013. By 1975, the level of urbanization reached 61 percent in Brazil, 55 percent in Poland, and 66 percent in Russia. In Portugal, the level of urbanization was relatively low but was beginning to rise steadily.

From the 1960s to the 1980s, the semi-periphery was at the center of global political instability. In Latin America, several democratically elected progressive governments were overthrown. Military authoritarian regimes ruled much of Latin America in the 1970s and the 1980s.

In 1968, the short-lived democratic experiment of Czechoslovakia (known as the "Prague Spring") was crushed by the Soviet invasion. In 1970, massive workers' protests erupted in Poland protesting against the rise of food prices. In 1974, revolution broke out in Portugal. By 1975, the last three fascist regimes in Europe (Spain, Portugal, and Greece) were overthrown. In 1979, Iran's Pahlavi dynasty was overthrown by the Islamic Revolution. In 1980, "Solidarity" emerged as a powerful working class movement in Poland.

In the 1970s, both the core countries and the semi-peripheral countries were pressured by rising labor and energy costs. While the core countries could transfer

Table 4.7 The Capitalist World System, 1975

	Per Capita GDP (1990 Int. $)	Per Capita GDP (% of World Average)	Population (% of World Total)	GDP (% of World Total)
Core	**13461**	**329%**	**16.5%**	**54.3%**
United States	16284	398%	5.3%	21.1%
Australia	13170	322%	0.3%	1.1%
France	12957	317%	1.3%	4.2%
Germany	12041	295%	1.9%	5.7%
United Kingdom	11847	290%	1.4%	4.0%
Austria	11646	285%	0.2%	0.5%
Japan	11344	278%	2.7%	7.6%
Italy	10742	263%	1.4%	3.6%
Semi-Periphery	**5854**	**143%**	**19.2%**	**27.5%**
Saudi Arabia	11787	288%	0.2%	0.5%
Spain	8346	204%	0.9%	1.8%
Argentina	8122	199%	0.6%	1.3%
Portugal	6517	159%	0.2%	0.4%
USSR	6135	150%	6.3%	9.4%
Iran	5883	144%	0.8%	1.2%
Hungary	5805	142%	0.3%	0.4%
Mexico	5158	126%	1.5%	1.9%
South Africa	4271	104%	0.6%	0.7%
Brazil	4187	102%	2.7%	2.7%
Turkey	3895	95%	1.0%	0.9%
Periphery	**1155**	**28%**	**64.3%**	**18.2%**
Indonesia	1497	37%	3.2%	1.2%
Africa*	1205	29%	9.6%	2.8%
India	897	22%	14.9%	3.3%
China	871	21%	22.5%	4.8%

Source: Maddison (2010).

* Africa does not include South Africa.

capital to new leading industries to re-establish monopolistic profits, the semi-peripheral countries were stuck with their obsolete industries.

There was a temporary glut of global financial capital as the "petrodollars" (the massive oil revenue accumulated by the Middle East oil exporters) flowed into the western banks. Induced by the temporarily low interest rates, the semi-peripheral and peripheral countries borrowed massive amounts of foreign debt to sustain economic growth.

But when the US Federal Reserve raised the interest rate in 1979 (in effect, the United States withdrew surplus capital from the rest of the world to finance its

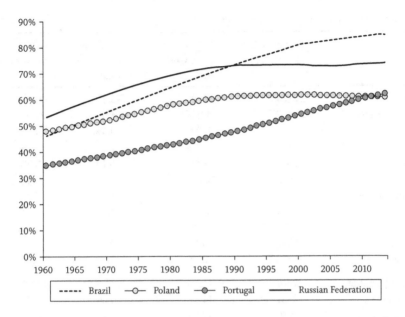

Figure 4.1 Urbanization in Semi-Peripheral Countries (Urban Population as % of Total Population, 1960–2013)

Source: World Bank (2014).

hegemonic revival and domestic class warfare, see Silver and Slater 1999: 214–215), debt crisis broke out, plunging the global South and East into economic and social catastrophes.

In Latin America and Eastern Europe, partly under the pressure of the United States and international financial institutions (the International Monetary Fund and the World Bank) and partly on their own initiatives, the ruling elites undertook "structural adjustments" that dismantled the socialist or import-substitution industrial structures. De-industrialization led to massive declines of living standards and, at least in the short run, destroyed the economic and social power of the semi-peripheral working classes.

Table 4.8 shows the population, GDP, and per capita GDP of various regions of the capitalist world system in 2000. From 1975 to 2000, the average per capita GDP of the former Soviet Union fell from 150 percent of the world average to 74 percent; the average per capita GDP of Eastern Europe fell from 132 percent of the world average to 99 percent; and the average per capita GDP of the eight large Latin American countries fell from 124 percent of the world average to 106 percent (data are from Maddison 2010).

By the early 2000s, Eastern European countries had become suppliers of cheap labor force to Western Europe; Russia and Latin America had been transformed into energy and raw materials exporters in the capitalist world system.

Table 4.8 The Capitalist World System, 2000

	Per Capita GDP (1990 Int. $)	Per Capita GDP (% of World Average)	Population (% of World Total)	GDP (% of World Total)
Core	**22174**	**367%**	**15.3%**	**56.1%**
United States	28467	471%	4.6%	21.9%
Australia	21732	360%	0.3%	1.1%
Japan	20738	343%	2.1%	7.2%
Austria	20691	343%	0.1%	0.5%
France	20422	338%	1.0%	3.4%
United Kingdom	20353	337%	1.0%	3.3%
Germany	18944	314%	1.4%	4.2%
Italy	18774	311%	0.9%	3.0%
Spain	15622	259%	0.7%	1.7%
Portugal	13813	229%	0.2%	0.4%
Semi-Periphery	**6778**	**112%**	**13.2%**	**14.8%**
Argentina	8581	142%	0.6%	0.9%
Saudi Arabia	7650	127%	0.4%	0.5%
Mexico	7275	120%	1.6%	2.0%
Hungary	7132	118%	0.2%	0.2%
Turkey	6446	107%	1.1%	1.2%
Brazil	5532	92%	2.9%	2.7%
Russian Federation	5277	87%	2.4%	2.1%
Periphery	**2452**	**41%**	**71.5%**	**29.0%**
Iran	4838	80%	1.0%	0.8%
South Africa	3890	64%	0.7%	0.5%
China	3421	57%	20.8%	11.8%
Indonesia	3276	54%	3.4%	1.8%
India	1892	31%	16.5%	5.2%
Africa*	1303	22%	12.6%	2.7%

Source: Maddison (2010).

* Africa does not include South Africa.

Unequal Exchange: China and the United States

To overcome the major crisis in the 1970s, global capitalist elites pursued several strategies. In the core, capital was transferred from mass-producing manufacturing industries to information technologies and the financial sector. The semi-peripheral countries were restructured to function as new suppliers of energy, raw materials, and cheap labor force. Most importantly, the industrial capital in the core and the semi-periphery needed to be relocated to a new geographic area with a large cheap labor force. China became the main beneficiary of global capital relocation in the late twentieth century.

The basic function of the peripheral regions in the capitalist world system is to generate large economic surplus to be extracted by the core regions. The extraction of economic surplus takes place through unequal exchange: the peripheral regions export commodities embodying a comparatively greater amount of labor in exchange for commodities imported from the core regions embodying a comparatively smaller amount of labor (Wallerstein 1979: 71).

The "labor term of trade" tells the degree to which a country gains or loses through unequal exchange in the capitalist world system. It is defined as the ratio of the labor time embodied in the goods imported by a country (of a certain amount of monetary value) over the labor time embodied in the goods exported by the country (of the same amount of monetary value). For example, in 2012, one million dollars of goods exported by China on average contained 60.7 "worker-years" of direct and indirect labor input (the annual labor of 60.7 average workers). For the same year, one million dollars of goods imported by China on average contained 32.8 "worker-years" of direct and indirect labor input. It follows that China's average labor term of trade in 2012 was 32.8 / 60.7 = 0.54; that is, each unit of Chinese labor exported on average could exchange for 0.54 unit of imported labor in the world market. Appendix B of this chapter explains the calculation of the labor terms of trade.

Figure 4.2 compares the average labor term of trade in the United States and China from 1990 to 2012. If a country's average labor term of trade is greater than

Figure 4.2 Average Labor Term of Trade (United States and China, 1990–2012)

Source: World Bank (2014). For the calculation of labor terms of trade, see Appendix B of Chapter 4.

one, it means that the country benefits from unequal exchange, extracting surplus from the rest of the world. If a country's average labor term of trade is smaller than one, it means that the country suffers from unequal exchange, generating surplus to be extracted by the rest of the world.

Being the world's hegemonic power, the United States has the highest average labor term of trade among the world's large economies. In the 1990s, the United States experienced a temporary revival of its hegemonic power. In 2003, when the United States embarked on the invasion of Iraq and there was widespread talk of the United States becoming a new "empire," the US average labor term of trade peaked at 6.4. Since then, American hegemony has been in decline. By 2012, the US average labor term of trade fell to 4.7.

Since the 1990s, China's average labor term of trade has improved dramatically. In 1990, China's average labor term of trade was only 0.07. By 2000, it improved to 0.20. By 2012, it improved to 0.54.

Figure 4.3 shows China's labor term of trade by geographical regions. In the early 1990s, China had unfavorable labor term of trade (less than one) against every other region in the world. China in the early 1990s was clearly a peripheral economy within the capitalist world system. By 2012, China had become a net "exploiter" in its trade with East Asian, South Asian, and African peripheral economies. However,

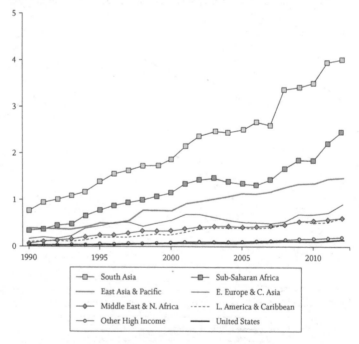

Figure 4.3 China's Labor Terms of Trade (By Geographical Regions, 1990–2012)

Source: World Bank (2014). For the calculation of labor terms of trade, see Appendix B of Chapter 4. The geographical regions other than the United States and "other high income" countries refer to "developing economies" only.

China's labor term of trade was only 0.14 against the United States and 0.20 against other "high income economies" (which include all the core countries, high-income oil exporters in the Middle East, and several semi-peripheral economies in Latin America and Eastern Europe). China's terms of trade against the Middle East, Eastern Europe and Latin America remained unfavorable. Overall, China continues to be a peripheral economy within the capitalist world system.

However, within about a decade, China's average labor term of trade is likely to approach or exceed one. China's labor terms of trade are likely to turn favorable against not only all the peripheral economies but also most of the semi-peripheral economies. By then, China will become a semi-peripheral state. Given China's enormous economic and demographic size, China's entry into the semi-periphery will have fundamental implications for the operations of the capitalist world system and may suggest that the successive "spatial fixes" as a historical strategy to revive the capitalist world system has reached its limit.

China and the Limit to Spatial Fix

Table 4.9 shows the population, GDP, and per capita GDP of various regions of the capitalist world system in 2013. Data for this table are from the World Bank's *World Development Indicators* (World Bank 2014).

Historically, the surplus value in the capitalist world system was concentrated in the core and the core regions had been the center of global capitalist accumulation. Both the core share of the gross world economic product and the core average per capita GDP as a ratio of the world average reached their peak in 2000 (see Table 4.8). However, since then, the long-term historical trend towards widening disparity between the core and the periphery has been reversed. Between 2000 and 2013, the core average per capita GDP as a ratio of the world average declined from 367 percent to 303 percent. Between 1975 and 2013, the periphery's average per capita GDP as a ratio of the world average rose from 28 percent to 54 percent. The more even distribution of the world surplus value across different geographical regions will undermine (rather than strengthen) the stability of the capitalist world system.

Figure 4.4 compares the net gain for the United States and the net loss for China through unequal exchange from 1990 to 2012, measured in million "worker-years" of labor embodied in trade. Net gain from unequal exchange refers to the economic surplus a country extracts through unequal exchange. Net loss from unequal exchange refers to the economic surplus a country loses through unequal exchange. See Appendix B of this chapter for the measurement of unequal exchange.

The US net gain from unequal exchange peaked in 2006 at 56 million worker-years of labor embodied. For the year of 2006, the US net gain from unequal exchange was equivalent to 38 percent of the US total labor employed. Had the US not been able to extract the economic surplus from the periphery through unequal exchange, about two-fifths of the US labor force would have to be withdrawn from their current

Table 4.9 The Capitalist World System, 2013

	Per Capita GDP (2011 Int. $)	Per Capita GDP (% of World Average)	Population (% of World Total)	GDP (% of World Total)
Core	**42066**	**303%**	**13.6%**	**41.3%**
United States	51451	371%	4.4%	16.5%
Austria	43085	311%	0.1%	0.4%
Australia	42810	309%	0.3%	1.0%
Germany	42045	303%	1.1%	3.4%
France	35969	259%	0.9%	2.4%
Japan	35481	256%	1.8%	4.6%
United Kingdom	35013	252%	0.9%	2.3%
Italy	32929	237%	0.8%	2.0%
Spain	30892	223%	0.7%	1.5%
Semi-Periphery	**19518**	**141%**	**13.8%**	**19.4%**
Saudi Arabia	52068	375%	0.4%	1.5%
Portugal	24882	179%	0.1%	0.3%
Russian Federation	23564	170%	2.0%	3.4%
Poland	22513	162%	0.5%	0.9%
Turkey	18647	134%	1.1%	1.4%
Mexico	16291	117%	1.7%	2.0%
Iran	15090	109%	1.1%	1.2%
Brazil	14555	105%	2.8%	3.0%
Periphery	**7512**	**54%**	**72.6%**	**39.3%**
South Africa	12106	87%	0.7%	0.6%
China	11525	83%	19.1%	15.8%
Indonesia	9254	67%	3.5%	2.3%
India	5238	38%	17.6%	6.6%
Sub-Saharan Africa*	2714	20%	12.4%	2.4%

Source: World Bank (2014).

* Sub-Saharan Africa does not include South Africa.

economic activities and redirected to the production of essential consumer goods and raw materials which the United States currently imports from the periphery. This would reduce the US overall economic output by about two-fifths.

Figure 4.4 shows that China's net loss from unequal exchange has been about one and a half times the US net gain. Given that the United States accounts for about 40 percent of the core regions' total economic output (see Table 4.9), the economic surplus extracted from China probably accounts for more than a half of the core regions' total net gain from unequal exchange. However, as China's labor term of trade approaches one, the enormous economic surplus that China currently supplies to the core through unequal exchange could completely vanish in about a decade.

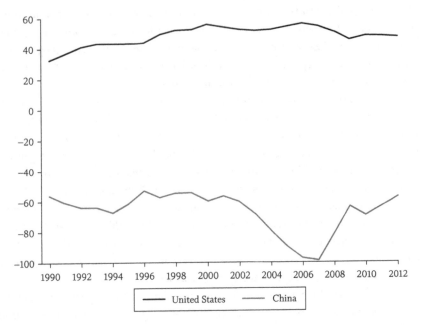

Figure 4.4 Net Gain or Loss from Unequal Exchange (Million Worker-Years of Labor, 1990–2012)

Source: World Bank (2014). For the measurement of unequal exchange, see Appendix B of Chapter 4.

Within the capitalist world system, there is not another large geographic area that can substitute China and generate economic surplus on a similar magnitude. The remaining large peripheral areas in South Asia and Sub-Saharan Africa have been under intense exploitation by the capitalist world system for about two centuries. Widespread political instability affects both regions. Ecologically and socially, the two regions may have reached the limits in bearing the rising burden of global capitalist exploitation.

Without the large economic surplus generated by the periphery, the core regions will be deprived of the economic resources they need to "subsidize" the comparatively high living standards of the working classes and the middle classes within the core regions. Political and social stability within the core regions will be jeopardized.

In the long run, capitalist accumulation tends to drive up labor and resources costs, leading to falling profit rate and malfunctioning of the capitalist world system. Historically, the capitalist world system has relied upon geographical expansion or "spatial fix" as the principal strategy to contain rising labor and resources costs.

In the first half of the twentieth century, global capitalist restructuring led to the mobilization of labor force and natural resources in Eastern European and Latin American semi-peripheral countries, which joined the core countries in the pursuit of rapid capital accumulation during the postwar "golden age."

By the 1970s, both the core and the semi-periphery were under pressure from rising labor and resources costs. For the first time in capitalist history, it became necessary to mobilize the labor force and natural resources in a large geographical area in the periphery (primarily China's cheap labor force and massive coal reserves) in order to re-accelerate global capital accumulation.

In the short run, the mobilization of China (China's capitalist transition and the economic rise of China) helped to lower the global labor cost and made a major contribution to the revival of the global profit rate. In the long run, China's participation in global capital accumulation has fundamentally transformed China's social structure. As the Chinese working class and urban middle class begin to demand higher living standards as well as political and social rights, China is likely to face a major crisis similar to the crisis faced by the Eastern European and Latin America semi-peripheral countries in the 1970s and the 1980s. But unlike in the late twentieth century, now there is not another large geographical area that can provide both a large cheap labor force and a large environmental space under politically stable conditions to underpin a new round of global capitalist restructuring.

Moreover, as China enters into the semi-periphery, both the population and the geographical areas that participate in high levels of energy and resources consumption will be greatly expanded. This will not only drive up global resources costs but also deplete the remaining global environmental space. Global ecological collapse will be inevitable unless fundamental social transformation takes place in the not very distant future.

The capitalist world system has reached the limit of spatial fix.

5

THE NEXT ECONOMIC CRISIS

Figure 5.1 compares the historical profit rates of the United States (from 1929 to 2013) and China (from 1990 to 2012). The United States has been the hegemonic power of the capitalist world system since the mid-twentieth century. Since the 1950s, US profit rates have fluctuated between 10 and 15 percent. By comparison, from 1990 to 2010, the Chinese business sector's profit rates moved in the range of 20–30 percent, about twice the level of US profit rates.

The very high profit rates allowed China to become the primary beneficiary of global capital relocation in the late twentieth and the early twenty-first century. As industrial capital was relocated from high-cost core regions to low-cost peripheral regions (especially China), the global average profit rate was pulled up and the tendency towards a falling rate of profit was temporarily reversed.

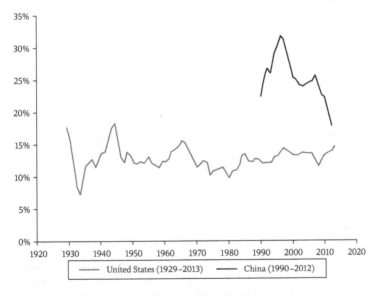

Figure 5.1 Profit Rate (United States and China, 1929–2013)

Sources: For the US profit rates from 1929 to 2013, see Figure 3.2 and Appendix of Chapter 3. China's profit rates from 1990–2012 are calculated using data from various issues of *China Statistical Yearbook* (National Bureau of Statistics 2013 and earlier years), see Appendix of this chapter. For the United States, the profit rate is defined as the ratio of the total capitalist profit over the net stock of private non-residential fixed assets. For China, the profit rate is defined as the ratio of the total capitalist profit over the business sector's net stock of fixed capital.

However, as China emerges as the new center of global capital accumulation, the tendency towards rising wage, taxation, and capital cost that undermined global capitalism during the twentieth century begins to operate in China. Since 2007, the Chinese profit rate has fallen rapidly. In a few years, the decline of the profit rate will begin to undermine the foundation of Chinese capitalism and bring the global capitalist system into the next major crisis.

The Output–Capital Ratio and the Profit Share

Chapter 3 explains that the profit rate is determined by the output–capital ratio and the profit share. Figure 5.2 compares the long-term movement of the output–capital ratio (ratio of gross domestic product to the business sector capital stock) in the United States (from 1929 to 2013) and China (from 1990 to 2012).

Since the 1950s, the US output–capital ratio has mostly fluctuated between 0.8 and 1. In the early 1980s and in 2009, American capitalism was in deep economic crisis and the output–capital ratio fell below 0.8. In 1990, China's output–capital ratio was about the same as the US output–capital ratio. China's output–capital ratio declined during the 1990s, stabilized in the early 2000s, and improved during the global economic boom from 2005 to 2007. But since 2007, China's output–capital

Figure 5.2 Output–Capital Ratio (United States and China, 1929–2013)

Sources: The US output–capital ratio is defined as the ratio of gross domestic product over the net stock of private non-residential fixed assets. Data are from BEA (2014). China's output–capital ratio is defined as the ratio of gross domestic product over the business sector's net stock of fixed capital. For estimates of China's capital stock, see Appendix of this chapter.

ratio has declined rapidly. China's output–capital ratio is now approaching levels comparable to the US output–capital ratios during the Great Depression.

China's low output–capital ratios reflect China's position in the capitalist world economy. Being a large peripheral economy specializing in manufacturing exports, Chinese capitalism needs to make heavy investment in industrial equipment and infrastructure to function as the world's leading industrial producer.

Figure 5.3 compares the long-term movement of the profit share (share of total capitalist profit in the gross domestic product) in the United States (from 1929 to 2013) and China (from 1990 to 2012).

The US profit share fell from 23 percent in 1929 to less than 13 percent in 1945. From the 1950s to the 1970s, the US profit share fluctuated between 13 and 15 percent. Since then, the US profit share has tended to increase through the business cycles of the 1980s, the 1990s, the 2000s, and the 2010s. By 2013, the US profit share rose to near 18 percent.

In the 1990s, China's profit share rose sharply as China began to privatize state-owned enterprises and lay off tens of millions of state sector workers. China's profit share peaked in 1997 at more than 43 percent. In the early 2000s, China's profit share stabilized around 36 percent. This was much higher than the American and the

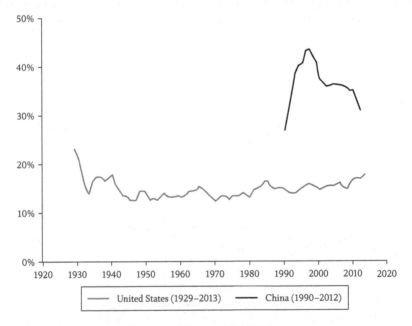

Figure 5.3 Profit Share (United States and China, 1929–2013)

Sources: The profit share is defined as the ratio of the total capitalist profit to gross domestic product. Total capitalist profit is defined as gross domestic product less wage cost (labor incomes), taxation cost (indirect business taxes and corporate profit taxes), and capital cost (depreciation of fixed capital). Individual income taxes on capitalists are not deducted from the total capitalist profit. For the United States, data are from BEA (2014). For estimates of China's profit share, see Appendix of this chapter.

British profit share in the twentieth century and is comparable to the British profit share in the early nineteenth century (see Table 3.1 and 3.2). But now there is some indication that the era of super exploitative Chinese capitalism is coming to an end. By 2012, China's profit share fell to 31 percent.

Figure 5.4 shows the movement of wage cost, taxation cost, and capital cost (depreciation of fixed capital) as a share of China's gross domestic product (GDP) from 1990 to 2012.

China's labor income (wage cost) fell sharply from 47 percent of GDP in 1990 to 32 percent in 1998. From 2000 to 2010, the labor income share stabilized around 34–35 percent. In 2010, China's labor income share was about 60 percent of the labor income share in the core capitalist countries. However, in 2011 and 2012, China's labor income share rose rapidly. By 2012, China's labor income share recovered to 38 percent.

China's taxation cost (the sum of indirect business taxes and business income tax) declined from 15 percent of GDP in 1990 to less than 10 percent in 1996. Since then, taxation cost has risen steadily relative to China's GDP. By 2012, taxation cost reached 18 percent of GDP. China's taxation cost as a share of GDP is relatively high by international comparison. It is about twice as high as the American taxation cost share and is also higher than the British taxation cost share (see Table 3.1 and 3.2). But the comparison does not include individual income taxes paid by capitalists.

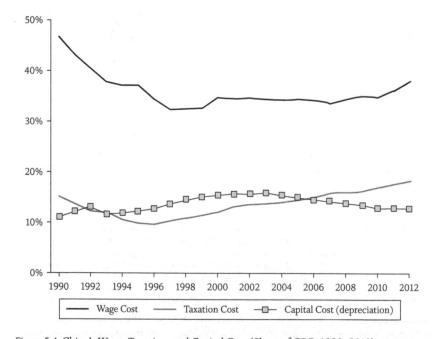

Figure 5.4 China's Wage, Taxation, and Capital Cost (Share of GDP, 1990–2012)

Sources: Data are from the National Bureau of Statistics of China (2013 and earlier years). For estimates of China's wage cost, taxation cost, and capital cost, see Appendix of this chapter.

China's capital cost (depreciation of fixed capital) as a share of GDP rose from 11 percent in 1990 to 16 percent in 2003. But by 2012, it declined to 13 percent.

As the Chinese working class begins to get organized, the capitalist class increases its demands on the state, and the state has to pay for the growing environmental cost, both the wage cost and the taxation cost are set to rise in the future. The capital cost may resume rising as China's output–capital ratio keeps falling (if the ratio of capital stock to economic output rises and the depreciation rate stays constant, depreciation as a share of economic output will rise). Chinese capitalism has entered into the era of profit squeeze.

Profit Rate, Marginal Profit Rate, and Capital Accumulation

The profit rate measures the rate of return on the existing capital stock. To evaluate the trend of profit rate, it is useful to measure and study the "marginal profit rate," or the incremental rate of return on newly invested capital:

Marginal Profit Rate = Change in Profit / Change in Capital Stock

Change in capital is the same as the net investment of new capital stock. If both the numerator and the denominator in the above formula are divided by profit, the following equation can be derived:

Marginal Profit Rate = (Change in Profit/Profit) / (Net Investment/Profit) = The Profit's Growth Rate / The Ratio of Accumulation

The "ratio of accumulation" is defined as the ratio of net investment to capitalist profit. It shows the share of capitalist profit that is used for capitalist accumulation rather than capitalist consumption. It follows that:

The Profit's Growth Rate = The Ratio of Accumulation * Marginal Profit Rate

Thus, if the marginal profit rate is multiplied by the ratio of accumulation, it results in the profit's growth rate.

On the other hand, if the (average) profit rate is multiplied by the ratio of accumulation, it results in the capital stock's growth rate:

Capital Stock's Growth Rate = Change in Capital Stock / Capital Stock = Net Investment / Capital Stock = (Net Investment/Profit) * (Profit/Capital Stock) = Ratio of Accumulation * Profit Rate

Thus, if the average profit rate is greater than the marginal profit rate, capital stock would grow more rapidly than the profit and the profit rate would fall. If the average profit rate is smaller than the marginal profit rate, capital stock would grow less rapidly than the profit and the profit rate would rise. When the average profit rate equals the marginal profit rate, the capital stock growth rate would be the same as the profit's growth rate and the profit rate would be at equilibrium:

Equilibrium Profit Rate = (Average) Profit Rate = Marginal Profit Rate = The Profit's Growth Rate / The Ratio of Accumulation

Figure 5.5 illustrates the determination of the equilibrium profit rate in a hypothetical economic model. In this hypothetical model, the profit's growth rate is assumed to be 5 percent and the ratio of accumulation is assumed to be 50 percent. If the profit rate is less than 10 percent, the growth rate of capital stock would be less than 5 percent, the capital stock would grow less rapidly than the profit, and the profit rate would rise. If the profit rate is greater than 10 percent, the growth rate of capital stock would be greater than 5 percent, the capital stock would grow more rapidly than the profit, and the profit rate would fall. Either way, the profit rate would converge towards 10 percent, which is the equilibrium profit rate (10% = 5% / 50%).

Profit equals the economic output multiplied by the profit share. Thus, the profit's growth rate equals the economic growth rate plus the rate of change of the profit share. This has important implications for the long-term future of capitalism. Rising resources costs and ecological constraints will impose limits on economic growth; rising wages, taxation, and capital costs will reduce the profit share

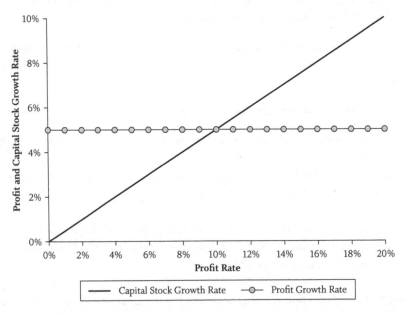

Figure 5.5 Determination of Equilibrium Profit Rate (Profit's Growth Rate = 5%; Ratio of Accumulation = 50%)

Sources: The author's assumptions and calculation.

(implying negative change of the profit share). In the long run, ecological limits on growth and rising costs will push the profit's growth rate towards zero (in Figure 5.5, the profit's growth rate curve would move all the way down towards zero). As the ratio of accumulation is normally positive (at least a fraction of the capitalist profit would be used for accumulation rather than consumption), it follows that there will be a long-term tendency for the equilibrium profit rate to fall towards zero.

Marx's hypothesis of the tendency for the rate of profit rate to fall may be validated by the coming structural crisis of global capitalism in the twenty-first century.

Profit and Accumulation: United States and China

Figure 5.6 shows the long-term movement of the profit's growth rate, the ratio of accumulation, and the marginal profit rate in the United States for the period 1929/1939–2003/2013. The profit's growth rate refers to the growth rate of real profits. Real profits are profits in current dollars deflated by the price index of capital stock. All variables are shown in ten-year moving averages to smooth out short-term fluctuations. Before 1945, the marginal profit rates cannot be calculated because of negative ratios of accumulation during the 1930s and the early 1940s.

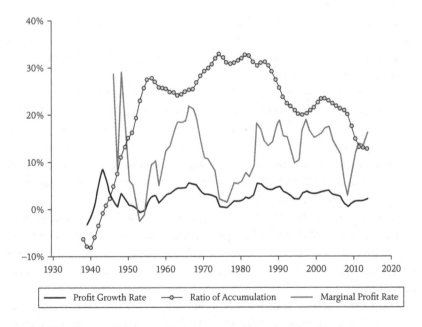

Figure 5.6 Profit and Accumulation (United States, 1929/39–2003/13)

Sources: The profit's growth rate refers to growth rate of real profits. Real profits are profits in current dollars deflated by the price index of private non-residential fixed capital. All variables are shown in ten-year moving averages to smooth out short-term fluctuations. Original data are from the BEA (2014).

During the postwar economic boom (from the mid-1950s to the mid-1960s), the US profit growth rates exceeded 5 percent. By the mid-1970s, American capitalism was in deep crisis and the profit growth collapsed. Under the Reagan administration, US profit growth experienced a strong recovery. Since then, American capitalism has struggled with declining economic growth rates. Under neoliberalism, profit share has increased. But the increase of profit share has not been sufficient to offset the negative effects of declining economic growth rates. The US ten-year average profit growth rate decelerated from 5.5 percent for the period 1974–1984 to only 0.1 percent for the period 1998–2008. For the period 2003–2013, the ten-year average profit growth rate recovered to 2.1 percent.

Despite the slow pace of profit growth, American capitalism has ironically benefited from low ratios of accumulation. Given a certain profit growth rate, a lower ratio of accumulation implies higher marginal profit rate and in the long run, higher average profit rate. In the 1960s and the 1970s, when American capitalism focused on "material expansion," the US ratio of accumulation averaged about 30 percent. By the 1990s, the US ratio of accumulation declined to about 20 percent. For the period 2004–2013, on average only 13 percent of US capitalist profit was spent on capital accumulation. The decline of the US ratio of accumulation reflects the financialization of American capitalism and the relocation of industrial capital from the United States to the peripheral regions.

In the early 1950s, the sharp declines of US marginal profit rates were caused by unusually high capitalist profits during World War II (and therefore the profit growth between 1943–1944 and 1953–1954 was negative). In the mid-1960s, the US marginal profit rates exceeded 20 percent.

The marginal profit rate collapsed in the 1970s, fluctuated between 10 and 20 percent from the 1980s to the early 2000s, and collapsed again during 2007–2009. Since the Great Recession, the US marginal profit rate has recovered strongly and reached 16 percent by 2013.

Figure 5.7 shows the profit's growth rate, the ratio of accumulation, and the marginal profit rate in China for the period 1990–2012. In Figure 5.7, annual numbers rather than multi-year averages are shown.

Figure 5.7 shows that Chinese capitalism has behaved very differently from American capitalism. While American capitalism has focused on financial accumulation, Chinese capitalism has become the center of global industrial production and depends on heavy investment in industrial equipment and infrastructure to sustain capital accumulation.

From 1990 to 2005, China's ratio of accumulation mostly fluctuated around 40 percent (with the exception of 1993 when the Chinese economy experienced high inflation and trade deficit). This was higher than the typical US ratios of accumulation during the postwar years of "material expansion," but not excessively high. China's ratio of accumulation rose to about 50 percent during 2006–2008. Since 2009,

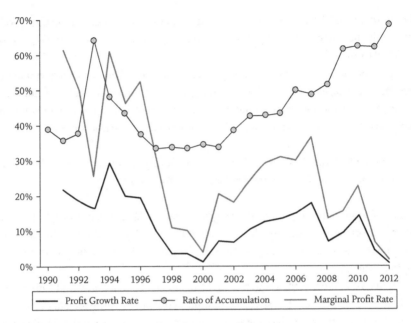

Figure 5.7 Profit and Accumulation (China, 1990–2012)

Sources: Profit growth rate refers to growth rate of real profit. Real profit is total capitalist profit in current prices deflated by fixed investment price index. Original data are from National Bureau of Statistics of China (2013 and earlier years).

Chinese capitalism has relied upon massive investment to sustain economic growth and the ratio of accumulation surged to 69 percent by 2012.

From 1991 to 1996, China's profit growth rates and marginal profit rates were very high. Profit growth rates fluctuated around 20 percent and marginal profit rates fluctuated around 50 percent. In the late 1990s, profit growth decelerated sharply as massive privatization reduced the working class purchasing power and depressed domestic demand. Staring with 2001, when China entered into the World Trade Organization, China's profit growth accelerated. By 2007, the profit growth rate reached 18 percent and the marginal profit rate reached 37 percent.

However, after 2007, both profit's growth rate and marginal profit rate fell sharply. In 2012, profit's growth rate fell to 1 percent and the marginal profit rate fell to 1.5 percent. The sharp decline of profit's growth rate and marginal profit rate raises serious questions regarding the future of Chinese capitalism.

Growth Accounting and the Falling Rate of Profit

The equilibrium profit rate is the profit growth rate divided by the ratio of accumulation. Profit growth rate equals the economic growth rate plus the rate of change of the profit share. In the long run, if the profit share stabilizes (and therefore the profit share's rate of change equals zero), the equilibrium profit rate will be determined by the economic growth rate and the ratio of accumulation.

In neoclassical economics, a common approach when analyzing economic growth is to disaggregate overall economic growth into the contribution from labor input, the contribution from capital input, and the contribution from technological progress ("total factor productivity"). This is known as "growth accounting":

Economic Growth Rate = Contribution of Labor Input + Contribution of Capital Input + Total Factor Productivity Growth Rate

Contribution of labor input equals the growth rate of labor input multiplied by the labor share of national income (the labor weight). Contribution of capital input equals the growth rate of capital input multiplied by the capital share of national income (the capital weight).

Table 5.1 compares the growth accounting for the United States and China from 1950 to 2013. For the United States, labor input is measured by the total hours worked in the business sector and the capital input is measured by the real net stock of private

Table 5.1 Analyzing Economic Growth in the United States and China, 1950–2013

	Economic Growth	Labor Growth	Capital Growth	Labor Contribution	Capital Contribution	Total Factor Productivity
US:						
1950–1960	3.6%	1.1%	3.2%	0.7%	1.1%	1.8%
1960–1970	4.3%	1.1%	4.2%	0.8%	1.4%	2.1%
1970–1980	3.2%	1.7%	3.7%	1.1%	1.2%	0.8%
1980–1990	3.3%	1.7%	3.1%	1.1%	1.1%	1.2%
1990–2000	3.4%	1.7%	3.0%	1.1%	1.1%	1.3%
2000–2010	1.6%	−0.9%	1.9%	−0.6%	0.7%	1.6%
2010–2013	2.0%	1.9%	1.4%	1.2%	0.5%	0.3%
China:						
1980–1990	9.3%	6.9%	12.1%	3.7%	5.7%	−0.1%
1990–2000	10.4%	3.4%	12.8%	1.4%	7.7%	1.4%
2000–2010	10.5%	2.9%	12.9%	1.1%	7.9%	1.5%
2010–2012	8.5%	2.8%	14.2%	1.2%	8.1%	−0.9%

Sources: For the United States, labor input is measured by business sector total hours worked and capital input is the real net stock of private nonresidential fixed assets. Labor is assigned a weight of 0.67, 0.67, 0.67, 0.65, 0.65, 0.64, and 0.62 for the 1950s, 1960s, 1970s, 1980s, 1990s, 2000s, and 2010s respectively. For China, labor is measured by non-agricultural employment and capital is measured by the real business sector capital stock. Labor weight is 0.53, 0.40, 0.39, and 0.43 for the 1980s, 1990s, 2000s, and 2010s respectively. Capital weight is simply labor weight less than one. These weights correspond to labor's and capital's share in the gross domestic product at factor cost. Data for the United States are from BEA (2014) and Economic Report of the President (2010 and 2014). Data for China are from National Bureau of Statistics (2013 and earlier years).

non-residential fixed assets. For China, labor input is measured by non-agricultural employment (because non-agricultural workers in China have much higher labor productivity than agricultural workers) and capital input is measured by the business sector real capital stock.

In the United States, growth rates of total factor productivity were about 2 percent when the United States benefited from the many inventions that originated from the "second industrial revolution." The growth rate of total factor productivity slowed down to 0.8–1.3 percent from the 1970s to the 1990s as the beneficial effects of the second industrial revolution faded. In the decade 2000–2010, the US total factor productivity growth rate accelerated to 1.6 percent, reflecting the relatively short-lived "third industrial revolution." However, since 2010, total factor productivity growth has nearly stopped. Robert Gordon, a leading neoclassical economist, wonders whether this would indicate the beginning of the end of technological progress (Gordon 2012).

From an ecological perspective, modern economic growth is based on the consumption of non-renewable resources (especially fossil fuels) and the relentless exploitation of the earth's ecological systems. From this perspective, the rapid growth of total factor productivity in the 1950s and the 1960s was largely based on the exploitation of cheap oil. The growth of total factor productivity in the early 2000s could be seen as the by-product of global capital relocation, which transferred much of the environmental and social costs from the core to the periphery.

In China, the total factor productivity growth rate averaged 1.4–1.5 percent in the 1990s and the 2000s. However, since 2010, China's total factor productivity has declined.

Neoclassical growth accounting is derived from the marginal productivity theory of distribution, which claims that in a competitive capitalist economy, "factors of production" (labor, capital, and land) receive incomes corresponding to their respective marginal productivity. On the other hand, Marxist political economy has always argued that productive labor alone is the source of value of commodities and capitalist incomes (profits and rents) are simply different forms of surplus value derived from the extraction of workers' surplus labor.

Nevertheless, neoclassical growth accounting could provide some interesting statistical information if one is interested in the empirical relationship between economic growth and the growth rates of labor and capital inputs.

In a capitalist economy, the growth of national income is distributed between wages and profits and the pattern of distribution has an impact on both the real wage and the profit rate.

The "labor contribution" in the growth accounting formula tell us the part of economic growth that needs to be committed to the payment of labor income assuming that the real wage stays constant and the total wages grow at the same proportion as the labor input. Similarly, the "capital contribution" represents the part of economic growth that needs to be committed to the payment of capital income assuming that the profit rate stays constant and total profits grow at the same proportion as the capital input.

If economic growth rate were greater than the sum of "labor contribution" and "capital contribution," there would be a "residual" which is called "total factor productivity" growth by neoclassical economics. The residual may be distributed between labor and capital, so that both the real wage and the profit rate can rise. Alternatively, the residual may be completely used up by either the growth of real wage or the growth of the profit rate.

For example, suppose that the total factor productivity growth rate is 2 percent, it is equally divided between the growth of labor income and the growth of capital income, the labor weight is 0.6 and the capital weight is 0.4. This would allow real wage to grow by 1 / 0.6 = 1.7 percent and the profit rate to grow by 1 / 0.4 = 2.5 percent.

However, if the real wage grows by 3.4 percent (rather than 1.7 percent), then the growth of real wage would have used up the entire growth of total factor productivity, leaving no room for profit rate growth.

Now suppose that the real wage grows by 3.4 percent but the total factor productivity growth rate declines to 1 percent. In this case, the profit rate will have to fall by 2.5 percent. Thus, a decline of the total factor productivity growth rate makes it more likely for the profit rate to fall.

In the long run, the growth rate of the capital stock should converge towards the economic growth rate (on the determination of the equilibrium output–capital ratio, see Chapter 2). Thus, in the long run, economic growth rate will be determined by the "total factor productivity" growth rate, the labor input growth rate, and the labor weight. This is known to neoclassical economics as the "steady-state" growth rate:

Long Run Steady-State Economic Growth Rate = Labor Input Growth Rate + Total Factor Productivity Growth Rate / Labor Weight

Suppose that in the future, China's total factor productivity growth rate will be 1 percent. The Chinese population is aging rapidly and China's working-age population is already in decline. The transfer of labor force from the agricultural sector to the non-agricultural sector will eventually come to an end. Thus, in the long run, both China's total labor force and the non-agricultural labor force will stop growing.

If the labor input growth rate is zero and the labor weight is 0.5, then China's long run steady-state economic growth rate will be 1 / 0.5 = 2 percent. If this is also China's profit growth rate and the ratio of accumulation is 0.7, then China's long run equilibrium profit rate will be 2.9 percent. Can a capitalist economic system operate stably with an average profit rate as low as 2.9 percent?

When Britain was the hegemonic power of the capitalist world system, British profit rates were often more than 25 percent. When the British profit rate fell to 10–15 percent in the early 1920s, it signaled the beginning of the "terminal crisis" of British hegemony. By the 1970s, British capitalism entered into a period of deep economic crisis and intense class conflicts as the economy-wide profit rate fell below 10 percent (see Figure 3.1).

In American economic history, the profit rate fell below 10 percent only during the Great Depression and briefly in 1980. On both occasions, American capitalism and global capitalism were in deep crisis. During the Great Recession of 2008–2009, the US profit rate fell to about 12 percent (see Figure 3.2 and 5.1).

Based on the historical experience of British and American capitalism, the leading capitalist economy (the economy functioning as the center of global capital accumulation) probably needs to have average profit rates significantly above 10 percent for the global capitalist system to operate with a reasonable level of economic and political stability.

China's profit rate was 18 percent in 2012. But China's profit rate has fallen rapidly. If China's economic growth rate gradually declines towards its long-term "steady-state" growth rate, what will happen to China's profit rate?

Figure 5.8 shows the historical and projected profits rates of the Chinese economy from 2000 to 2030. Under the projection, China's profit rate will fall below 12 percent after 2022 and fall below 10 percent after 2028.

The projection shown in Figure 5.8 is likely to be too optimistic. It assumes that China's total factor productivity will grow by 1 percent a year; non-agricultural employment will increase by 10 million each year between now and 2030, and gross profit (including both capitalist profit and the depreciation of fixed capital) will have a constant share of GDP at 40 percent.

In reality, both China's total factor productivity and non-agricultural employment may stop growing by the 2020s and rising wage and taxation cost is likely to result in falling gross profit share in the future.

Falling Profit Rate and Economic Crisis

The above projection assumes that China's profit rate will decline gradually as the economic growth rate falls towards the "steady-state" growth rate. In the real world of capitalist economy, both the profit rate and other economic variables are subject to wild fluctuations. If the profit rate falls below a certain threshold, capitalist investment may collapse. The collapse of investment may lead to rapid decline of the profit rate, leading to further declines of investment and profits. The vicious circle will continue as the capitalist economy sinks into a major crisis.

This can be illustrated by the following formula:

Wages + Profits + Taxes = Consumption + Investment + Government Spending + Net Exports

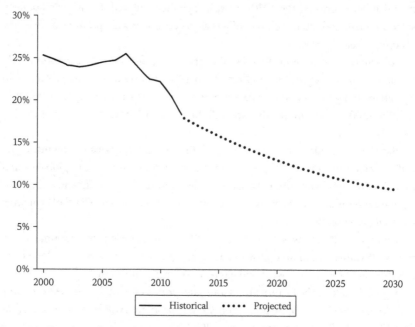

Figure 5.8 China's Profit Rate (Historical and Projected, 2000–2030)

Sources: For China's profit rate from 2000 to 2012, see Figure 5.1. Projections from 2013 to 2030 are based on the author's assumptions and calculation. Some key assumptions include: the total factor productivity will grow by 1 percent each year; non-agricultural employment will grow by 10 million each year; labor weight is 0.5; gross profits (including profits and depreciation) will have a constant share of GDP at 40 percent; and the ratio of accumulation will stay constant at 70 percent.

On the left side of the equation, the sum of wages, profits, and taxes equals total national income. On the right side, the sum of consumption, investment, government spending, and net exports equals total national expenditures. The above equation says that the total national income must equal total national expenditures. Rearrange the terms:

Profits = Investment + (Consumption – Wages) + (Government Spending – Taxes) + Net Exports

Consumption less wages roughly equals the household sector spending less the household sector income. The household sector spending less income is the household sector deficit. Government spending less government income (taxes) is the government sector deficit. Net exports represent a country's trade surplus, which is the same as the rest of the world's trade deficit. Thus, the above equation says that capitalist profit is determined by the sum of investment, household sector deficit, government sector deficit, and the foreign sector deficit.

Capitalist investment is motivated by the pursuit of profit. However, because of the fundamental uncertainty about the future, it is impossible for individual capitalists to make rational calculations of future profit rates. When capitalists are driven by optimistic "animal spirits," investment may rise to levels substantially above what can be justified by the underlying profit rate. On the other hand, when capitalists lose confidence, investment may suddenly collapse. Therefore, capitalist investment is fundamentally unstable, subject to large and violent fluctuations (Keynes 1964[1936]: 147–164).

If the profit rate falls below a certain threshold, capitalist confidence may be fatally undermined, leading to a large and rapid decline of investment. Figure 5.9 illustrates the historical relationship between profit rate and private investment in the US economy.

During the Great Depression, the US profit rate fell below 10 percent. The US net domestic private investment (including net non-residential fixed investment, net residential fixed investment, and change of inventories) fell from 7.5 percent of GDP in 1929 to –9.4 percent of GDP in 1932, a massive swing by 17 percent of GDP within just three years.

After World War II, the government sector was greatly expanded and Keynesian macroeconomic policies were regularly conducted to stabilize the capitalist economy. However, the decline of the profit rate from the mid-1960s to the early 1980s led to two deep recessions in 1974–1975 and in 1981–1982. In 1974, the profit rate fell to just above 10 percent and net private investment fell from 9.5

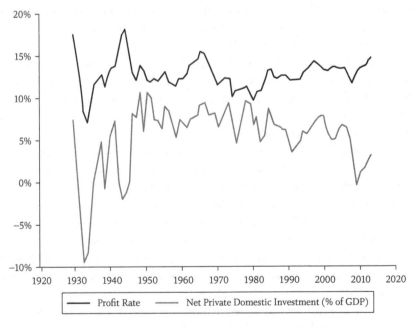

Figure 5.9 Profit Rate and Private Investment (United States, 1929–2013)

Sources: For US profit rates from 1929 to 2013, see Figure 3.2 and Appendix of Chapter 3. Net private domestic investment and GDP are from BEA (2014).

percent of GDP in 1973 to 4.6 percent of GDP in 1975. In 1980, the profit rate fell below 10 percent and net private investment fell from 9.5 percent in 1979 to 4.8 percent in 1982.

In the neoliberal era, as American capitalism became financialized and industrial capital was relocated, net private investment as a share of GDP tended to fall in the 1980s and the 1990s despite rising profit rates. During the last business cycle, the profit rate fell from 13.6 percent in 2006 to 11.6 percent in 2008. But net private investment collapsed, falling from 6.8 percent of GDP in 2005 to –0.3 percent of GDP in 2009. For the first time after World War II, US net private investment turned negative.

Based on the historical experience of American capitalism, when the profit rate fell to the range of 10–12 percent, private investment was likely to collapse, sending the economy into a deep recession. Using US historical experience as a guide, the Chinese economy is likely to enter into a major crisis in the 2020s when China's profit rate falls to 10–12 percent.

Can the Chinese profit rate be stabilized and maintained at a level that is sufficiently high to prevent major economic crisis? The equilibrium profit rate is determined by the profit's growth rate divided by the ratio of accumulation. In principle, the equilibrium profit rate can be raised either by raising the profit's growth rate or by lowering the ratio of accumulation.

The Chinese government is currently pursuing a new round of liberalization and privatization. According to neoliberal economists, liberalization and privatization will help to improve the allocation of resources, raise economic efficiency, and potentially deliver a higher growth rate of "total factor productivity."

Historical experience from China and other capitalist countries suggests that any acceleration of "total factor productivity" growth rate is likely to be short-lived. Moreover, the next two chapters will argue that the coming peak of world oil production and the escalating ecological crisis will impose fundamental constraints on China's and global economic growth.

How about lowering the ratio of accumulation? If China's long-run "steady-state" growth rate is 2 percent, then the ratio of accumulation will have to be lowered to 20 percent in order to stabilize the equilibrium profit rate at 10 percent.

China's business sector net investment is currently about 21 percent of GDP. If China's profit share of GDP eventually stabilizes at 20 percent (still higher than the current British or US profit share), then a ratio of accumulation of 20 percent implies that business sector net investment will be 4 percent of GDP. Thus, to stabilize China's profit rate at 10 percent, business sector net investment needs to fall by 17 percent of GDP.

If business sector net investment falls by 17 percent of GDP, what can replace the missing demand? One possibility is for business sector net investment to be replaced by household consumption. At the aggregate level, household consumption is mainly determined by labor income. In 2012, household consumption was

37 percent of China's GDP and labor income was 38 percent of China's GDP. For household consumption to rise by 17 percent of GDP, the labor income share of GDP needs to rise accordingly. However, if 17 percent of GDP were to be redistributed from the capitalist class to the working class, this would represent a massive reduction of the profit share and the profit rate. By itself, this would precipitate a major capitalist crisis.

If business sector net investment were to be replaced by government spending without a corresponding increase in government tax revenue, the government sector deficit and debt would surge. In fact, the Chinese economy is already struggling with unsustainable business and local government debts.

Debt and Economic Crisis

Big government has become indispensable for the normal operations of modern capitalist economies. During recessions, the government increases deficit, helping to offset part of the decline of private investment and stabilize capitalist profits. In the postwar years, the big government sector and Keynesian macroeconomic policies have helped the core capitalist countries to prevent major economic depressions from happening again (Minsky 2008[1986]).

However, under big government capitalism, a large portion of the investment risk has become socialized. While society as a whole (through big government) now pays for the investment risks, investment decisions continue to be made by the private capitalists who receive all the profits from investment. The socialization of investment risks without socialization of investment is an important contradiction of the modern capitalist system (Pollin and Dymski 1994; Li, M. 2009).

Without social control over investment, private capitalists are encouraged to undertake increasingly more risky investment financed by rising levels of debt. In the United States, non-financial sector debt has risen relative to GDP since the 1980s.

Figure 5.10 compares the non-financial sector debt to GDP ratios in the United States and China from 1980 to 2013.

From the second half of the 1980s to the 1990s, US total non-financial sector debt (including household debt, non-financial business debt, state and local government debts, and federal government debt) stayed around 180 percent of the US GDP. After 2000, the US non-financial sector debt surged as the US economic the housing bubble drove expansion. By 2007, on the eve of the economic crisis, the US non-financial sector debt reached 236 percent of GDP.

During and after the Great Recession, households and private businesses dramatically increased savings to pay down debts. Household sector debt peaked at 95 percent of GDP in 2007 and fell to 78 percent of GDP by 2013. Non-financial business sector debt peaked at 79 percent of GDP in 2008 and fell to 76 percent of GDP by 2010 (but rose to 81 percent of GDP by 2013). The private sector's repairing of balance sheets was made possible by the dramatic increase in US federal

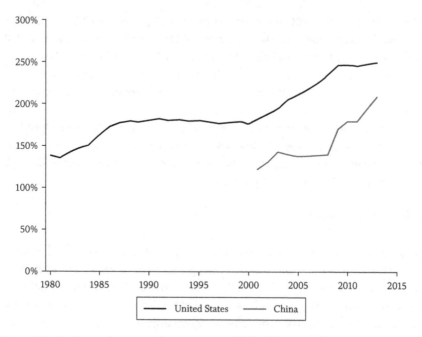

Figure 5.10 Nonfinancial Sector Debt to GDP Ratio (United States and China, 1980–2013)

Sources: Federal Reserve (2014) and National Bureau of Statistics of China (2013 and earlier years). China's non-financial sector debt in 2001 was assumed to be the sum of the total balances of the banking sector loans and the central government debt. Starting with 2002, the annual growth of non-financial sector debt is calculated as the "total social financing" less non-financial corporate business sector's net sales of equities plus change in the central government debt.

government debt, which surged from 35 percent of GDP in 2007 to 74 percent of GDP in 2013 (data are from Federal Reserve 2014).

In China, total non-financial sector debt was relatively stable from 2003 to 2008, with debt–GDP ratios fluctuating around 140 percent. In 2009, the Chinese government responded to the global economic crisis by encouraging local governments and state-owned enterprises to undertake massive investment programs financed by bank loans. From 2008 to 2013, China's non-financial sector debt surged from 140 percent of GDP to 209 percent of GDP.

Chinese central government debt is about 15 percent of GDP. Excluding the central government debt, China's total debt of households, non-financial businesses, and provincial and local governments reached 194 percent of GDP by 2013. By comparison, in 2007, the total debt of US households, non-financial businesses, and state and local governments was 191 percent of GDP.

Debt–GDP ratio cannot keep rising forever. Long-term debt–GDP ratio is determined by the ratio of the current borrowing as a share of GDP divided by the long-term nominal GDP growth rate. In 2013, China's non-financial sector borrowing reached 31 percent of GDP. China's current nominal GDP growth rate is about 10 percent. Given these ratios, China's non-financial sector debt will eventually rise above 300 percent of GDP!

Can China's debt–GDP ratio be stabilized without a major economic crisis? Suppose that the objective is to stabilize the non-financial sector debt–GDP ratio at 200 percent (a level that may be too high). If the long-term nominal GDP growth rate is 10 percent, then the non-financial sector borrowing needs to be lowered from about 30 percent of GDP to 20 percent of GDP.

How can non-financial sector borrowing be lowered relative to GDP? Let us first consider a "soft landing" scenario, which assumes that China will have ten years' time starting in 2014 to make the required adjustment.

If 30 percent of China's GDP is currently financed by an increase in debt, then about 70 percent of GDP does not directly depend on debt financing. Assuming that the part of GDP that is not directly dependent on debt financing can keep growing by 10 percent a year, then by the end of the ten-year period (or by 2023), this part of GDP will have grown to 182 percent of China's GDP in 2013 ($0.7 * 1.1^{10} = 1.82$). By 2023, non-financial sector borrowing should fall to 20 percent of GDP and the part of GDP that is not directly dependent on debt financing should account for 80 percent of GDP. Thus, by 2023, China's nominal GDP should be 227 percent of China's nominal GDP in 2013 ($1.82 / 0.8 = 2.27$), implying an average annual growth rate of 8.5 percent over the ten years (corresponding to an average annual growth rate of real GDP by about 6.5 percent, assuming that the inflation rate will be 2 percent).

However, does China have ten years to achieve the "soft landing" adjustment? Given the decline of the profit rate from 2013 to 2023, can China manage to avoid a sudden and large decline of business investment and borrowing? In fact, under the above "soft landing" scenario, China's non-financial sector debt is set to rise to 260 percent of GDP by 2020–2023 as the projected non-financial sector borrowings are large enough so that the debt continues to grow more rapidly than GDP until 2023. Such a debt level would have exceeded US debt levels during and after the Great Recession. High debt–GDP ratios in combination with a falling rate of profit will almost guarantee that the Chinese economy will be hit by a major economic and financial crisis.

Now consider a more realistic scenario. Suppose that non-financial sector borrowing accounts for 30 percent of China's GDP in 2014 and 2015. The Chinese economy starts to restructure in 2016 and the non-financial sector borrowing will fall to 20 percent of GDP by 2020. During the period of adjustment (2016–2020), the part of GDP that is not directly dependent on debt financing keeps growing by 10 percent each year. Under this scenario, China's non-financial sector borrowing will fall from 30 percent of GDP to 20 percent of GDP over five years (rather than ten years). During the period of adjustment, China's average annual growth rate of nominal GDP will be 7 percent (corresponding to an average annual growth rate of real GDP of about 5 percent). Nevertheless, under the second scenario, the non-financial sector debt–GDP ratio will rise to 231 percent by 2015 and 266 percent by 2020, and only begin to fall after 2020.

Both of the above two scenarios assume that China can maintain a long-term nominal GDP growth rate of 10 percent. Given the resources and environmental constraints, China's long-term economic growth rate is unlikely to be higher than 2–3 percent, implying growth rate of nominal GDP of 4–5 percent. Experiences of the United States, Europe, and Japan also suggest that economies hit by major financial crisis are likely to suffer from a structural downward shift in trend economic growth rate. If China's long-term nominal GDP growth rate is 5 percent, then non-financial sector borrowing will have to be lowered to 10 percent of GDP in order to stabilize the debt–GDP ratio at 200 percent.

Suppose that China is hit by a major financial crisis after 2015 and the non-financial sector borrowing falls sharply from 30 percent of GDP in 2015 to 10 percent of GDP in 2020. The part of GDP that is not directly dependent on debt financing grows by 5 percent each year from 2016 to 2020. Under this "hard landing" scenario, China's nominal GDP will shrink in 2016 and 2017 and will not exceed the 2015 level until 2021. The Chinese economy will suffer from a deep and prolonged recession and the non-financial sector debt–GDP ratio will surge to 314 percent of GDP by 2020.

The Next Global Economic Crisis

Being a large peripheral economy specializing in manufacturing exports, it is necessary for China to maintain heavy investment in industrial equipment and infrastructure. As a result, the Chinese capitalist economy has very high ratios of accumulation by the international standard.

As the Chinese population ages and the transfer of labor force from agriculture to non-agriculture approaches the limit, China's labor input growth is set to slow down. Resources and ecological constraints will limit China's future growth of "total factor productivity." If some positive growth of "total factor productivity" can be maintained, China's economic growth rate will approach 2–3 percent in the long term. Chapter 6 and 7 will argue that in the long run, very low economic growth rate and possibly negative economic growth will be required to maintain ecological sustainability. On the other hand, as wage, taxation, and capital costs rise, the profit share will decline and the profit's growth rate will be lower than the economic growth rate.

The combination of these developments implies that China's economy-wide profit rate is likely to approach or fall below 10 percent by the 2020s, leading to a major economic crisis. But with the rapid escalation of China's debt–GDP ratios, a major financial and economic crisis before 2020 is a distinct possibility.

Since 2008, China has replaced the United States to become the main driving engine of the global capitalist economy. For the period 2003–2013, China accounted for 31 percent of global economic growth (see Figure 1.1). Given China's current economic weight, if the Chinese economy simply stops growing, it could drag the global economy into the next recession.

In the neoliberal era, many governments have pursued fiscal austerity policies. Rising inequality has depressed mass consumption. Large parts of the global economy suffer from insufficient "effective demand." Many countries attempt to pursue an export-led strategy of economic growth. However, for the world as a whole, it is not possible for all countries to run trade surpluses.

Before the Great Recession of 2008–2009, the United States functioned as the world's "borrower of last resort." The United States ran large trade deficits, allowing the rest of the world to pursue export-led growth.

Table 5.2 compares the trade balances of the world's major regions (in billion US dollars) in selected years between 2000 and 2012. From 2000 to 2006, the US trade deficit expanded from about 380 billion dollars to 760 billion dollars, leading the expansion of global effective demand. US trade deficits allowed the Euro Area, Japan, China, the Russian Federation, and the Middle East to run large trade surpluses, fueling the global economic boom before 2008.

Figure 5.11 shows the trade balances of the world's major regions as a percentage of world GDP (in current US dollars) from 2000 to 2012. Since 2000, three regions (Europe and Central Asia, East Asia and the Pacific, and the Middle East and North Africa) have consistently run large trade surpluses. In 2006–2007, at the peak of the last global business cycle, total surpluses from the three regions reached 1.9 percent of world GDP. This represented the total amount of excess production generated from these regions that had to be absorbed by the rest of the world.

From 2000 to 2005, US trade deficits were roughly comparable to the total trade surpluses of Europe, East Asia, and the Middle East. In 2006, the US trade deficit absorbed 81 percent of the three regions' trade surpluses. In 2007, the US trade deficit absorbed 66 percent of the three regions' trade surpluses.

Between 2007 and 2012, the East Asian trade surplus shrank from 1.0 percent of world GDP to 0.4 percent of world GDP; the European and Central Asian trade surplus expanded from 0.4 percent of world GDP to 0.8 percent of world GDP; and the Middle East trade surplus expanded from 0.5 percent of world GDP to 0.8 percent of world GDP. Thus, Europe and the Middle East have replaced East Asia as the primary sources of trade surpluses.

The surge of the European trade surplus reflected the European economic crisis and the collapse of Europe's internal demand. The Middle East oil exporters benefited from the high oil prices from 2008 to 2012. China's investment boom and Japan's rising energy imports (after the 2011 Fukushima nuclear incident) contributed to the reduction of the East Asian trade surplus.

In 2012, total surpluses from the three regions reached 2.0 percent of world GDP, slightly above the previous peak observed in 2007. By this measure, the global trade imbalance has not been corrected.

North America is the only region that has consistently run large trade deficits since 2000. The rest of the world (Latin America, Sub-Saharan Africa, and South Asia) has had small surpluses or deficits. South Asia began to run significant trade

Table 5.2 Trade Balances of the World's Major Regions (billion US dollars, 2000–2012)

	2000	2002	2004	2006	2008	2010	2012
North America	−339	−393	−571	−728	−688	−550	−585
United States	−380	−425	−615	−762	−713	−519	−547
Canada and Other	41	32	44	34	25	−32	−38
Europe and Central Asia	98	206	260	241	283	351	576
Euro Area	39	165	194	117	120	159	315
United Kingdom	−28	−44	−60	−65	−60	−51	−53
Russian Federation	52	37	72	126	153	123	148
Other	35	47	54	63	69	120	166
East Asia and Pacific	173	183	250	412	469	504	298
China	29	37	51	209	349	223	232
Japan	69	53	91	55	9	66	−118
Other	76	92	108	148	110	215	184
Middle East and North Africa	79	48	127	288	388	255	577
L. America and Caribbean	−14	16	51	79	1	26	−51
Sub-Saharan Africa	13	2	−0	25	21	15	37
South Asia	−11	−11	−20	−52	−99	−106	−174
World Imports Less Exports	3	−54	−97	−265	−371	−510	−652

Source: World Bank (2014).

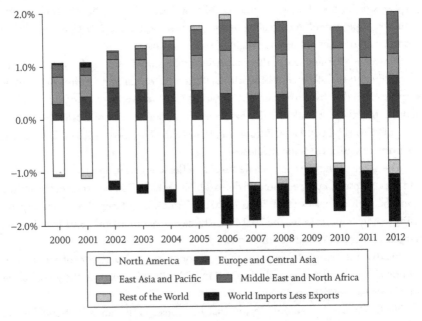

Figure 5.11 Trade Balance as % of World GDP (Major Regions, 2000–2012)

Sources: World Bank (2014).

deficits after 2008. In 2012, South Asia's trade deficit reached 170 billion dollars (about 0.2 percent of world GDP).

Theoretically, world total exports should equal total imports. But there are always statistical discrepancies. These discrepancies are shown as "World Imports Less Exports" in Table 5.2 and Figure 5.11. Before 2005, the discrepancies were reasonably small. In 2005, the world total exports were greater than the total imports by 150 billion dollars. In 2007, the "discrepancy" already helped to "absorb" 34 percent of the total trade surpluses from Europe, East Asia, and the Middle East. This indicates possible large illegal capital flows. One possibility is that some capital inflows into the "emerging markets" were misrepresented as exports to get around official capital controls. Another possibility is that some goods were illegally imported to avoid tariffs and other trade restrictions.

Since then, the discrepancy has steadily expanded. By 2012, the world total exports were greater than the total imports by an incredibly large 650 billion dollars or 0.9 percent of world GDP. In 2012, 45 percent of total trade surpluses from Europe, East Asia, and the Middle East were "absorbed" by this mysterious source of "statistical discrepancy."

While the global trade imbalance has regained the previous peak level, the composition of the imbalance has changed. Now about one-half of total trade surpluses from the world's main surplus-generating regions are not absorbed by the official imports of any nation-state. Instead, they are probably accounted for by illegal trade and capital flows. This change in the composition of the global trade imbalance could greatly increase the instability of the global economy when it is hit by the next major crisis.

In the last business cycle, the US economic growth rate peaked at 3.8 percent in 2004 and decelerated to 2.7 percent in 2006. The US economy entered into recession in late 2007 and did not begin to recover until late 2009. In 2009, the US economy contracted by 2.8 percent. From 2006 to 2009, the US economic growth rate fell by 5.5 percentage points. In 2006, the United States still accounted for 19 percent of the gross world economic product. US economic deceleration from 2006 to 2009 directly subtracted about one percentage point from the world economic growth.

In 2005–2006, the US trade deficit peaked at about 1.5 percent of world GDP. This is the largest trade imbalance that has been experienced by a major economy in modern world economic history. During the Great Recession, US imports fell sharply. By 2009, the US trade deficit shrank to less than 0.7 percent of world GDP. By reducing imports from the rest of the world, the reduction of the US trade imbalance amounted to a 0.8 percent subtraction of the world income.

Overall, the US recession itself and the correction of the US trade imbalance subtracted about two percentage points from world GDP. The American economic crisis destroyed global capitalist confidence and led to further declines of investment and consumption in the rest of the world. The global economy decelerated from a positive growth rate of 5.5 percent in 2007 to a contraction of 0.3 percent in 2009. The total reduction of global economic growth rate was about 6 percent, or three times the direct reduction caused by the American economic crisis.

Based on the US experience of postwar recessions, when the profit rate fell to 10–12 percent, business investment would fall by 5–10 percent of GDP. China's current investment–GDP ratio is more than twice as high as the US investment–GDP ratio before the Great Recession. Thus, when China's profit rate falls to 10–12 percent, China's investment could fall by 10–20 percent of GDP. In the previous sections, it has been argued that to stabilize China's profit rate or to stabilize China's debt–GDP ratio, China's investment may need to fall by 15–20 percent of GDP.

As China's investment (broadly defined, including productive and residential investment) is now about one-half of China's GDP, a reduction of investment by 10–20 percent of GDP would translate into a reduction of economic growth rate by 5–10 percentage points.

The Chinese economy was 16 percent of the gross world economic product in 2013. When China enters into the coming economic crisis, the Chinese economy may account for 20 percent of the gross world economic product. Thus, a reduction of the Chinese economic growth rate by 5–10 percentage points would translate into a direct reduction of global economic growth rate by 1–2 percentage points.

If China's investment falls by 10–20 percent of GDP, the Chinese demand for foreign capital goods and raw materials will decline accordingly. Chinese imports are about 3 percent of world GDP (in current US dollars) but may rise to 5 percent of world GDP when China enters into the economic crisis. If Chinese imports fall by 10–20 percent, it would subtract world income by 0.5–1 percentage point.

Overall, a major crisis of the Chinese economy would directly subtract 1.5–3 percentage points from the global economic growth rate. The global economy currently grows at about 3–4 percent a year. Global recession is usually defined as negative growth of world average per capita real GDP (IMF 2009: 11–14). Given the current global population growth rate, global economy would be in recession if the world economic growth rate falls below 1 percent. Thus, the direct effects from the Chinese economic crisis alone could drag the global capitalist economy into the next recession.

But a major crisis of the Chinese economy will cause major disruptions of the global commodity chains and fatally undermine the international capitalist confidence. The experience of 2008–2009 demonstrated that the overall damage to the global economy could be several times the direct effects resulting from the leading capitalist economy's major crisis.

When China enters into its major economic crisis, the ensuing global economic crisis could turn out to be far more damaging than the Great Recession of 2008–2009. In the past, global capitalism has managed to recover from major crises by undertaking restructuring without changing the basic institutional framework of capitalism. However, in the twenty-first century, global capitalism will have to confront not only the traditional economic and social contradictions but also the rapidly escalating ecological contradictions. In particular, the global carbon dioxide emissions from fossil fuels burning are currently on a path that threatens to bring about the worst climate catastrophes.

6

CLIMATE CHANGE, PEAK OIL, AND THE GLOBAL CRISIS

All economic activities involve physical and chemical transformations that directly and indirectly consume energy. Figure 6.1 shows the close relationship between global economic growth and energy consumption growth for the period 1991–2014. World primary energy consumption grew in every year during 1991–2014 except in 2009, when the global economy suffered the deepest economic crisis since World War II. For global economic growth rates above 1 percent, on average, an increase in global economic growth rate by one percentage point was associated with an increase in the world's primary energy consumption growth rate by 0.89 percentage points.

The core capitalist economies normally need to grow by about 3 percent a year to avoid rising unemployment and social instability (assuming a growth rate of labor force of 1 percent and a growth rate of labor productivity of 2 percent). Many peripheral and semi-peripheral economies need an economic growth rate of 4–5 percent to absorb the rural surplus labor force. On average, the global capitalist economy currently needs to grow by about 3.5 percent a year to avoid rising global unemployment. To sustain a global economic growth rate of 3.5 percent, world primary energy consumption needs to grow by about 2 percent a year.

In 2014, the world's total primary energy consumption reached 12.9 billion tonnes of oil equivalent. Oil was still the world's largest energy source, accounting for 32.6 percent of total primary energy consumption. Natural gas accounted for 23.7 percent, coal accounted for 30 percent, nuclear accounted for 4.4 percent, hydro accounted for 6.8 percent, and other renewables accounted for 2.5 percent. Fossil fuels (oil, natural gas, and coal) accounted for 86 percent of the world's total primary energy consumption in 2014.

By comparison, in 2000, oil accounted for 38.2 percent of the world's total primary energy consumption. Natural gas accounted for 23.3 percent, coal accounted for 25.3 percent, nuclear accounted for 6.2 percent, hydro accounted for 6.4 percent, and other renewables accounted for 0.6 percent. In 2000, the share of fossil fuels in the world's total primary energy consumption was 87 percent (data are from BP 2015).

Between 2000 and 2014, the global economy practically did not reduce its dependence on fossil fuels. In term of physical volume, coal made the largest contribution to world energy consumption growth, outpacing the combined

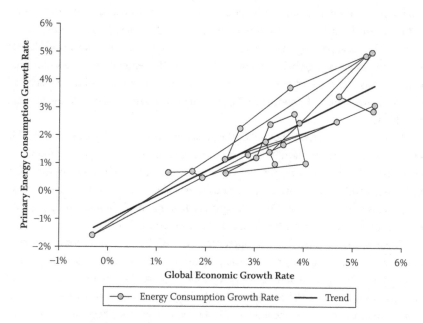

Figure 6.1 Global Economic Growth and Energy Consumption Growth (1991–2014)

Sources: World economic growth rates from 1991 to 2013 are from the World Bank (2014), updated to 2014 using data from IMF (2015). World primary energy consumption growth rates are from BP (2015). Linear regression result: primary energy consumption growth rate = −0.011 + 0.895 * global economic growth rate (regression R-square: 0.739).

growth of natural gas, hydro, and other renewables. Coal accounted for 43 percent of the total energy consumption growth between 2000 and 2014.

Fossil fuels are non-renewable resources. Current evidence suggests that the world's total production of oil, natural gas, and coal may peak before the mid-twenty-first century. The consumption of fossil fuels results in emissions of carbon dioxide and other greenhouse gases that threaten to bring about global ecological catastrophes. To prevent the climate catastrophes, it is imperative for human society to rapidly reduce the consumption of fossil fuels and achieve decarbonization of the global economy in a few decades. The question is whether decarbonization of the global economy can be achieved within the basic framework of global capitalism.

The Impending Climate Catastrophes

For the ten-year period 2005–2014, global land and ocean surface temperatures averaged 14.6°C (degrees Celsius). This was 0.8°C higher than the global average temperature during 1880–1889 and 0.6°C higher than during 1971–1980 (NASA 2015).

If global warming rises above 2°C (relative to the pre-industrial era), sea level could rise by several meters, submerging many coastal areas around the world. Arctic summer sea ice will disappear. As the Arctic sea ice helps to reflect back sunlight, the disappearing of the summer sea ice would result in a warmer Arctic ocean and accelerate global warming. About 10–30 percent of the species that currently exist on the earth may become extinct, greatly reducing biodiversity and increasing the chance of a sudden collapse of the earth's ecological systems (Hansen et al. 2013).

If global warming rises above 3°C, the Amazon rainforest will be destroyed. This could lead to a further warming of 1.5°C as the carbon stored in the rainforest is released into the atmosphere. Southern Africa, Australia, Mediterranean Europe, and the Western United States would turn into deserts. Sea level could rise by 25 meters as ice sheets in Greenland and West Antarctica disintegrate. Billions of people would become environmental refugees (Spratt and Sutton 2008: 26–32).

Humans have a core body temperature near 37°C. The maximum "wet-bulb temperature" (the temperature with 100 percent relative humidity) that humans can tolerate for a short period of time is about 35°C. If the wet-bulb temperature exceeds 35°C for several hours, the human body will begin to experience hyperthermia as dissipation of the metabolic heat generated by the human body becomes impossible. In practice, people have to work and undertake activities outside their homes. Thus, the practically tolerable maximum wet-bulb temperature is likely to be several degrees lower than the theoretical maximum of 35°C (Sherwood and Huber 2010).

Currently, the highest annual maximum wet-bulb temperature observed anywhere on earth is about 30°C. This may be taken as the practically acceptable maximum wet-bulb temperature for human inhabitation under the conditions of active work and outside living. About 60 percent of the world population currently lives in areas where the annual maximum web-bulb temperature is 26°C or higher. Thus, if the global average temperature rises by more than 5°C from the current level (or more than 6°C from the pre-industrial level), more than half of the world will become practically uninhabitable for human beings.

The currently available scientific evidence suggests that if global warming rises above 3°C (relative to the pre-industrial era), there may be runaway global warming that will be out of human control. According to James Hansen, one of the world's leading climate scientists, if global warming rises above 3°C, various "slow feedback" mechanisms (such as vegetation change and ice sheet disintegration) will begin to operate, taking the eventual long-term warming to more than 6°C (Hansen 2009: 140–171). In that case, much of the world will become uninhabitable for human beings. To prevent climate catastrophes that would destroy human civilization as we know it, it is absolutely imperative for the world to undertake the necessary economic and social transformations that will limit long-term global warming to no more than 3°C.

To provide a sufficiently large margin of safety to prevent very dangerous climate change, it would be desirable for the world to be committed to emissions reduction that will limit global warming to no more than 2°C. But given the current trajectory of the global economy and energy consumption, for all practical purposes, global warming of no more than 2°C is already out of reach.

The Emissions Budget

Figure 6.2 shows the relationship between global average surface temperature (shown in ten-year moving averages) and cumulative global carbon dioxide emissions from fossil fuels burning. From 1751 to 2000, the world's cumulative emissions of carbon dioxide from fossil fuels burning were 1.04 trillion tonnes. From 1880/1889 to 1991/2000, the global ten-year average surface temperature increased from 13.8°C to 14.4°C, or an increase by 0.6°C. From 2001 to 2014, the world's cumulative emissions of carbon dioxide from fossil fuels burning were 438 billion tonnes (or 42 percent of the cumulative emissions before 2000). From 1991/2000 to 2005/2014, the global ten-year average surface temperature increased by 0.2°C.

Since the late nineteenth century, there has been a near linear relationship between the global cumulative carbon dioxide emissions and global ten-year average surface temperatures. From 1880/1889 to 2005/2014, on average, an

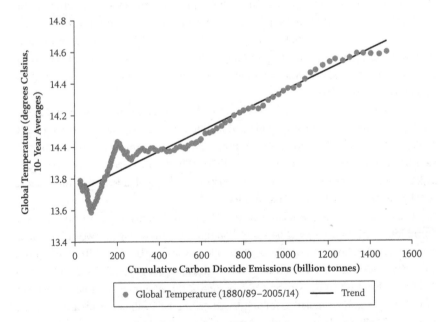

Figure 6.2 Global Carbon Dioxide Emissions and Global Temperature (1880–2014)

Sources: Global carbon dioxide emissions from fossil fuels burning from 1751 to 2012 are from EPI (2013a), updated to 2014 using data from BP (2015). Global average surface temperatures from 1880 to 2014 are from NASA (2015). Linear regression result: global average temperature (ten-year moving averages) = 13.712 + 0.643 * trillion tonnes of cumulative global carbon dioxide emissions (regression R-square: 0.924).

increase in cumulative global carbon dioxide emissions by 100 billion tonnes was associated with an increase in global ten-year average temperature by 0.064°C.

In recent years, global warming has temporarily slowed. The ten-year period ending in 2014 had an average temperature that was slightly above the ten-year periods ending in 2010 and 2011. The slow-down of global warming is caused mainly by short-term cooling of the Pacific Ocean and the growth of atmospheric aerosols. The relative cooling or warming of the Pacific Ocean can play a dominant role in the year-to-year variability of the global temperature, but has little impact on the long-term trend. The growth of atmospheric aerosols is probably mainly caused by China's massive coal consumption. Coal consumption generates carbon dioxide emissions that lead to global warming in the long run. However, in the short run, coal consumption generates air pollutants that have cooling effects. Over longer periods (periods longer than a decade), the warming effects from human generated greenhouse gases will dominate both the variability of the Pacific Ocean and the short-term cooling effects from aerosols (Hansen, Sato, and Ruedy 2014).

The Fifth Assessment Report (AR5) of the United Nations Intergovernmental Panel on Climate Change (IPCC) projects several scenarios of climate change corresponding to alternative pathways of carbon dioxide emissions from 2012 to 2100. The scenarios are represented by their approximate radiative forcing in year 2100 relative to 1750 (a measure of the warming effects of the human generated greenhouse gases). RCP 2.6, RCP 4.5, RCP 6.0, and RCP 8.5 refer to "representative concentration pathways" corresponding to average radiative forcing of 2.6 watts, 4.5 watts, 6.0 watts, and 8.5 watts per square meter of the earth surface in 2100 respectively (IPCC 2013).

Under RCP 2.6, the mean cumulative carbon dioxide emissions from 2012 to 2100 (from fossil fuels burning) will be 990 billion tonnes (with a range between 510 billion tonnes and 1.5 trillion tonnes). Projected global warming by 2081–2100 will be 1.0°C from 1986–2005 or 1.6°C from 1850–1900 (with a likely range of 0.9°C to 2.3°C). Thus, under RCP 2.6, there is a possibility that global warming may exceed 2°C by the end of the twenty-first century.

Under RCP 4.5, the mean cumulative carbon dioxide emissions from 2012 to 2100 (from fossil fuels burning) will be 2.9 trillion tonnes (with a range between 2.2 trillion tonnes and 3.7 trillion tonnes). The projected global warming by 2081–2100 will be 1.8°C from 1986–2005 or 2.4°C from 1850–1900 (with a likely range of 1.7°C to 3.2°C). Under RCP 4.5, global warming will continue beyond 2100. Assuming a climate sensitivity of 0.75°C per watt of radiative forcing based on the paleoclimate evidence ("climate sensitivity" tells the long-term global warming that would result from a permanent increase in radiative forcing on the earth surface, see Hansen 2009: 28–58), a radiative forcing of 4.5 watts per square meter implies a long-term global warming of 3.4°C. This would be sufficient to set in force runaway global warming that may eventually lead to climate catastrophes making much of the world uninhabitable for human beings.

Under RCP 6.0, the mean cumulative carbon dioxide emissions from 2012 to

2100 (from fossil fuels burning) will be 3.9 trillion tonnes (with a range between 3.1 trillion tonnes and 4.6 trillion tonnes). Projected global warming by 2081–2100 will be 2.2°C from 1986–2005 or 2.8°C from 1850–1900 (with a likely range of 2.0°C to 3.7°C). Under RCP 6.0, global warming will approach 3°C by 2100.

Under RCP 8.5, the mean cumulative carbon dioxide emissions from 2012 to 2100 (from fossil fuels burning) will be 6.2 trillion tonnes (with a range between 5.2 trillion tonnes and 7 trillion tonnes). Projected global warming by 2081–2100 will be 3.7°C from 1986–2005 or 4.3°C from 1850–1900 (with a likely range of 3.2°C to 5.4°C). Under RCP 8.5, major climate catastrophes will begin to fall upon humanity by the late twenty-first century.

Figure 6.3 compares the world's historical carbon dioxide emissions from fossil fuels burning from 2000 to 2014 and the projected emissions under RCP 2.6, 4.5, 6.0, and 8.5 from 2012 to 2100.

In 2011, world carbon dioxide emissions were about 34 billion tonnes. To achieve RCP 2.6, the world would need to have started emissions reduction in 2012 and maintain an annual reduction rate of 3 percent each year from 2012 to 2100. By 2100, world carbon dioxide emissions need to decline to about 2 billion tonnes, with a cumulative decline of 93 percent from the level in 2011.

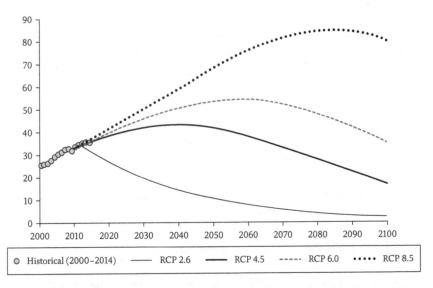

Figure 6.3 World Carbon Dioxide Emissions (Historical and Projected, Billion Tonnes, 2000–2100)

Sources: Historical carbon dioxide emissions from fossil fuels burning from 2000 to 2014 are from BP (2015). The emissions pathways for RCP 2.6, 4.5, 6.0, and 8.5 are calculated by this author assuming that the cumulative carbon dioxide emissions from 2012 to 2100 will be about 1, 3, 4, and 6 trillion tonnes respectively.

To achieve RCP 4.5, world carbon dioxide emissions need to peak in 2040 at about 43 billion tonnes. By 2100, world carbon dioxide emissions need to decline to about 17 billion tonnes, with a cumulative decline of 60 percent from the peak level.

To achieve RCP 6.0, world carbon dioxide emissions need to peak in the late 2050s at about 54 billion tonnes. By 2100, world carbon dioxide emissions need to decline to about 36 billion tonnes, with a cumulative decline of 33 percent from the peak level.

For RCP 8.5, world carbon dioxide emissions will keep growing until the mid-2080s when emissions rise to 84 billion tonnes. After the mid-2080s, world carbon dioxide emissions will decline slowly and fall to 80 billion tonnes by 2100.

From 2000 to 2014, world carbon dioxide emissions from fossil fuels burning rose from 25.5 billion tonnes to 35.5 billion tonnes. In recent years, world carbon dioxide emissions roughly followed the pathway of RCP 4.5.

The World Is Set for More Than 2°C Warming

To limit long-term global warming to no more than 2°C, the world needs to follow the emissions pathway of RCP 2.6. For RCP 2.6 to be achieved, the world needs to reduce carbon dioxide emissions by 3 percent each year from 2012 to 2100. In fact, world carbon dioxide emissions grew by an average annual rate of 2.4 percent between 2000 and 2014 (BP 2015). During the global recession of 2009, world carbon dioxide emissions only declined by 1.8 percent.

World carbon dioxide emissions depend on the total level of economic output (gross world economic product or world GDP) and the emission intensity of world GDP, which is defined as the ratio of world carbon dioxide emissions over world GDP:

World Carbon Dioxide Emissions = World GDP * Emission Intensity

In terms of their growth rates:

Growth Rate of Carbon Dioxide Emissions = World Economic Growth Rate + Emission Intensity Growth Rate

To write the same formula in the form of reduction rate:

Reduction Rate of Carbon Dioxide Emissions = Emission Intensity Reduction Rate – World Economic Growth Rate

From 2000 to 2014, world carbon dioxide emissions grew by an average annual rate of 2.4 percent and world GDP grew by an average annual rate of 3.7 percent. The implied average annual rate of reduction of emission intensity was 1.3 percent.

If the world economy grows by 3 percent a year and the reduction rate of emissions needs to be 3 percent, then the reduction rate of emission intensity will have to be 6 percent! Is this at all possible?

A basic fact that is often neglected by the technology optimists is that the current global economy is built upon capital infrastructure that is heavily dependent on fossil fuels. Regardless of how rapidly technology advances at the frontier, most of the new technologies need to be incorporated into new buildings and equipment. But the existing capital goods last many years and can only be replaced slowly. Typically only 4–5 percent of old capital stock is replaced each year.

Suppose that 5 percent of the old capital stock is depreciated and new capital investment exactly replaces the depreciated capital stock. In this case, there is no growth of capital stock. Suppose that new capital stock incorporates major technical innovations so that the new capital stock has an average emission intensity that is 50 percent lower than the old capital stock's emission intensity. This is roughly equivalent to assuming that all new electric power plants have zero emissions (currently electric power plants account for about 40 percent of total carbon dioxide emissions). But the new capital stock is only 5 percent of the total capital stock and the remaining 95 percent of the capital stock continues to use the old technologies. Thus, for the entire economy, the average emission intensity is only 2.5 percent lower than the previous emission intensity (5% * 50% = 2.5%).

Now suppose that the economy grows by 3 percent. To support the economic growth, capital stock also grows by 3 percent and the new capital stock now accounts for 8 percent of total capital stock (replacement of 5 percent of the old capital stock plus a net growth of capital stock by 3 percent). Again assuming that the new capital stock has an average emission intensity that is 50 percent lower than the old capital stock's emission intensity, the emission intensity of the entire economy will decline by 4 percent (8% * 50% = 4%). However, the economic growth rate is 3 percent. Thus, total emissions will decline by only 1 percent.

In reality, it is highly unlikely for new capital stock to incorporate new technologies that reduce the emission intensity by 50 percent. The observed emission intensity reduction rates of the global economy imply emission intensity reduction rates for the new capital stock of about 25 percent (see Figure 7.1 in Chapter 7).

The above reasoning suggests that it is basically impossible for the global economy to achieve an annual reduction rate of emission intensity of 6 percent over a multi-decade long period. Thus, under conditions of unlimited economic growth, it is not possible for the world to achieve the emissions reduction required to limit global warming to no more than 2°C relative to the pre-industrial era. In fact, even if the world immediately commits to zero economic growth, it would be nearly impossible for the world to achieve an annual emissions reduction rate of 3 percent each year between now and the end of the twenty-first century.

As global warming approaches 2°C, some forms of dangerous climate change will be unavoidable by the second half of the twenty-first century. The question is whether humanity can manage to avoid the worst climate catastrophes that may destroy human civilization. The answer to this question partly depends on the amounts of economically recoverable fossil fuels.

Peak Oil

Oil is the lifeblood of the global economy. According to the International Energy Agency's *Key World Energy Statistics*, in 2012, oil accounted for 93 percent of the world's total transportation fuels, 72 percent of the chemical industry feedstocks, 12 percent of the industrial sector fuels, 14 percent of the fuels used by the agricultural, residential, and commercial sectors, and 5 percent of the fuels used for electricity generation (IEA 2014).

Before the global economic crisis of 2008–2009, there was widespread discussion of a possible peak of world oil production in the near term (Long 2014). However, world oil production has increased steadily since 2009.

From 2008 to 2014, world oil production (including crude oil and natural gas liquids) increased from 3,989 million tonnes to 4,221 million tonnes (or from 82.8 million barrels per day to 88.7 million barrels per day) (BP 2015). Thus, during the six-year period, world oil production increased by 232 million tonnes or by 5.9 million barrels per day.

During the same six-year period, US oil production increased from 302 million tonnes to 520 million tonnes (or from 6.8 million barrels per day to 11.6 million barrels per day). US oil production increased by 218 million tonnes or by 4.8 million barrels per day.

Thus, in term of tonnes or energy content, virtually the entire growth of world oil production from 2008 to 2014 can be accounted for by the growth of US oil production. In term of barrels or physical volume, the US accounted for 81 percent of the total growth of world production of crude oil and natural gas liquids.

US oil production growth has been driven by the "shale oil" boom. Shale oil is also known as "tight oil," referring to the oil trapped in rocks with low permeability. Traditionally, it was too expensive to be developed. In recent years, US oil companies have used new technologies, such as hydraulic fracturing and horizontal drilling, which were first developed for the production of "shale gas." The new technologies and the high oil prices have made it economically profitable to extract the shale oil resources (Aleklett 2012: 109–111).

Figure 6.4 shows US historical oil production and the future production projected by the US Energy Information Administration (EIA). EIA's *Annual Energy Outlook 2014* projected that US oil production would peak in 2019 (EIA 2014a). In *Annual Energy Outlook 2015*, EIA revised its projections of future US oil production. According to EIA's latest "reference case" scenario, US oil production is projected to grow from 520 million tonnes in 2014 to 650 million tonnes in 2020. After 2020, US oil production is projected to decline slowly and will fall to 597 million tonnes by 2040 (EIA 2015).

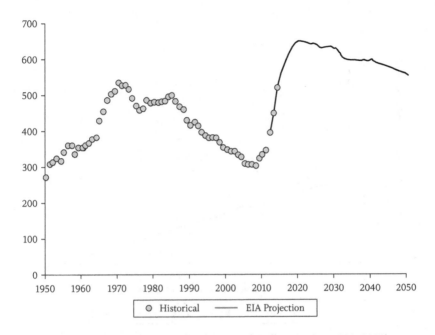

Figure 6.4 US Oil Production (Historical and Projected, Million Tonnes, 1950–2050)

Sources: US oil production from 1950 to 1964 is from Rutledge (2007). US oil production from 1965 to 2014 is from BP (2015). Projected US oil production from 2012 to 2040 is based on the EIA's "reference case" scenario (EIA 2015), extended to 2050 based on the trend.

In a report published by the Post Carbon Institute, David Hughes (a long-time Canadian geologist), projects that US shale oil production is likely to peak before 2020. Using detailed data from US shale oil production, Hughes concludes that EIA's official forecasts are likely to be too optimistic. Although US oil production will enjoy robust growth in the short run, the production level will be substantially below EIA's forecast by 2040 (Hughes 2014).

Outside the United States, oil production has stagnated. Russia, the world's second largest oil producer, is approaching peak oil production (Patterson 2014). Western sanctions on Russia are preventing Russia from receiving western capital and advanced drilling equipment. If the sanctions are not lifted, Russia could face a 20 percent decline in oil production by 2020 (Chazan and Farchy 2014). Tony Hayward, the former chief executive of BP (one of the largest multinational oil and gas companies in the world), warned that "The world has been lulled into a false sense of security because of what's going on in the US." According to Hayward, the world would struggle to find new sources of oil supply when US oil production peaks again (Chazan 2014).

Figure 6.5 shows the Hubbert linearization analysis of world (excluding the United States) oil production. Hubbert linearization analysis is named after the American geologist M. King Hubbert. It projects the ultimately recoverable amount of

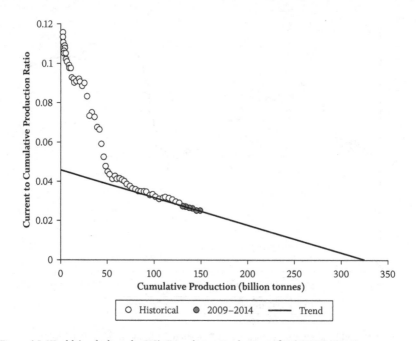

Figure 6.5 World (excluding the US) Cumulative Production of Oil (1950–2014)

Sources: World historical oil production is from Rutledge (2007) and BP (2015). For the linear trend from 1995 to 2013, regression R-square is 0.959.

non-renewable resources based on the observed relationship between current production and cumulative production (Hubbert 1982).

As cumulative oil production rises, the ratio of current production to cumulative production tends to fall. By observing the declining trend of the current production to cumulative production ratios, one can estimate the ultimately recoverable amount of oil by identifying where the cumulative oil production would be as the current production to cumulative production ratio falls to zero (for more discussion on Hubbert linearization, see Li, M. 2014: 76–78).

The linear trend from 2009 to 2014 (regression R-square is 0.959) indicates that the ultimately recoverable amount of oil resources for the world (excluding the United States) will be about 327 billion tonnes. World (excluding the United States) cumulative production of oil up to 2014 was about 149 billion tonnes. According to the Hubbert linearization model, peak production is likely to happen when about a half of the ultimately recoverable resources have been produced. World (excluding the United States) annual oil production is about 3.7 billion tonnes. At this rate, world (excluding the United States) cumulative oil production will exceed 163 billion tonnes (half of 327 billion tonnes) by 2018.

Figure 6.6 shows historical and projected oil production for the world (excluding the United States) from 1950 to 2050. World (excluding the United States) oil production is projected to peak in 2018 with a production level of 3,747 million

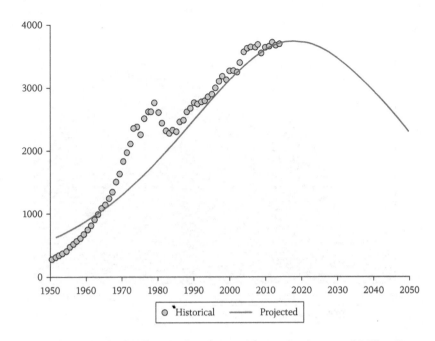

Figure 6.6 World (excluding the US) Oil Production (Historical and Projected, Million Tonnes, 1950–2050)

Sources: World historical oil production is from Rutledge (2007) and BP (2015). Projected oil production is based on the parameters derived from the linear regression shown in Figure 6.5.

tonnes. By 2050, world (excluding the United States) oil production is projected to fall to 2,308 million tonnes.

For the world as a whole, the projected ultimately recoverable oil resources in the United States and the rest of the world add up to 409 billion tonnes. The world's cumulative oil production up to 2014 was 180 billion tonnes. The projections imply that the world's remaining recoverable oil resources will be 229 billion tonnes. By comparison, BP's *Statistical Review of World Energy* reports that the world's "proved oil reserves" in 2014 were 240 billion tonnes (BP 2015). The "proved oil reserves" reported by BP include the official oil reserves reported by the OPEC countries (Organization of Petroleum Exporting Countries), which have been inflated for political purposes (Aleklett 2012: 45–49).

The world's biofuels production increased from 9 million tonnes of oil equivalent in 2000 to 71 million tonnes of oil equivalent in 2014, with an average annual growth of 4.4 million tonnes of oil equivalent. I assume that the world's biofuels production will grow by 5 million tonnes of oil equivalent each year from 2015 to 2050.

Figure 6.7 shows the historical and projected world production of liquid fuels from 1950 to 2050. "Liquid fuels" are broadly defined to include crude oil, natural gas liquids, and biofuels. World total liquid fuels production is projected to peak in 2020

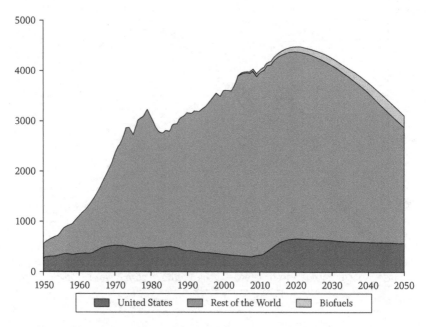

Figure 6.7 World Production of Liquid Fuels (Million Tonnes of Oil Equivalent, 1950–2050)

Sources: World historical oil production is from Rutledge (2007) and BP (2015). Historical biofuels production from 1990 to 2014 is from BP (2015). For projected oil production, see Figure 6.4 and 6.6.

at 4,493 million tonnes of oil equivalent. By 2050, world total liquid fuels production is projected to decline to 3,113 million tonnes of oil equivalent.

Oil and Economic Growth

Oil provides liquid fuels and chemical industrial inputs that cannot be easily substituted by other forms of energy. If global oil production begins to fall, the shortage of liquid fuels could become a binding constraint on global economic growth.

Figure 6.8 shows the historical relationship between the annual change in world oil consumption (including all liquid fuels) and the world economic growth rate from 1991 to 2014. Since 1991, world oil consumption has grown each year except in 1993 and 2008–2009. For global economic growth rates above 1 percent, on average, an increase in global economic growth rate by one percentage point was associated with an annual increase in world oil consumption by 470,000 barrels per day. From 1990 to 2014, on average, world oil consumption grew by 1.06 million barrels per day annually.

Between 2020 and 2050, world liquid fuels production is projected to decline from 4,493 million tonnes to 3,113 million tonnes, with an average annual decline

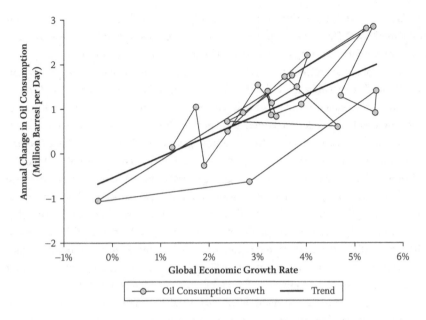

Figure 6.8 Global Economic Growth and Oil Consumption Growth (1991–2014)

Sources: World economic growth rates from 1991 to 2013 are from the World Bank (2014), updated to 2014 using data from the IMF (2015). World oil consumption is from BP (2015). Linear regression result: oil consumption growth = −0.529 + 0.469 * global economic growth rate (regression R-square: 0.514).

of 46 million tonnes, which corresponds to an average annual decline of 1 million barrels per day. Based on the historical relationship between world oil consumption growth and the global economic growth rate, an annual decline of oil consumption by 1 million barrels per day corresponds to a contraction of the global economy by about 1 percent a year.

Based on this rough estimate, peak oil will have a devastating impact on the global economy. It should be noted that this rough estimate is based on the historical relationship and does not take full account of future possibilities of technical change. In the future, as world oil production declines and the oil price rises, higher oil prices may encourage more rapid substitution of other energies for oil. Can the substitution of other energies for oil help to sustain normal global economic growth?

To sustain a normal global economic growth rate of 3.5 percent (the average global economic growth rate in recent years), world oil consumption needs to rise by about 50 million tonnes each year (approximately 1 million barrels per day). Oil may be substituted by natural gas. To substitute 50 million tonnes of oil, it would take 55 billion cubic meters of natural gas, which equals 1.6 percent of world natural gas production in 2014 but 74 percent of the average annual growth of world natural gas production from 2000 to 2014.

Existing natural gas production is already committed to other industrial and residential uses. Thus, the natural gas that is used to substitute oil will have to come from additional natural gas production. The above calculation suggests that just to substitute for about 1 million barrels per day of oil consumption, natural gas production growth needs to accelerate by about 70 percent! In addition, cars, buses, and trucks need to be remodeled to operate with natural gas. Trillions of dollars of additional investment will be needed to build natural gas pipelines and fueling stations.

Liquid fuels can be made from natural gas. The advantage of gas-to-liquids technology is that the liquid fuels made from natural gas can be used directly in the existing oil-based infrastructure, saving the massive investment on infrastructure transformation. But gas-to-liquids transformation involves substantial energy losses. For example, the Chevron Corporation describes a process that can convert 325 million cubic feet of natural gas (with an energy equivalent of 61,000 barrels of oil) into 33,000 barrels of synthetic diesel, implying a net energy loss of 46 percent (Chevron 2014). At this rate, to substitute 50 million tonnes of oil, it would take about 93 million tonnes of oil equivalent or 103 billion cubic meters of natural gas.

Liquid fuels can also be made from coal. Coal has many varieties with a wide range of quality and energy content. On average, 1 tonne of coal has the same energy content as about 0.5 tonne of oil. Coal-to-liquids transformation involves an energy loss of about 50 percent. South Africa relies upon coal-to-liquids to meet about one-third of its petroleum product demand. On average, it took about 0.7–1 tonne of coal to make one barrel of synthetic fuel (Höök and Aleklett 2009). This corresponds to a conversion ratio of 5–7 tonnes of coal for 1 tonne of oil. To substitute 50 million tonnes of oil, it would take 250–350 million tonnes of coal. Each tonne of coal consumption results in about 2 tonnes of carbon dioxide emissions. To substitute 50 million tonnes of oil each year from 2021 to 2050, it would require 7.5–10.5 billion tonnes of additional coal consumption, which would result in 15–21 billion tonnes of additional carbon dioxide emissions.

Biomass is the only renewable energy that can be converted to liquid fuels without major technical obstacles. Currently, biofuels are mainly made from corn, sugarcane, and palm oil that compete with food supply. In 2013, the United States produced 28.4 million tonnes of biofuels, accounting for only 0.7 percent of the world's total oil consumption (BP 2015). In the same year, the United States used 127 million tonnes of corn for fuel ethanol production, accounting for 5.3 percent of the world grain production (EPI 2014). At this rate, just to provide 5 percent of the world oil consumption, it would use up about 37 percent of the world grain production.

In the transportation sector, electric vehicles may replace the passenger cars and buses fueled by petroleum products. The lithium requirement for fully electric cars with a range of 100 miles varies between 3 kilograms per battery and 13 kilograms per battery. If electric cars were to have a range comparable to today's typical gasoline-fueled cars (about 300 miles), the lithium requirement needs to be between 9 kilograms per battery and 39 kilograms per battery (Gaines and Nelson 2009).

The world's current car fleet is about 800 million (Oak Ridge National Laboratory 2014). Assuming that the lithium requirement for electric vehicles will be 10 kilograms per battery, it would take 8 million tonnes of lithium to replace the world's current car fleet with electric vehicles. The world lithium production in 2013 was 35,000 tonnes. Currently, about 30 percent of the world lithium consumption is used for batteries and only a fraction of the lithium consumption for batteries is used for electric vehicles (USGS 2014). If the entire world's annual lithium production (at the rate of 2013 production) is used to make batteries for electric vehicles, it will take about 230 years just to replace the world's current car fleet with electric vehicles. This has not taken into account the growth of the world car fleet as a function of world economic growth. Nor has it taken into account the additional lithium consumption that will be needed to replace worn-out lithium batteries.

In 2010, the world's total motor gasoline consumption was 22.1 million barrels per day, accounting for 25 percent of world petroleum consumption (EIA 2014b). Assuming that in 2013, 25 percent of world oil consumption is used for fuel consumption by passenger cars, the total fuel consumption by passenger cars would be about 1,050 million tonnes. On average, each car in the world consumes about 1.25 tonnes of fuel a year.

To replace 50 million tonnes of passenger car fuel with electricity, would require replacing 40 million gasoline-fueled cars with electric vehicles. The total lithium consumption required to produce 40 million electric vehicles will be 400,000 tonnes, or 11 years of the world's current annual production of lithium.

Natural Gas

Natural gas plays a crucial role in meeting the energy demand of the industrial and residential sectors. According to the International Energy Agency's *Key World Energy Statistics*, in 2012, natural gas accounted for 20 percent of the world's industrial sector fuels, 23 percent of chemical industry feedstocks, 19 percent of the fuels used by agricultural, residential, and commercial sectors, and 4 percent of transportation fuels (IEA 2014).

Natural gas-fired electric power plants accounted for 23 percent of the world's electricity generation in 2012. As the gas-fired turbines can be turned on or off quickly, natural gas-fired plants play a very important role in meeting the peak demand for electric power as well as helping to balance against fluctuations of intermittent electric power sources, such as wind and solar electric power.

According to the International Energy Agency, the world's remaining "technically" recoverable natural gas resources amount to 750 trillion cubic meters (about 675 billion tonnes of oil equivalent), including 420 trillion cubic meters of conventional gas resources and 330 trillion cubic meters of shale gas and other unconventional gas resources (IEA 2012).

Only a fraction of the technically recoverable natural gas resources will prove to be economically recoverable and the development of unconventional natural gas resources may involve substantial environmental costs. Aleklett (2012: 243–247) estimates that the world's cumulative production of natural gas up to 2100 will be 340 billion tonnes of oil equivalent. BP's *Statistical Review of World Energy* reports that the world's "proved natural gas reserves" in 2013 were 187 trillion cubic meters or 168 billion tonnes of oil equivalent (BP 2015).

The United States is the world's largest natural gas producer. Figure 6.9 shows historical and projected US natural gas production from 1950 to 2050. US natural gas production reached the first peak in 1971. Since 2005, US natural gas production has grown rapidly, driven by the shale gas boom. In 2014, the United States produced 668 million tonnes of oil equivalent of natural gas, accounting for 21 percent of world natural gas production (BP 2015). According to the US Energy Information Administration, US natural gas production is projected to rise to 921 million tonnes of oil equivalent by 2040 (EIA 2015).

US cumulative natural gas production up to 2014 was 31 billion tonnes of oil equivalent. A Hubbert linearization analysis applied to the EIA projection implies that the US's ultimately recoverable natural gas resources will be 130 billion tonnes of oil equivalent and the remaining recoverable natural gas resources will be 99 billion tonnes of oil equivalent. US natural gas production will not peak until 2054.

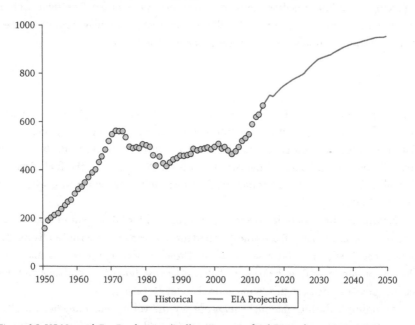

Figure 6.9 US Natural Gas Production (Million Tonnes of Oil Equivalent, 1950–2050)

Sources: US natural gas production from 1950 to 1964 is from EIA (2014c). US natural gas production from 1965 to 2014 is from BP (2015). Projected US natural gas production from 2012 to 2040 is based on the EIA's "reference case" scenario (EIA 2015), extended to 2050 based on the trend.

Shale gas production consumes a massive amount of fresh water. Outside the United States, production of shale gas is likely to be limited by the shortage of fresh water. According to a report by the World Resources Institute, 38 percent of the world's shale gas resources are in areas that suffer from high or extremely high levels of water stress (Reig, Luo, and Proctor 2014).

Figure 6.10 shows the Hubbert linearization analysis of the world (excluding the United States) natural gas production. The linear trend from 2009 to 2014 (regression R-square is 0.723) indicates that the ultimately recoverable natural gas resources for the world (excluding the United States) will be about 188 billion tonnes of oil equivalent. World (excluding the United States) cumulative production of natural gas up to 2014 was 65 billion tonnes of oil equivalent. The implied remaining recoverable natural gas resources are 123 billion tonnes of oil equivalent.

Figure 6.11 shows historical and projected natural gas production for the world (excluding the United States) from 1950 to 2050. World (excluding the United States) natural gas production is projected to peak in 2025 with a production level of 2,769 million tonnes of oil equivalent. By 2050, world (excluding the United States) natural gas production is projected to fall to 1,711 million tonnes of oil equivalent.

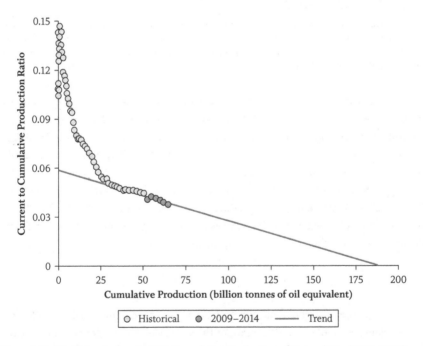

Figure 6.10 World (excluding the US) Cumulative Production of Natural Gas (1950–2014)

Sources: World's historical natural gas production from 1900 to 1969 is estimated from carbon dioxide emissions from natural gas burning (data are from EPI 2013b). Historical natural gas production from 1970 to 2014 is from BP (2015). For the linear trend from 2009 to 2014, regression R-square is 0.723.

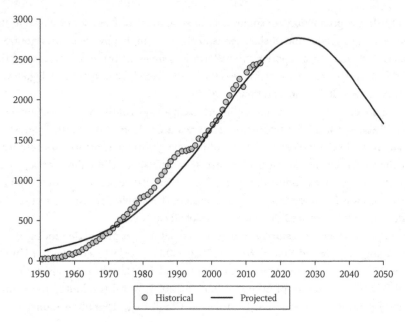

Figure 6.11 World (excluding the US) Natural Gas Production (Million Tonnes of Oil Equivalent, 1950–2050)

Sources: World's historical natural gas production from 1950 to 1969 is estimated from carbon dioxide emissions from natural gas burning (data are from EPI 2013b). Historical natural gas production from 1970 to 2014 is from BP (2015). Projected natural gas production is based on the parameters derived from the linear regression shown in Figure 6.10.

For the world as a whole, projected ultimately recoverable natural gas resources in the United States and the rest of the world add up to about 318 billion tonnes of oil equivalent. The world's cumulative natural gas production up to 2014 was 96 billion tonnes of oil equivalent. The projections imply that the world's remaining recoverable natural gas resources will be 222 billion tonnes of oil equivalent.

Figure 6.12 shows the historical and projected world natural gas production from 1950 to 2050. World natural gas production is projected to peak in 2029 at 3,587 million tonnes of oil equivalent. By 2050, world natural gas production is projected to decline to 2,669 million tonnes of oil equivalent.

Coal

Coal is the world's largest fuel source of electricity generation. Coal-fired electric power plants accounted for 40 percent of the world's electricity generation in 2012. In addition, coal provided 29 percent of the world's industrial sector fuels, 5 percent of chemical industrial feedstocks, and 4 percent of the fuels used in the agricultural, residential, and commercial sectors (IEA 2014). Coking coal is an essential input for steel production. In 2010, about 720 million tonnes of coal was used in steel

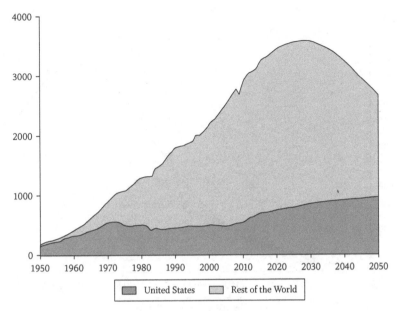

Figure 6.12 World Natural Gas Production (Million Tonnes of Oil Equivalent, 1950–2050)
Sources: See Figure 6.9 and 6.11.

production (world steel production in 2010 was 1.4 billion tonnes) (World Coal Association 2014).

China is the world's largest coal producer. In 2014, China produced 3,874 million tonnes of coal (1,845 million tonnes of oil equivalent), accounting for 47 percent of the world's total coal production (BP 2015).

According to BP's *Statistical Review of World Energy*, China's coal reserves are 114.5 billion tonnes (including 62.2 billion tonnes of bituminous coal and 52.3 billion tonnes of sub-bituminous coal and lignite). BP has not updated its reported coal reserves for China in many years. According to the *China Statistical Yearbook 2014*, China's coal "reserve base" was 236 billion tonnes at the end of 2013. China's cumulative coal production up to 2013 was 68 billion tonnes. I assume that China's ultimately recoverable coal resources will be 304 billion tonnes.

Figure 6.13 shows China's historical and projected coal production from 1950 to 2050. China's coal industry association predicts that China's coal production will decline by 5 percent in 2015 due to falling demand from electric power and steel industries (China Coal Industry Association 2015a). However, a separate report from the coal industry association points out that China's annual coal production capacity has reached 5 billion tonnes (China Coal Industry Association 2015b). I assume that China's coal production will resume growth after 2015. China's coal production is projected to peak in 2033 with a production level of 4,977 million tonnes. China's coal production will decline to 3,648 million tonnes by 2050.

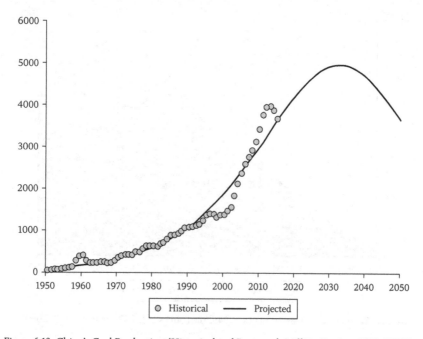

Figure 6.13 China's Coal Production (Historical and Projected, Million Tonnes, 1950–2050)

Sources: China's historical coal production before 1981 is from Rutledge (2007). China's coal production from 1981 to 2014 is from BP (2015). Projection of China's coal production is based on the assumption that China's ultimately recoverable coal resources will be 304 billion tonnes.

The United States is the world's second largest coal producer. In 2014, the US produced 907 million tonnes of coal (508 million tonnes of oil equivalent), accounting for 13 percent of the world's total coal production. According to BP's *Statistical Review of World Energy*, US coal reserves are 237.3 billion tonnes, including 108.5 billion tonnes of anthracite and bituminous coal and 128.8 billion tonnes of sub-bituminous coal and lignite (BP 2015).

Figure 6.14 shows the historical and projected US coal production from 1950 to 2050. The US coal production peaked in 2008 at 1,063 million tonnes. According to the US Energy Information Administration's projection, the US coal production will rise to 967 million tonnes by 2020 and will stay around 1 billion tonnes between 2020 and 2040 (EIA 2015).

A Hubbert linearization analysis applied to the EIA projection implies that the US's ultimately recoverable coal resources will be 187 billion tonnes. The US's cumulative coal production up to 2014 was 73 billion tonnes. This implies that the US's remaining recoverable coal resources will be 114 billion tonnes.

In 2014, the rest of the world (the world excluding China and the United States) produced 3,384 million tonnes of coal (1,781 million tonnes of oil equivalent). According to BP's *Statistical Review of World Energy*, the rest of the world's coal reserves are 539.7 billion tonnes, including 232.5 billion tonnes of anthracite

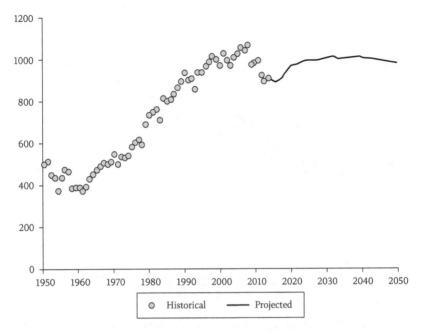

Figure 6.14 US Coal Production (Historical and Projected, Million Tonnes, 1950–2050)

Sources: The US's historical coal production before 1981 is from Rutledge (2007). The US coal production from 1981 to 2014 is from BP (2015). Projected US coal production from 2012 to 2040 is based on the EIA's "reference case" scenario (EIA 2015), extended to 2050 based on the trend.

and bituminous coal and 307.2 billion tonnes of sub-bituminous coal and lignite (BP 2015).

The rest of the world's cumulative production of coal up to 2014 was 206 billion tonnes. Figure 6.15 shows the rest of the world's historical and projected coal production from 1950 to 2050, assuming that the rest of the world's ultimately recoverable coal resources will be 746 billion tonnes. The rest of the world's coal production is projected to rise to 4,192 million tonnes by 2050 and will not peak until 2057.

Figure 6.16 shows historical and projected world coal production from 1950 to 2050. World coal production is projected to peak in 2034, with a production level of 9,916 million tonnes. World coal production will decline to 8,825 million tonnes by 2050.

Nuclear Energy

In 2014, world consumption of nuclear electricity was 2,537 terawatt-hours (574 million tonnes of oil equivalent, converted based on the "thermal equivalent" assumption that 1 million tonnes of oil equivalent = 4.4194 terawatt-hours of electricity). Between 2000 and 2014, world nuclear electricity consumption declined

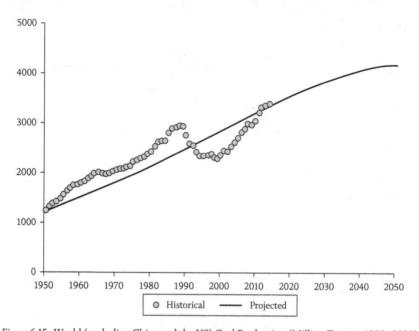

Figure 6.15 World (excluding China and the US) Coal Production (Million Tonnes, 1950–2050)

Sources: The historical coal production from 1950 to 1980 is from Rutledge (2007). Coal production from 1981 to 2014 is from BP (2015). Projected coal production is based on the assumption that the ultimately recoverable coal resources of the world (excluding China and the United States) will be 746 billion tonnes.

by 45 terawatt-hours (BP 2015). In 2012, nuclear electricity accounted for 11 percent of the world electricity generation (IEA 2014).

Current nuclear technology is based on nuclear fission reactions (obtaining energy liberated by fission of atoms). Uranium is the basic raw material for nuclear fission reactions. In 2014, the world's total uranium requirements for nuclear power plants are estimated to be about 66,000 tonnes (World Nuclear Association 2014). World uranium production is about 58,000 tonnes. The difference was made up by "secondary sources" (supplies from civilian and military uranium stockpiles).

According to the 2011 edition of the "Red Book" (an official report on uranium resources), the world's identified uranium resources are about 7 million tonnes (Nuclear Energy Agency 2012). At the current consumption rate, the world's identified uranium resources can last about 120 years.

As of October 2014, the world had 376 gigawatts of nuclear electric power plants. 75 gigawatts of nuclear power plants are currently under construction, 191 gigawatts are being planned, and 331 gigawatts are being proposed (World Nuclear Association 2014).

If all of the currently constructed, planned, and proposed nuclear power plants become operable in the next thirty years, the world will need to install on average about 20 gigawatts of new nuclear power plants each year.

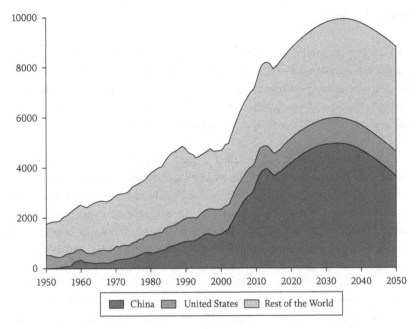

Figure 6.16 World Coal Production (Historical and Projected, Million Tonnes, 1950–2050)

Sources: See Figure 6.13, 6.14, and 6.15.

I assume that the world will install 20 gigawatts of new nuclear power plants each year from 2014 to 2050, but 2 percent of existing nuclear power plants will close every year. I also assume that the nuclear power plants have an average capacity utilization rate of 80 percent.

Hydro, Geothermal, and Biomass

In 2014, the world consumption of hydro electricity was 3,885 terawatt-hours (879 million tonnes of oil equivalent). From 2000 to 2014, world consumption of hydro electricity grew from 602 million tonnes to 879 million tonnes of oil equivalent, with an average annual growth of 20 million tonnes of oil equivalent (BP 2015). In 2012, hydro accounted for 16 percent of the world electricity generation (IEA 2014).

In 2014, the world consumption of geothermal and biomass electricity was 509 terawatt-hours (115 million tonnes of oil equivalent). From 2000 to 2014, world consumption of geothermal and biomass electricity grew from 45 million tonnes to 115 million tonnes of oil equivalent, with an average annual growth of 5 million tonnes of oil equivalent (BP 2015).

I assume that the world consumption of hydro, geothermal, and biomass electricity will grow by 25 million tonnes of oil equivalent each year from 2015 to 2050.

Wind and Solar

In 2014, world consumption of wind electricity was 706 terawatt-hours (160 million tonnes of oil equivalent). From 2000 to 2014, world consumption of wind electricity grew at an average annual rate of 25.5 percent. In 2014, the world consumption of solar electricity was 186 terawatt-hours (42 million tonnes of oil equivalent). From 2000 to 2014, the world consumption of solar electricity grew at an average annual rate of 44.9 percent.

Up to 2014, the world had installed 373 gigawatts of wind power generating capacity. In 2014, the observed world average capacity utilization rate for the wind power generating capacity was 22 percent. Up to 2014, the world had installed 180 gigawatts of solar power generating capacity. In 2014, the observed world average capacity utilization rate for the solar power generating capacity was 12 percent. In 2014, the observed world average capacity utilization rate for wind and solar power generating capacity combined was 18 percent (BP 2015).

Figure 6.17 shows the relationship between the total annual installation of wind and solar power generating capacity and the "annual growth to installation ratios" which are the ratios of the annual growth of the annual installation over the total annual installation. As the total annual installation rises, the annual growth to installation ratio tends to fall.

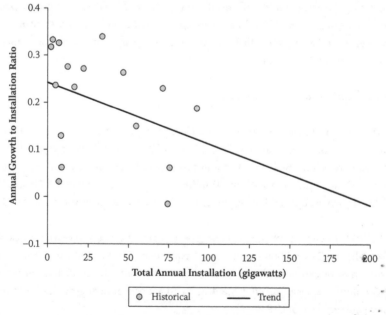

Figure 6.17 World Annual Installation of Wind and Solar Power (1998–2014)

Sources: Data for wind and solar power generating capacity from 1996 to 2014 are from BP (2015). For the linear trend from 1998 to 2014, regression R-square is 0.126.

The world is still in the early phase of wind and solar development. The observed annual growth to installation ratios are scattered around and the regression R-square is low. Nevertheless, a preliminary downward trend of the annual growth to installation ratios can be identified. Where the trend meets the horizontal zero line, it indicates that the long-term maximum annual installation rate of wind and solar power generating capacity will be about 186 gigawatts. By comparison, in 2011, the world net installation of all types of electric power plants was 245 gigawatts (EIA 2014b).

Figure 6.18 shows the historical and projected world total annual installation of wind and solar power generating capacity from 1998 to 2050. The world total annual installation of wind and solar power increased from 75 gigawatts in 2013 to 92 gigawatts in 2014. The projection shown in Figure 6.19 indicates that the world total annual installation of wind and solar power will continue to grow rapidly and will rise above 180 gigawatts after 2030. From 2030 to 2050, the world total annual installation of wind and solar power will stabilize around 186 gigawatts. By 2050, the total wind and solar electric power generating capacity is projected to rise to about 6,800 gigawatts.

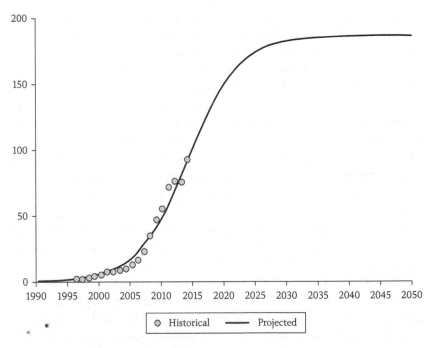

Figure 6.18 World Annual Installation of Wind and Solar Power (Historical and Projected, Gigawatts, 1997–2050)

Sources: Data for wind and solar power generating capacity from 1996 to 2014 are from BP (2015). Projected annual installation is based on the parameters derived from the linear regression shown in Figure 6.17.

I assume that from 2015 to 2050, the world's annual consumption of wind and solar electricity will be proportional to the total installation of wind and solar electric power generating capacity. The future wind and solar electric power plants are assumed to have an average capacity utilization rate of 20 percent.

The Limits to Wind and Solar Electricity

In the medium term and possibly in the long term (if there is no major breakthrough in technology for electricity storage), the intermittency problem will be a major obstacle to the growth of wind and solar electricity. Consider an electric power system that has a maximum demand of 2 gigawatts, that is, the peak demand of electricity is at the rate of 2 million kilowatt-hours per hour. Suppose that within the same system, the "base-load" demand for electricity is 1 gigawatt. That is, electricity demand at constant or slowly varying rates is up to 1 gigawatt. The base-load demand for electricity can only be met by nuclear or conventional thermal electric power plants.

In this system, the maximum generating capacity of intermittent electric power (such as wind and solar power) would be 1 gigawatt. If the generating capacity of intermittent electric power is greater than 1 gigawatt (the difference between the maximum electricity demand and the base-load electricity demand), then there will be times when the intermittent power plants generate more electricity than the demand. The extra electricity will have to be dumped.

In addition, the system will need to have 1 gigawatt of fossil fuel-based electric power plants (ideally natural gas-fired power plants) to balance against fluctuations of intermittent sources of electric power and to make up for any shortfalls when the combined generation of base-load and intermittent electric power plants falls short of the electricity demand. Thus, in this hypothetical electric power system, the penetration of wind and solar electricity is limited to about one-third of the total generating capacity (the total generating capacity in the system includes 1 gigawatt of base-load capacity, 1 gigawatt of intermittent capacity, and 1 gigawatt of balancing capacity).

In 2011, the world's total electric power generating capacity was about 5,300 gigawatts. The world's total electric power generating capacity grew at an average annual rate of 3.2 percent from 1980 to 2011 (EIA 2014b).

Assuming that the world electric power generating capacity grows at the rate of 3.5 percent a year from 2012 to 2050, the world's total electric power generating capacity will rise to about 20,300 gigawatts by 2050. If one-third of total electric power generating capacity in 2050 will be intermittent electric power plants, then the total wind and solar electric power generating capacity will be 6,800 gigawatts by 2050, the same as the projection shown in the last section.

In the long term, the growth of wind and solar electricity will be limited by the availability of land and precious metals. According to Carlos de Castro and several other researchers, the global geographical-technical potential of wind electricity will be less than 1 terawatt in terms of electric power, which corresponds to the electricity generated by 4,000 gigawatts of wind generating capacity with an average capacity utilization rate of 25 percent. When land and materials constraints are taken into account, the maximum long-term potential of solar electric power will be in the range of 2–4 terawatts in terms of electricity power, which corresponds to the electricity generated by 14,000–28,000 gigawatts of solar generating capacity assuming an average capacity utilization rate of 15 percent (Castro, Mediavilla, Miguel, and Frechoso 2011, 2013).

The Structural Crisis of Global Capitalism

Figure 6.19 shows the historical and projected world primary energy consumption from 1950 to 2050. The projected world primary energy consumption is the sum of the projected world oil production (including biofuels), world natural gas production, world coal production (converted to oil equivalents), world nuclear electricity consumption, world consumption of hydro, geothermal, and biomass electricity, and world consumption of wind and solar electricity.

World primary energy consumption is projected to peak in 2038 at 16.4 billion tonnes of oil equivalent. After 2038, the growth of nuclear and renewable energies

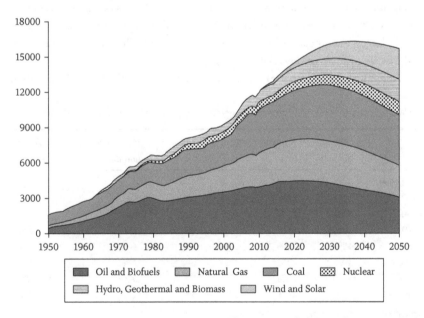

Figure 6.19 World Primary Energy Consumption (Million Tonnes of Oil Equivalent, 1950–2050)

Sources: World energy consumption data from 1965 to 2014 are from BP (2015). For the historical period 1950–1964 and for the projections from 2014 to 2050, consumption is assumed to equal production for each type of energy. For coal production, coal production in China, the United States, and the rest of the world is converted into tonnes of oil equivalent by multiplying tonnes of coal by 0.48, 0.56, and 0.47 respectively.

will be insufficient to offset the decline of fossil fuels. By 2050, the world's total primary energy consumption is projected to decline to 15.8 billion tonnes of oil equivalent.

Table 6.1 shows the changing structure of world energy consumption from 1950 to 2050. Oil was the energy foundation of the global economic expansion over the second half of the twentieth century. In the 1970s, oil accounted for almost one-half of the world's total energy consumption. In the 1990s, oil accounted for nearly 40 percent of world energy consumption. The oil share of world energy consumption declined to about one-third by 2010. Currently, oil is still the world's largest energy source but will be overtaken by coal in 2030. The oil share is projected to fall to about one-quarter by the 2030s and one-fifth by 2050.

Natural gas's share of world energy consumption rose above 20 percent after 1980 as the oil price shocks in the 1970s encouraged substitution of natural gas for oil. Natural gas now accounts for about a quarter of world energy consumption. World natural gas consumption is projected to peak in the late 2020s. By 2050, natural gas is projected to fall to 17 percent of the world energy consumption.

Coal dominated world energy consumption in the nineteenth century and the first half of the twentieth century. By the 1990s, the coal share of world energy consumption fell to about one-fourth. However, during the first decade of the twenty-first century, coal experienced a spectacular revival as China's rapid industrialization was driven by the massive consumption of coal. Coal is projected to regain the title of world's largest energy source by 2030. By 2050, coal will still account for one-quarter of the world primary energy consumption.

The contribution of nuclear energy was insignificant in the 1970s. By the 1990s,

Table 6.1 Structure of World Primary Energy Consumption (% of Total), 1950–2050

	Oil and Biofuels	Natural Gas	Coal	Nuclear	Hydro, Geothermal and Biomass	Wind and Solar
Historical:						
1950	34%	11%	55%	n.a.	n.a.	n.a.
1960	39%	15%	46%	n.a.	n.a.	n.a.
1970	46%	18%	30%	0%	5%	n.a.
1980	45%	20%	27%	2%	6%	0%
1990	39%	22%	27%	6%	6%	0%
2000	38%	23%	25%	6%	7%	0%
2010	33%	24%	30%	5%	7%	1%
Projected:						
2020	31%	24%	29%	5%	8%	4%
2030	27%	22%	29%	5%	9%	8%
2040	23%	20%	29%	6%	10%	12%
2050	20%	17%	27%	7%	12%	17%

Sources: See Figure 6.19.

the nuclear share of world energy consumption rose to 6 percent. Since then, the world's nuclear energy consumption has stagnated. In Figure 6.19 and Table 6.1, it is assumed that the nuclear share of world energy consumption will rise from 5 percent in 2010 to 7 percent in 2050. However, safety and security concerns as well as a shortage of uranium resources will impose constraints on the growth of nuclear energy. The projected growth of nuclear energy consumption may prove to be too optimistic.

Hydro, geothermal, and biomass electricity currently account for about 7 percent of world energy consumption. In Figure 6.19 and Table 6.1, it is assumed that their contribution to world energy consumption will grow steadily in the coming decades so that their share of world energy consumption will rise to 12 percent by 2050.

Wind and solar electricity currently account for less than 2 percent of world energy consumption. In Figure 6.19 and Table 6.1, it is assumed that wind and solar electricity will experience very rapid growth in the coming decades and their share of world energy consumption will rise to 17 percent by 2050. The intermittency problem and the shortage of precious metals used as key inputs in the manufacturing of wind and solar equipment may impose constraints on the growth of wind and solar electricity.

Figure 6.20 shows the historical and projected world economic growth rates from 1951 to 2050. World economic growth rates from 2015 to 2050 are projected using the projected world primary energy consumption (shown in Figure 6.19) and the historical relationship between world energy consumption growth and the world economic growth rate (shown in Figure 6.1).

The section on "Oil and Economic Growth" argues that peak oil may have a devastating impact on global economic growth. In Figure 6.20, it is implicitly assumed that other forms of energy can substitute for oil without much difficulty. This assumption may prove to be too optimistic. Nevertheless, global economic growth rate is projected to fall below 2 percent by 2030, fall below 1 percent by 2040, and approach 0.7 percent by 2050. By comparison, during the period 1913–1950, a period of major crisis of global capitalism that included the Great Depression and two world wars, the average annual growth rate of the global economy was 1.8 percent. After World War II, the world economic growth rate fell below 2 percent on several occasions: in 1975, 1981–1982, 1991–1993, and 2009.

Based on historical experience, a prolonged period during which the global average economic growth rate stays below 2 percent may be considered a period of major crisis of global capitalism. As the world economic growth rate falls below 2 percent, the global capitalist system is likely to suffer from persistent economic and political instabilities. By this definition, the projections shown in Figure 6.20 imply that global capitalism will enter into a new major crisis after about 2030.

To the extent that the coming major crisis can no longer be resolved within the basic institutional framework of capitalism, it will prove to be the structural or the terminal crisis of global capitalism.

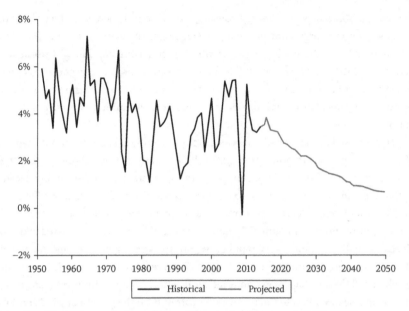

Figure 6.20 World Economic Growth Rate (Historical and Projected, 1951–2050)

Sources: Historical world economic growth rates from 1951 to 2013 are from Maddison (2010) and World Bank (2014), updated to 2014 using data from the IMF (2015). World economic growth rates in 2015 and 2016 are projected using data from the IMF (2015). The projected future economic growth rates from 2017 to 2050 are calculated using the projected world primary energy consumption (shown in Figure 6.19) and the historical relationship between the world energy consumption growth rate and the world economic growth rate (shown in Figure 6.1).

Averting Climate Catastrophes?

Figure 6.21 shows the historical and projected world carbon dioxide emissions from fossil fuels burning from 1950 to 2100. The carbon dioxide emissions are calculated from historical and projected world oil consumption, natural gas consumption, and coal consumption. The carbon dioxide emissions are calculated using standard global average conversion factors: 1 tonne of oil emits 3.07 tonnes of carbon dioxide; 1 tonne of oil equivalent of natural gas emits 2.35 tonnes of carbon dioxide; 1 tonne of oil equivalent of coal emits 3.96 tonnes of carbon dioxide (BP 2015).

Table 6.2 summarizes the historical and projected average annual growth rates of world economic output (gross world product), world primary energy consumption, and world carbon dioxide emissions for each decade from the 1950s to the 2040s.

World carbon dioxide emissions are projected to peak in 2029 at 39.9 billion tonnes. World carbon dioxide emissions are projected to decline at an average annual rate of 0.7 percent in the 2030s and 1.5 percent in the 2040s. World carbon dioxide emissions will fall to 32.0 billion tonnes by 2050 and fall to 11.7 billion tonnes by 2100.

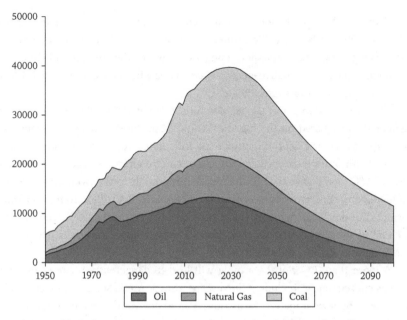

Figure 6.21 World Carbon Dioxide Emissions (Historical and Projected, Million Tonnes, 1950–2100)

Sources: World carbon dioxide emissions from fossil fuels burning are calculated from the historical and projected world oil consumption, world natural gas consumption, and world coal consumption. 1 tonne of oil is assumed to emit 3.07 tonnes of carbon dioxide; 1 tonne of oil equivalent of natural gas is assumed to emit 2.35 tonnes of carbon dioxide; 1 tonne of oil equivalent of coal is assumed to emit 3.96 tonnes of carbon dioxide. These are standard global average conversion factors (BP 2015).

Table 6.2 Gross World Product, Energy Consumption, and Carbon Dioxide Emissions, Average Annual Growth Rates (%), 1950–2050

	Gross World Product	Primary Energy Consumption	Carbon Dioxide Emissions
Historical:			
1950–1960	4.7%	5.6%	5.3%
1960–1970	5.0%	5.8%	4.6%
1970–1980	3.8%	3.0%	2.7%
1980–1990	3.1%	2.1%	1.6%
1990–2000	3.0%	1.4%	1.2%
2000–2010	3.7%	2.6%	2.8%
Projected:			
2010–2020	3.4%	1.9%	1.4%
2020–2030	2.3%	1.0%	0.4%
2030–2040	1.4%	0.1%	−0.7%
2040–2050	0.8%	−0.4%	−1.5%

Sources: See Figure 6.19, 6.20, and 6.21.

Given the above projections, the cumulative world carbon dioxide emissions from 2012 to 2100 will be 2.4 trillion tonnes. The cumulative emissions are more than twice as high as the total emissions budget required by the scenario of RCP 2.6 and within the range of cumulative emissions associated with the scenario of RCP 4.5 (see the section on "The Emissions Budget").

The present global average temperature is about 0.8°C higher than the pre-industrial time. Based on the historical trend from the late nineteenth century to the early twenty-first century, an increase in cumulative carbon dioxide emissions by 1 trillion tonnes is associated with an increase in global average temperature by about 0.6°C (see Figure 6.2). If this relationship holds in the twenty-first century, an increase in cumulative carbon dioxide emissions by 2.4 trillion tonnes is likely to result in an additional increase in global average temperature by 1.4°C. Thus, towards the end of the twenty-first century, global average temperature may rise to about 2.2°C higher than the pre-industrial time.

A more than 2°C global warming will lead to dangerous climate change with serious consequences, including the disappearing of Arctic summer sea ice, the rise of sea level by several meters, extinction of up to one-third of the currently existing species, and increased risks of ecological collapse.

The carbon dioxide emitted will stay in the atmosphere for thousands of years. Global warming will continue beyond the twenty-first century. In 2013, the atmospheric concentration of carbon dioxide reached 396 parts per million (ppm) (NOAA 2014). This represents an increase by 118 ppm from the pre-industrial level (278 ppm).

If the cumulative carbon dioxide emissions in the rest of the twenty-first century are 2.4 trillion tonnes and suppose that about one-half of the emissions can be absorbed by the oceans and the terrestrial ecological systems, about 1.2 trillion tonnes of carbon dioxide will stay in the atmosphere (over the period 1950–2010, about 56 percent of the carbon dioxide emissions from fossil fuels burning stayed in the atmosphere, see Hansen 2009: 119–120). This will result in an increase in the atmospheric concentration of carbon dioxide by about 150 ppm (7.8 billion tonnes of carbon dioxide = 1 ppm). Atmospheric concentration of carbon dioxide will rise to about 550 ppm by the end of the twenty-first century. Taking into account other greenhouse gases, the atmospheric concentration of carbon dioxide equivalent may rise to 600–650 ppm (depending on the levels of other greenhouse gases).

This would represent more than a doubling of the atmospheric concentration of greenhouse gases from the pre-industrial era. A doubling of atmospheric greenhouse gases implies radiative forcing of 4 watts per square meter (Hansen 2009: 46). Thus, atmospheric concentration of carbon dioxide equivalent to more than 600 ppm implies long-term global warming of 3°C or higher. As the global warming rises above 3°C, sea level may rise by more than 25 meters, billions of people may become environmental refugees, Amazon rainforests will be destroyed, and dangerous climate feedbacks may be initiated that may eventually make much of the world uninhabitable for human beings.

Therefore, despite the drastic reduction of fossil fuels consumption projected in this chapter after 2030, the cumulative carbon dioxide emissions during the rest of the twenty-first century will be large enough to cause dangerous climate change and there is a not insignificant chance that the worst climate catastrophes may eventually fall upon humanity.

The current projections assume that the world production of oil, natural gas, and coal will peak before the mid-twenty-first century. The projections implicitly assume that the massive amounts of unconventional oil and natural gas resources will be mostly left underground.

The world's total extra heavy oil resources (known as "tar sands") are more than 3 trillion barrels or about 400 billion tonnes. Currently, only about one-tenth of these extra heavy oil resources are considered recoverable. In addition, the world has about 3 trillion barrels of oil resources contained in oil shale (oil shale contains "kerogen" and is the source rock of conventional oil; it is not the same as "shale oil") (Aleklett 2012: 99–100; 106–109).

If the unconventional oil resources are fully exploited, it will lead to 2.4 trillion tonnes of additional carbon dioxide emissions.

According to the International Energy Agency, the world has about 330 trillion cubic meters of technically recoverable unconventional natural gas resources (IEA 2012). If the unconventional natural gas resources are fully exploited, there will be 700 billion tonnes of additional carbon dioxide emissions.

If all of the above oil and natural gas resources are exploited over the rest of the twenty-first century, the cumulative carbon dioxide emissions between now and the end of the century will amount to 5.5 trillion tonnes. The cumulative emissions will fall within the range associated with the scenario of RCP 8.5 (see Figure 6.3). Towards the end of the twenty-first century, major climate catastrophes will begin to destroy the material foundation of human civilization.

7

THE UNSUSTAINABILITY OF CHINESE CAPITALISM

Capitalist economy is based on the pursuit of profit. The long-term equilibrium profit rate is determined as the ratio of the profit's long-term average growth rate over the long-term average ratio of accumulation. The profit's growth rate equals the economic growth rate plus the rate of change of the profit share in the economic output. The ratio of accumulation is the ratio of capitalist net investment to the total profit (see Chapter 5). In a capitalist economy, the ratio of accumulation is typically positive as capitalist competition forces capitalist individuals and states to use a portion of the profit for capital accumulation. In the long term, if the economic growth rate approaches zero and the profit share stabilizes, the profit's growth rate will approach zero. As a result, the profit rate will approach zero. To the extent that a capitalist economy cannot function with a zero profit rate, the capitalist system will enter into a structural crisis that cannot be resolved within its own institutional framework.

In reality, leading capitalist economies may need to have profit rates above 10 percent to prevent major economic and political crises. From 1913 to 1950, global capitalism suffered from a system-wide major crisis that included the Great Depression and two world wars. During the same period, global economy grew at an average annual rate of 1.8 percent (Maddison 2010), or just below 2 percent. Assuming a ratio of accumulation of 20 percent and a constant profit share, a long-term average economic growth rate of 2 percent is consistent with a long-term equilibrium profit rate of 10 percent.

Within the current global capitalist division of labor, Chinese capitalism specializes in manufacturing production. This requires China to make massive investments in industrial capital infrastructure. As a result, Chinese capitalism has had ratios of accumulation much higher than other major capitalist economies. Chapter 5 shows that China's ratio of accumulation is approaching 70 percent. With a ratio of accumulation of 70 percent, the Chinese economy needs to grow at a rate of more than 7 percent to keep the profit rate above 10 percent.

Theoretically, Chinese capitalism can adapt to lower economic growth rates by lowering the ratio of accumulation. But a lower ratio of accumulation would undermine the capacity of Chinese capitalism to deliver industrial goods to the global capitalist market. With a lower ratio of accumulation, labor productivity will grow less rapidly. If the Chinese workers' wages continue to grow more rapidly than labor productivity, the competitiveness of Chinese capitalism in the global market will be undermined. In addition, a lower ratio of accumulation implies a smaller share of investment in China's gross domestic product (GDP). To compensate for the lower investment share, household consumption needs to rise relative to China's GDP. But a higher household consumption share cannot be achieved without a major redistribution of national income from the capitalists to the workers. Such redistribution will accelerate the decline of the profit rate.

Given these dilemmas, in the short- and the medium-term, Chinese capitalism will struggle to lower the ratio of accumulation. Assuming that the Chinese capitalism can lower the ratio of accumulation to about 50 percent, the Chinese economy needs to grow at least 5 percent a year in order to keep the long-term profit rate above 10 percent (assuming a constant profit share).

All economic activities (including the so-called service sectors) involve some forms of physical and chemical transformations of the physical world. Rapid economic growth cannot happen without massive consumption of material resources and degradation of ecological systems. This raises the question of how long Chinese capitalism can maintain rapid economic growth without irreparably damaging China's and the global ecological systems.

Ecological Sustainability and the Limits to Growth

All economic activities directly or indirectly consume material resources. Agricultural and industrial activities directly transform natural resources through physical, chemical, or biological processes to produce material goods that meet human needs or desires. All services activities directly consume energy resources (in the form of electricity use, heating, cooling, and transportation fuels). In addition, for services activities to take place, buildings, equipment, and material supplies are needed. Service sector workers need to consume material goods. The production of capital goods, material supplies, and material consumer goods has to consume material resources.

Material resources include renewable resources and non-renewable resources. Within certain limits, renewable resources can be regenerated by nature's ecological systems within a certain period of time that is meaningful for human economic activities (for example, within a year). Renewable resources include fresh water, fish, forests, soil, and renewable energies. Non-renewable resources are mineral resources that cannot be regenerated by nature's ecological systems within a period of time that is meaningful for human economic activities. The geological deposits of non-renewable resources may be regarded as "fixed" from the point of view of human economic activities. Human consumption of non-renewable resources in any given period of time reduces the available resources for future generations.

In addition to consumption of material resources, all human economic activities inevitably generate various material by-products in solid, liquid, or gaseous forms.

These are pollutants that interfere with the natural operations of the ecological systems. Within certain limits, ecological systems can absorb the material by-products generated by human activities without undermining their own operations. However, beyond certain limits, the ecological systems will be overwhelmed by the excessive amounts of pollutants. Excessive pollution leads to ecological "overshoot." If the overshoot is not corrected within a short period of time, ecological systems will begin to fail and eventually collapse.

Ecological systems are the material foundation of all human civilizations. All human societies depend on ecological systems to provide material resources and to absorb pollution. Without the normal operations of ecological systems, no human society can last very long. Thus, ultimately, all human societies must live within the limits required by ecological sustainability.

For ecological systems to be sustainable, human consumption of renewable resources has to stay below the rates at which the renewable resources can be regenerated by the ecological systems and the human generation of pollutants has to stay below the rates at which the pollutants can be absorbed by the ecological systems. In addition, human societies need to gradually reduce the consumption of non-renewable resources and keep the consumption of non-renewable resources at minimal levels so that the lifetime of available non-renewable resources can be maximized (on the requirements of ecological sustainability, see Huesemann 2003).

The "IPAT formula" is a commonly used formula that helps to illustrate the relationship between economic growth and the environmental impact of human activities. In the formula, "I" stands for environmental impact, "P" stands for population, "A" stands for "affluence" or per capita GDP, and "T" stands for "technology" or environmental impact per unit of GDP:

$$I = P * A * T$$

In growth rate form, the formula can be re-written as:

Environmental Impact Growth Rate = Population Growth Rate + Per Capita GDP Growth Rate + Growth Rate of Environmental Impact per Unit of GDP

The sum of population growth rate and per capita GDP growth rate is the economic growth rate, and the growth rate of environmental impact per unit of GDP is the negative of the reduction rate of environmental impact per unit of GDP. Thus:

Environmental Impact Growth Rate = Economic Growth Rate – Reduction Rate of Environmental Impact per Unit of GDP

To achieve ecological sustainability, the environmental impact growth rate needs to approach zero if human economic activities have stayed below the limits of ecological systems but needs to be negative if human economic activities have already overshot the ecological limits.

Under capitalism, economic growth rate is normally positive as a result of the capitalist tendency to pursue endless accumulation of capital. Moreover, in the long term, positive economic growth rate is necessary to ensure that the long-term equilibrium profit rate stays positive. Thus, other things being equal, positive economic growth rate will inevitably lead to rising levels of environmental impact that will sooner or later overwhelm the earth's ecological systems. In this sense, capitalism is fundamentally incompatible with ecological sustainability.

On the other hand, the depletion of material resources leads to higher prices of resources that may encourage the capitalists to search for substitution or to use the resources more efficiently. Environmental degradation may force capitalist governments to impose regulations that help to alleviate the environmental consequences of capitalist economic activities. In fact, in many areas, the global average environmental impact per unit of GDP has declined over the past several decades. The observed decline of environmental impact per unit of GDP raises the question whether it is conceivable that "technological progress" would help to deliver both endless economic growth and ecological sustainability, leading to the wonderland of "green capitalism."

The last chapter explains that the pace of technological progress is fundamentally limited by the rate of infrastructure replacement (see the section on "The World Is Set for More Than 2°C Warming"). Most of the new technologies need to be incorporated into the new capital equipment and infrastructure. But each year only a fraction of the infrastructure and equipment can be replaced. If an economy each year replaces 5 percent of the old capital stock and the economic growth rate is 5 percent, then the total new capital stock would be 10 percent of the old capital stock. Even if the new capital stock reduces the environmental impact per unit of GDP by 50 percent, the total economy environmental impact per unit of GDP would only fall by 5 percent (10% * 50% = 5%). The growth rate of environmental impact equals economic growth rate less the reduction rate of environmental impact per unit of GDP. As the economic growth rate is 5 percent, the growth rate of environmental impact equals 0 percent (5% – 5% = 0%). That is, even though the new capital stock incorporates new technologies that reduce the environmental impact per unit of GDP by 50 percent (a highly optimistic assumption), the total economy reduction of environmental impact per unit of GDP is fully offset by economic growth so that in the end, there is no change in the overall level of environmental impact.

Figure 7.1 shows the relationship between global economic growth rate and the growth rate of what is probably the single most important global environmental impact, the carbon dioxide emissions from burning fossil fuels.

The linear trend indicates that over the period 1991–2014, there was an "autonomous" tendency for the world carbon dioxide emissions to fall by 1.6 percent

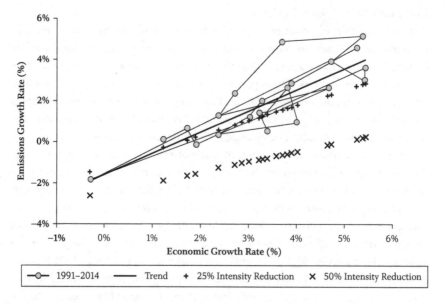

Figure 7.1 Global Economic Growth and Carbon Dioxide Emissions (1991–2014)

Sources: Gross world product in constant 2011 international dollars from 1990 to 2013 is from the World Bank (2014), updated to 2014 using data from the IMF (2015). Global carbon dioxide emissions from fossil fuels burning from 1990 to 2014 are from BP (2015). Linear regression results in the following trend relationship: Emissions Growth Rate = –0.016 + 1.023 * Economic Growth Rate (regression R-square = 0.717). The "25% Intensity Reduction" scenario assumes that the new capital's emission intensity falls by 25 percent relative to the old capital and the "50% Intensity Reduction" scenario assumes that the new capital's emission intensity falls by 50 percent relative to the old capital.

a year, a reduction that was associated with zero economic growth. Beyond zero economic growth, there was a one-to-one relationship between economic growth and emissions growth. For each increase in world economic growth rate by one percentage point, the emissions growth rate tended to rise by 1.02 percent.

The linear trend is compared with the hypothetical scenarios of "25% Intensity Reduction" and "50% Intensity Reduction." Under the "25% Intensity Reduction" scenario, new capital's emission intensity is assumed to be 25 percent lower than that of the old capital. Depreciation rate is assumed to be 5 percent. That is, each year the faction of new capital relative to old capital equals the sum of economic growth rate and 5 percent. Thus, the relationship between the emissions growth rate and the economic growth rate is as follows:

Emissions Growth Rate = Economic Growth Rate – Emission Intensity Reduction Rate

= Economic Growth Rate – (5% + Economic Growth Rate) * 25%

= –1.25% + 75% * Economic Growth Rate

Under the "50% Intensity Reduction" scenario, new capital's emission intensity is assumed to be 50 percent lower than that of the old capital. Depreciation rate is still assumed to be 5 percent. The relationship between the emissions growth rate and the economic growth rate is as follows:

Emissions Growth Rate = Economic Growth Rate – Emissions Intensity Reduction Rate
= Economic Growth Rate – (5% + Economic Growth Rate) * 50%
= –2.5% + 50% * Economic Growth Rate

At low economic growth rates, the observed trend for the period 1991–2013 roughly matches the hypothetical scenario of "25% Intensity Reduction." But at higher economic growth rates, there is a significant gap between the observed trend and the "25% Intensity Reduction" scenario. The "25% Intensity Reduction" scenario generally implies lower emissions growth rates. Under the "25% Intensity Reduction" scenario, a global economic growth rate of 3.5 percent (a growth rate that is required to prevent rising global unemployment) is associated with a growth rate of emissions of 1.4 percent. In other words, it would guarantee climate catastrophes.

The "50% Intensity Reduction" scenario leads to emissions growth rates far lower than the observed trend for all economic growth rates, suggesting that the scenario is based on highly optimistic assumptions. Even under the "50% Intensity Reduction" scenario, if the economic growth rate is maintained at 3.5 percent, the emission reduction rate will be only 0.75 percent.

Figure 7.1 illustrates the great difficulty (and even the impossibility) to achieve ecological sustainability under "normal" economic growth rates required for global capitalist stability.

The following sections will discuss the relationship between the growth of the Chinese capitalist economy and several aspects of environmental impact: the impact on non-renewable energy resources (oil, natural gas, and coal), the impact on renewable water resources, and the impact on ecological systems' absorptive capacity (air pollution and carbon dioxide emissions).

Oil and China's Economic Growth

In 2014, China's oil consumption reached 520 million tonnes (11.1 million barrels per day). Oil accounted for 17.5 percent of China's primary energy consumption in 2014. China is the world's second largest oil consumer (after the United States) and accounted for 12 percent of world oil consumption in 2014. From 2000 to 2014, China accounted for 47 percent of the total growth of world oil consumption.

Figure 7.2 shows the relationship between per capita real GDP (in constant 2011

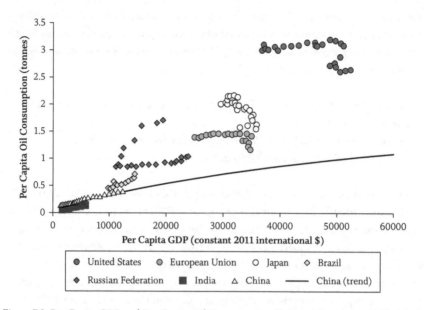

Figure 7.2 Per Capita GDP and Per Capita Oil Consumption (Selected Countries, 1990–2014)

Sources: Population and GDP per capita in constant 2011 international dollars from 1990 to 2013 are from the World Bank (2014), updated to 2014 using data from the IMF (2015). Oil consumption from 1990 to 2014 is from BP (2015). Oil consumption per capita is calculated using oil consumption divided by population. Logarithmic linear regression of China's per capita oil consumption and per capita GDP results in the following trend relationship over the period 1990–2014: ln(Per Capita Oil Consumption) = –7.068 + 0.651 * ln(Per Capita GDP) (regression R-square = 0.992).

international dollars) and per capita oil consumption for the world's seven largest economies (the United States, the European Union, Japan, China, India, Brazil, and the Russian Federation) from 1990 to 2014.

Among the world's largest economies, the United States has the highest per capita oil consumption. US per capita oil consumption peaked at 3.2 tonnes in 2004. US per capita oil consumption declined sharply during the Great Recession of 2008–2009. In 2014, US per capita oil consumption stood at 2.6 tonnes.

The European Union's per capita oil consumption peaked at less than 1.5 tonnes in 2005. By 2014, the European Union's per capita oil consumption fell to less than 1.2 tonnes as European economies struggled with financial instability. Japan's per capita oil consumption peaked at less than 2.2 tonnes in 1996. Since then, Japan's per capita oil consumption has declined due to economic stagnation and improvement in energy efficiency. In 2014, Japan's per capita oil consumption was 1.5 tonnes.

The former Soviet Union was the world's second largest oil consumer in the 1980s. In 1990, the Russian Federation's per capita oil consumption was 1.7 tonnes, higher than the European Union's per capita oil consumption in the same year. As the Soviet Union disintegrated, the Russian Federation underwent economic and social collapse. Russia's per capita oil consumption fell to 838 kilograms in 1998. By 2014, Russia's per capita oil consumption recovered to 1.03 tonnes.

In China, India, and Brazil, per capita oil consumption has grown in proportion with per capita GDP. From 1990 to 2014, China's per capita oil consumption grew from 99 kilograms to 381 kilograms, India's per capita oil consumption grew from 67 kilograms to 141 kilograms, and Brazil's per capita oil consumption grew from 429 kilograms to 705 kilograms.

Logarithmic linear regression of China's per capita oil consumption and per capita GDP finds that China's per capita oil consumption is highly correlated with China's per capita GDP. Over the period 1990–2014, on average, an increase in per capita GDP by one percentage point was associated with an increase in per capita oil consumption by 0.65 percentage points. China is currently more "oil efficient" (that is, having lower oil consumption per unit of GDP) than most of the largest economies in the world. Under the existing trend, even if China's per capita GDP rises to 50,000 dollars (in constant 2011 international dollars), China's per capita oil consumption would only rise to about 1 tonne, similar to Russia's per capita oil consumption today.

Figure 7.3 applies Hubbert linearization to China's cumulative oil production. Linear trend from 2009 to 2014 indicates that China's ultimately recoverable oil

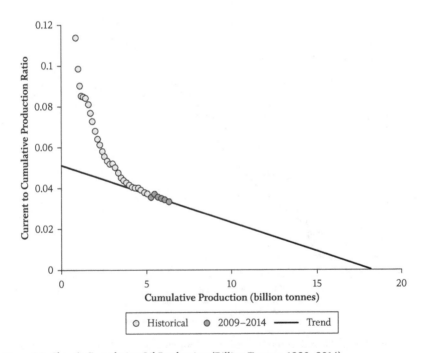

Figure 7.3 China's Cumulative Oil Production (Billion Tonnes, 1980–2014)

Sources: China's historical oil production from 1949 to 1964 is from the National Bureau of Statistics of China (2013 and earlier years). China's oil production from 1965 to 2014 is from BP (2015). For the linear trend from 2009 to 2014, regression R-square is 0.785.

resources will be 18.3 billion tonnes (regression R-square 0.785). China's cumulative oil production up to 2014 was 6.3 billion tonnes. Thus, the implied remaining recoverable oil resources are 12 billion tonnes. By comparison, China's official oil reserves were 2.5 billion tonnes in 2014 (BP 2015).

Figure 7.4 shows China's historical and projected oil production from 1950 to 2050. China is the world's fourth largest oil producer (after Saudi Arabia, the Russian Federation, and the United States). In 2014, China's oil production reached 211 million tonnes, accounting for 5 percent of world oil production. China's oil production is projected to peak in 2027, with a production level of 236 million tonnes.

Figure 7.5 shows the net oil imports of China and the United States as a share of world oil production from 1965 to 2014. The historical net oil imports shares are compared with three different scenarios of China's future net oil imports as a share of world oil production from 2015 to 2050. The three scenarios assume that China's future oil consumption will grow by 3 percent a year, grow by 1 percent a year, or fall by 1 percent a year from 2015 to 2050. Net oil imports are defined as oil consumption less oil production (including biofuels production).

US net oil imports rose above 10 percent of world oil production in 1973, when both the United States and the global capitalist economy were hit by a major crisis.

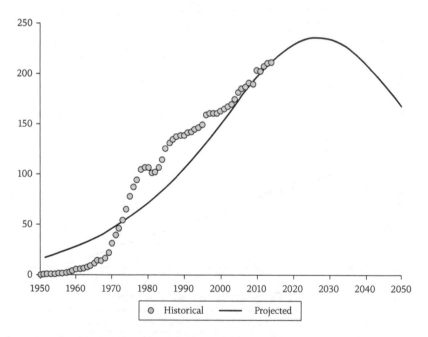

Figure 7.4 China's Oil Production (Historical and Projected, Million Tonnes, 1950–2050)

Sources: China's historical oil production from 1949 to 1964 is from the National Bureau of Statistics of China (2013 and earlier years). China's oil production from 1965 to 2014 is from BP (2015). Projection is based on the parameters derived from the linear trend shown in Figure 7.3.

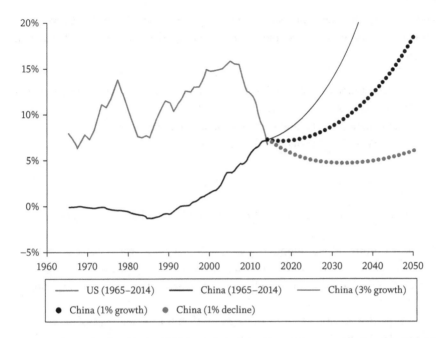

Figure 7.5 Net Imports as % of World Oil Production (China and the United States, 1965–2050)

Sources: Historical oil production and consumption are from BP (2015). Net oil imports are defined as oil consumption less oil production and biofuels production. To project China's future net oil imports, oil production is based on the projection shown in Figure 7.4 and China's biofuels production is assumed to grow from 2.1 million tonnes in 2014 to 5.7 million tonnes in 2050. Future world oil production (including biofuels) is based on the projection shown in Figure 6.7.

In the first half of the 1980s, the US net oil imports fell below 10 percent of world oil production as the United States managed to reduce oil consumption and the Alaska oil field contributed to a temporary revival of US oil production. From the 1990s to the early 2000s, US net oil imports grew rapidly. By 2005, US net oil imports peaked at 16 percent of world oil production. The growth of US net oil imports helped to push oil prices to record high levels that precipitated the global economy into the Great Recession. Since 2007, US oil consumption has declined and shale oil production has grown rapidly. As a result, US net oil imports fell from 15 percent of world oil production in 2007 to less than 7 percent of world oil production in 2014.

From the 1960s to the 1980s, China was a net oil exporter. In 1985, China's net oil exports peaked at 1.3 percent of world oil production. In 1993, China turned into a net oil importer. In 1998, China's net oil imports exceeded 1 percent of world oil production. Since then, China's net oil imports have surged. By 2014, China overtook the United States to become the world's largest oil importer.

Assuming that China's new capital can each year reduce oil intensity (oil consumption per unit of economic output) by 25 percent compared to the old capital and assuming that the depreciation rate is 5 percent, the relationship between the oil consumption growth rate and the economic growth rate can be calculated as follows:

Oil Consumption Growth Rate = Economic Growth Rate – Oil Intensity Reduction Rate
= Economic Growth Rate – (5% + Economic Growth Rate) * 25%
= –1.25% + 75% * Economic Growth Rate

Or,

Economic Growth Rate = (Oil Consumption Growth Rate + 1.25%) / 0.75

If China's future oil consumption grows by 3 percent a year (consistent with an economic growth rate of 5.7 percent), China's net oil imports will rise above 10 percent of world oil production by 2025 and rise above 15 percent of world oil production by the 2030s.

Any particular nation-state can have access to only a limited share of the world oil market. The United States, being the world's hegemonic power, saw its net oil imports above 15 percent of world oil production only in the early 2000s. Thus, 15 percent of world oil production may be taken as the practical maximum limit to a country's share in the world oil market. If China's net oil imports rise above 15 percent of world oil production, the potential economic costs (oil imports spending) and geopolitical tensions may become overwhelming, exceeding the capacity that the Chinese state can cope with.

If China's future oil consumption grows by 1 percent a year (consistent with an economic growth rate of 3 percent), China's net oil imports will rise above 10 percent of world oil production by the 2030s and rise above 15 percent of world oil production by the 2040s. In this scenario, the economic and geopolitical crisis may be postponed by about a decade. But eventually, China's oil consumption growth will be unsustainable.

If China's future oil consumption falls by 1 percent a year (consistent with an economic growth rate of 0.3 percent), China's net oil imports will fall below 5 percent of world oil production by the 2030s and will stay below 6 percent of world oil production by 2050. Thus, only under the condition of near zero economic growth, China's oil imports may be "sustainable" between now and the mid-twenty-first century.

Natural Gas and China's Economic Growth

In 2014, China's natural gas consumption reached 186 billion cubic meters (167 million tonnes of oil equivalent). Natural gas accounted for 5.6 percent of

China's primary energy consumption in 2014. China is the world's third largest natural gas consumer (after the United States and the Russian Federation) and accounted for 5.4 percent of world natural gas consumption in 2014. From 2000 to 2014, China accounted for 17 percent of the total growth of world natural gas consumption.

Figure 7.6 shows the relationship between per capita real GDP (in constant 2011 international dollars) and per capita natural gas consumption (in terms of oil equivalent) for the world's seven largest economies (the United States, the European Union, Japan, China, India, Brazil, and the Russian Federation) from 1990 to 2014.

Natural gas consumption generates about half as much carbon dioxide emissions per unit of energy as coal consumption and much less hazardous air pollutants. In advanced capitalist countries, natural gas is often used as the primary fuel for residential and commercial heating. In the electric power sector, natural gas-fired power plants play crucial roles in meeting the peak power demand and providing

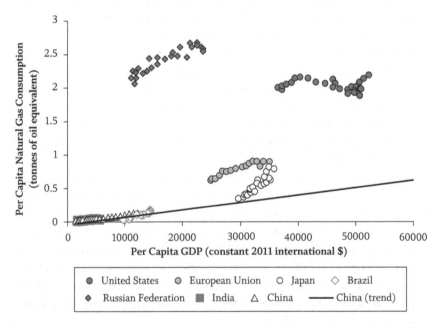

Figure 7.6 Per Capita GDP and Per Capita Natural Gas Consumption (Selected Countries, 1990–2014)

Sources: Population and GDP per capita in constant 2011 international dollars from 1990 to 2013 are from the World Bank (2014), updated to 2014 using data from the IMF (2015) Natural gas consumption from 1990 to 2014 is from BP (2015). Natural gas consumption per capita is calculated using natural gas consumption divided by population. Logarithmic linear regression of China's per capita natural consumption and per capita GDP results in the following trend relationship over the period 1990–2014: ln(Per Capita Natural Gas Consumption) = –13.449 + 1.180 * ln(Per Capita GDP) (regression R-square = 0.930).

back-up for intermittent renewable power plants (such as wind and solar power plants).

Among the world's largest economies, the Russian Federation has the highest per capita natural gas consumption. In 2013, Russia's per capita natural gas consumption was 2.6 tonnes of oil equivalent. US per capita natural gas consumption has fluctuated around 2 tonnes of oil equivalent since 1990. Since 2009, US natural gas consumption has grown steadily. By 2014, US per capita natural gas consumption reached 2.2 tonnes of oil equivalent. The European Union's per capita natural gas consumption grew steadily from 614 kilograms of oil equivalent in 1990 to 908 kilograms of oil equivalent in 2005. Since then, the European Union's natural gas consumption has fallen sharply as households and businesses struggle with economic crisis. By 2014, the European Union's per capita natural gas consumption declined to 685 kilograms of oil equivalent.

Despite economic stagnation, Japan's natural gas consumption has doubled over the past two decades. After the Fukushima nuclear accident in 2011, Japan shut down most of its nuclear power plants and increased the consumption of coal and natural gas to make up for the energy shortfalls. In 2014, Japan's per capita natural gas consumption reached 797 kilograms of oil equivalent.

In China, India, and Brazil, per capita natural gas consumption is much less than in the advanced capitalist countries but has grown rapidly. From 1990 to 2014, China's per capita natural gas consumption grew from 12 kilograms of oil equivalent to 112 kilograms of oil equivalent, India's per capita natural gas consumption grew from 12 kilograms of oil equivalent to 35 kilograms of oil equivalent, and Brazil's per capita natural gas consumption grew from 18 kilograms of oil equivalent to 177 kilograms of oil equivalent.

Logarithmic linear regression of China's per capita natural gas consumption and per capita GDP finds that China's per capita natural gas consumption is highly correlated with China's per capita GDP. Over the period 1990–2014, on average, an increase in per capita GDP by one percentage point was associated with an increase in per capita natural gas consumption by 1.2 percentage points. Under the existing trend, even if China's per capita GDP rises to 50,000 dollars (in constant 2011 international dollars), China's per capita natural gas consumption would only rise to about 500 kilograms of oil equivalent, much less than the per capita natural gas consumption in advanced capitalist countries today.

Figure 7.7 applies Hubbert linearization to China's cumulative natural gas production. The linear trend from 2009 to 2014 indicates that China's ultimately recoverable natural gas resources will be 9.2 billion tonnes of oil equivalent (regression R-square 0.740). China's cumulative natural gas production up to 2014 was 1.4 billion tonnes of oil equivalent. Thus, the implied remaining recoverable natural gas resources are 7.8 billion tonnes of oil equivalent. By comparison, China's official natural gas reserves were 3.5 trillion cubic meters or 3.2 billion tonnes of oil equivalent in 2014 (BP 2015).

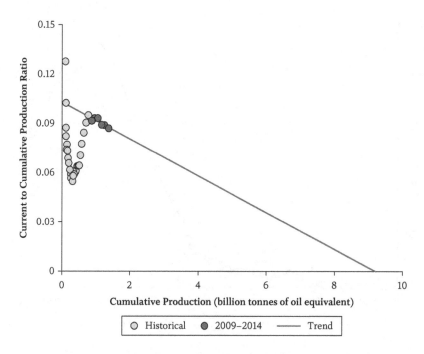

Figure 7.7 China's Cumulative Natural Gas Production (Billion Tonnes of Oil Equivalent, 1980–2014)

Sources: China's historical natural gas production from 1949 to 1969 is from the National Bureau of Statistics of China (2013 and earlier years). China's natural gas production from 1970 to 2014 is from BP (2015). For the linear trend from 2009 to 2014, regression R-square is 0.740.

Figure 7.8 shows China's historical and projected natural gas production from 1950 to 2050. China is the world's fifth largest natural gas producer (after the United States, the Russian Federation, Qatar, and Iran). In 2014, China's natural gas production reached 121 million tonnes of oil equivalent, accounting for 3.9 percent of world natural gas production. China's natural gas production is projected to peak in 2031, with a production level of 236 million tonnes of oil equivalent.

Figure 7.9 compares the natural gas net imports of China and the European Union as a share of world natural gas production from 1970 to 2014. The historical net import shares are compared with three different scenarios of China's future net natural gas imports as a share of world natural gas production from 2015 to 2050. The three scenarios assume that China's future natural gas consumption will grow by 5.5 percent a year, 3 percent a year, or 0.5 percent a year from 2015 to 2050. Net natural gas imports are defined as natural gas consumption less natural gas production.

The European Union is the world's largest natural gas net importer. In 2014, the European Union's natural gas net imports were 229 million tonnes of oil equivalent, equaling 7 percent of world natural gas production. Between 2005 and 2010, the

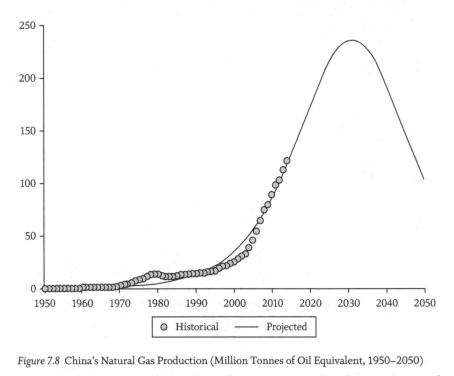

Figure 7.8 China's Natural Gas Production (Million Tonnes of Oil Equivalent, 1950–2050)

Sources: China's historical natural gas production from 1949 to 1969 is from the National Bureau of Statistics of China (2013 and earlier years). China's natural gas production from 1970 to 2014 is from BP (2015). Projection is based on the parameters derived from the linear trend shown in Figure 7.7.

European Union's natural gas net imports have been around 10 percent of world natural gas production (BP 2014).

The cheapest way to transport natural gas is through pipelines, which can only be constructed between countries on the same continent. On the Eurasian continent, China will have to rely upon Russia as the main source of natural gas supply. In 2014, Russia exported 202 billion cubic meters of natural gas (including 187 billion cubic meters of pipeline exports), or 5.8 percent of world natural gas production. About four-fifths of Russia's pipeline natural gas exports went to Europe (BP 2015).

Natural gas transported over the sea needs to be liquefied first. Liquefaction of natural gas is economically expensive and consumes a substantial amount of energy. International supply of liquefied natural gas is limited. In 2014, total world exports of liquefied natural gas were 333 billion cubic meters or 9.6 percent of world natural gas production. In Asia, China has to compete with Japan and South Korea for imports of liquefied natural gas. The two countries accounted for 52 percent of world liquefied natural gas imports in 2014 (BP 2015).

Given the above considerations, 10 percent of world natural gas production may be the maximum limit to China's future natural gas imports.

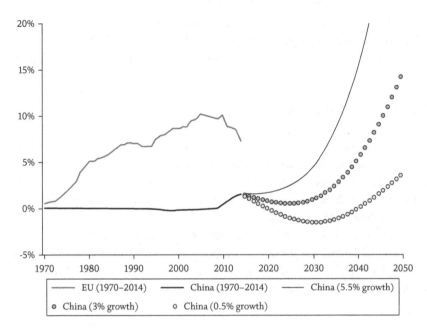

Figure 7.9 Net Imports as % of World Natural Gas Production (China and the European Union, 1970–2050)

Sources: Historical natural gas production and consumption are from BP (2015). Net natural gas imports are defined as natural gas consumption less natural gas production. To project China's future net natural gas imports, natural gas production is based on the projection shown in Figure 7.8. Future world natural gas production is based on the projection shown in Figure 6.12.

From the 1970s to the 1980s, China was self-sufficient in natural gas. In the 1990s and the early 2000s, China was a small net exporter of natural gas. China became a net importer of natural gas in 2007. By 2014, China's net imports of natural gas rose to 1.5 percent of the world natural gas production.

Given the near one-to-one correspondence between China's per capita natural gas consumption and per capita GDP, it is reasonable to assume that China's future natural gas consumption growth rate will be about the same as the economic growth rate.

If China's future natural gas consumption grows by 5.5 percent a year (corresponding to an economic growth rate of 5.5 percent), China's net natural gas imports will rise above 10 percent of world natural gas production by the late 2030s and rise above 15 percent of world natural gas production by 2040. Under this scenario, China may face a serious natural gas shortage by the 2030s. The shortage of natural gas will limit China's capacity to substitute natural gas for coal or to use natural gas-fired electric power to balance the intermittent renewable electric power.

If China's future natural gas consumption grows by 3 percent a year, China's net natural gas imports will rise above 5 percent of world natural gas production by 2040 and rise above 10 percent of world natural gas production by the late

2040s. If China's future natural gas consumption increases by 0.5 percent a year, China's net natural gas imports will decline in the coming years. China will become a net natural gas exporter by 2020 before turning into a net importer again by 2040.

Coal and China's Economic Growth

In 2014, China's coal consumption reached 1,962 million tonnes of oil equivalent. Coal accounted for 66 percent of China's primary energy consumption in 2014. China is the world's largest coal consumer and accounted for 51 percent of world coal consumption in 2014. From 2000 to 2014, China accounted for 86 percent of the total growth of world coal consumption.

Figure 7.10 shows the relationship between per capita GDP (in constant 2011 international dollars) and per capita coal consumption (in terms of oil equivalent) for the world's seven largest economies (the United States, the European Union, Japan, China, India, Brazil, and the Russian Federation) from 1990 to 2014.

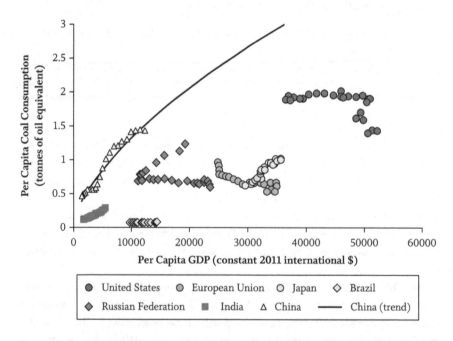

Figure 7.10 Per Capita GDP and Per Capita Coal Consumption (Selected Countries, 1990–2014)

Sources: Population and GDP per capita in constant 2011 international dollars from 1990 to 2013 are from the World Bank (2014), updated to 2014 using data from the IMF (2015). Coal consumption from 1990 to 2014 is from BP (2015). Coal consumption per capita is calculated using coal consumption divided by population. Logarithmic linear regression of China's per capita coal consumption and per capita GDP results in the following trend relationship over the period 1990–2014: ln(Per Capita Coal Consumption) = –5.560 + 0.638 * ln(Per Capita GDP) (regression R-square = 0.918).

From 1990 to 2007, US per capita coal consumption stayed just under 2 tonnes of oil equivalent. Since 2008, the US coal consumption has fallen sharply due to economic crisis and substitution by natural gas. In 2014, US per capita coal consumption stood at 1.42 tonnes of oil equivalent.

In 1990, the European Union's per capita coal consumption was near 1 tonne of oil equivalent. The European Union's coal consumption fell sharply in the 1990s, reflecting the economic restructuring of Eastern European former socialist states. In 2014, the European Union's per capita coal consumption was 531 kilograms of oil equivalent. Despite economic stagnation, Japan's per capita coal consumption has increased steadily since 1990. From 1990 to 2014, Japan's per capita coal consumption rose from 615 kilograms of oil equivalent to about 1 tonne of oil equivalent. Russia's per capita coal consumption was 1.2 tonnes of oil equivalent in 1990. Russia's coal consumption declined sharply in the 1990s because of economic collapse and substitution by natural gas. By 2014, Russia's per capita coal consumption fell to 593 kilograms of oil equivalent. Coal consumption is insignificant in Brazil. In 2014, Brazil's per capita coal consumption was 76 kilograms of oil equivalent.

Both China and India depend heavily on coal consumption to sustain economic growth. From 1990 to 2014, China's per capita coal consumption grew from 462 kilograms of oil equivalent to 1.44 tonnes of oil equivalent and India's per capita coal consumption grew from 110 kilograms of oil equivalent to 281 kilograms of oil equivalent.

Over the period 1990–2014, on average, an increase in China's per capita GDP by one percentage point was associated with an increase in per capita coal consumption by 0.64 percentage points. Under the existing trend, when China's per capita GDP increases to 50,000 dollars (in constant 2011 international dollars), China's per capita coal consumption would reach 4 tonnes of oil equivalent. This is unlikely to happen due to insufficient resources and environmental constraints.

China is the world's largest coal producer. In 2014, China produced 3.87 billion tonnes of coal (1.84 billion tonnes of oil equivalent). Assuming that China's ultimately recoverable coal resources will be 304 billion tonnes, China's coal production is projected to peak in 2033 with a production level of near 5 billion tonnes (see Figure 6.13).

Figure 7.11 compares the net coal imports of China and India as a share of world coal production from 1981 to 2014. Net coal imports are defined as coal consumption less coal production.

The figure shows three different scenarios of China's future net coal imports as a share of world coal production from 2015 to 2050. In all three scenarios, China's coal consumption is assumed to fall by 5 percent in 2015 (China's coal demand is likely to fall in 2015 due to the slowdown of heavy industries and the surge of hydroelectricity). Starting with 2016, the three scenarios assume that China's coal consumption will grow by 3 percent a year, grow by 1 percent a year, or decline

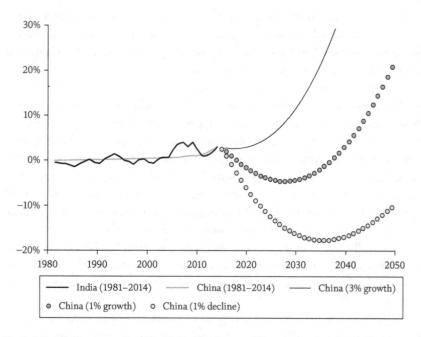

Figure 7.11 Net Imports as % of World Coal Production (China and India, 1981–2050)

Sources: Historical coal production and consumption are from BP (2015). Net coal imports are defined as coal consumption less coal production. To project China's future net coal imports, coal production is based on the projection shown in Figure 6.13. Future world coal production is based on the projection shown in Figure 6.16.

by 1 percent a year. Assuming that China's new capital reduces the coal intensity (coal consumption per unit of economic output) by 25 percent compared to the old capital, coal consumption growth rate of 3 percent, 1 percent, or –1 percent would correspond to economic growth rate of 5.7 percent, 3 percent, or 0.3 percent respectively.

India is the world's third largest coal consumer and one of the largest importers. In 2014, India's net coal imports were 117 million tonnes of oil equivalent, accounting for about 3 percent of world coal production. Other important net coal importers in the Asia-Pacific region include China, Japan, South Korea, and Taiwan. In 2014, China's net coal imports were 118 million tonnes of oil equivalent, Japan's were 126 million tonnes of oil equivalent, South Korea's were 84 million tonnes of oil equivalent, and Taiwan's were 41 million tonnes of oil equivalent. The total net coal imports of the five largest net coal importers in the Asia-Pacific region added up to 486 million tonnes of oil equivalent, about 12 percent of world coal production in 2014 (BP 2015).

Australia and Indonesia are the world's largest and second largest net coal exporter respectively. In 2014, Australia's net coal exports were 237 million tonnes of oil equivalent and Indonesia's were 221 million tonnes of oil equivalent. The total net coal exports from Australia and Indonesia were about as large as the total net imports from the five largest net coal importers in the Asia-Pacific region.

Other important coal exporters include the Russian Federation, South Africa, Colombia, and the United States. In 2014, Russia's net coal exports were 86 million tonnes of oil equivalent, South Africa's were 58 million tonnes of oil equivalent, Colombia's were 53 million tonnes of oil equivalent, and the US's were 54 million tonnes of oil equivalent (BP 2015). These coal suppliers are geographically far away from the Asian markets and Asian importers have to compete with European importers for coal exports from Russia, America, and Africa.

Given the conditions of the world coal market, if China's coal imports exceed 10 percent of world coal production, it is likely to impose an unbearable burden on the world coal market and cause major geopolitical tensions in the Asia-Pacific region.

In the 1980s, China was a net exporter of coal. Since 2002, China has consistently been a net coal importer. In 2014, China's net coal imports rose to 3 percent of world coal production. If China's future coal consumption grows by 3 percent a year, China's net coal imports as a share of world coal production will increase by 5 percent 2025 and will exceed 10 percent by 2030. If China's future coal consumption grows by 1 percent a year, China's coal trade balance will improve in the coming years. However, by the 2040s, China will again become a large net coal importer. If China's future coal consumption falls by 1 percent a year, China's coal trade balance will improve rapidly in the coming years. China will remain a large net coal exporter before 2050.

The Water Crisis

Seventy percent of the earth's surface is covered by water. However, 97.5 percent of the water on earth is salt water in seas and oceans. Only 2.5 percent is fresh water. Nearly 70 percent of the fresh water is frozen in the icecaps of Antarctica and Greenland. The rest of the fresh water mostly lies deep underground or exists as soil moisture, not available for human use.

Less than 1 percent of the world's total fresh water can be found in rivers, lakes, reservoirs, and shallow underground aquifers. This is the water that is regularly replenished by rains and snowfalls and is accessible for human use on a renewable basis (Global Change 2006).

Global annual runoff is the source of all human water withdrawals for agricultural, industrial, and municipal uses (in addition to withdrawal of non-renewable ground water). Global annual runoff of fresh water is estimated to be about 40,700 cubic kilometers. Excluding the runoff in geographically remote areas and the flood water that cannot be captured, the global available annual runoff is about 12,500 cubic kilometers.

Based on the 1990 estimate, the world's total human appropriation of runoff amounted to 6,780 cubic kilometers, or 54 percent of the global available annual runoff of freshwater. Human appropriation included 4,430 cubic kilometers of gross withdrawal and 2,350 cubic kilometers of pollution dilution. The world's total agricultural water use was estimated to be 2,880 cubic kilometers or 65 percent of the total gross withdrawal. Total industrial water use was estimated to be 975 cubic kilometers or 22 percent of the total gross withdrawal. Total municipal water use was estimated to be 300 cubic kilometers or 7 percent of the total gross withdrawal. The remaining water withdrawal was used to replenish reservoir losses (Global Change 2006).

Global water resources are highly unevenly distributed. Asia has 69 percent of the world population but only 36 percent of the global runoff. About one-third of the world population already lives in countries that experience water stress. By 2025, the total human appropriation may increase to 70 percent of the global available runoff, approaching the limit of available fresh water supply (Global Change 2006).

China's annual runoff is about 2,600 cubic kilometers (based on the multi-year average from 2000 to 2012) or 6 percent of the world total (National Bureau of Statistics of China 2013 and earlier years). China's population is about 19 percent of the world total. Thus, China's per capita water resources are only about one-third of the world average. Moreover, China's water resources are highly unevenly distributed. Southern China accounts for 53 percent of the national population but 80 percent of the country's naturally available water resources. Northern China accounts for 47 percent of the national population but less than 20 percent of water resources (China Water Risk 2010).

Subtracting water resources in remote areas and flood water that cannot be captured, China's annual available fresh water resources are estimated to be about 1,100 cubic kilometers (Baidu Baike 2014). In 2012, China's total gross water withdrawal was 614 cubic kilometers or 56 percent of the annual available fresh water resources. This does not include the annual runoff needed to dilute pollution. Assuming that the annual water use required for pollution dilution is 445 cubic meters per person (using the same rate as the global per capita water use for pollution dilution in 1990), China's water requirement for pollution dilution is about 600 cubic kilometers annually. Adding up the gross water withdrawal and the water requirement for pollution dilution, China's total water demand (about 1,200 cubic kilometers) has already exceeded the available fresh water resources.

Because of insufficient water available for pollution dilution, a large proportion of China's existing water resources are heavily polluted. About two-fifths of China's rivers and three-quarters of the lakes and reservoirs are considered to be unsuitable for drinking or fishing. More than three-quarters of the surface water flowing through Chinese cities is heavily polluted. About 4 million hectares or 7 percent of China's irrigated lands are irrigated with polluted water.

About 300 million people in rural China rely on unsafe drinking water and 190 million people in China drink water with unhealthy levels of hazardous materials. It is estimated that 100,000 people in China die annually due to water pollution-related diseases (China Water Risk 2010).

China's agricultural water use declined from 383 cubic kilometers in 2002 to 343 cubic kilometers in 2004. Since then China's agricultural water use has grown steadily. In 2013, China's agricultural water use reached 388 cubic kilometers, accounting for 63 percent of China's total water use (National Bureau of Statistics of China 2014b).

From 2000 to 2013, China's non-agricultural water use (including the industrial water use and the municipal water use) grew at an average annual rate of 2.3 percent. Figure 7.12 shows the relationship between China's economic growth and non-agricultural water use from 2001 to 2013.

In recent years, China has achieved rapid improvement of water efficiency (to reduce the water use per unit of economic output). The trend from 2001 to 2013

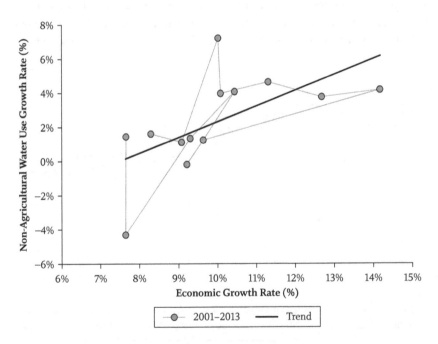

Figure 7.12 China's Economic Growth and Non-Agricultural Water Use (2001–2013)

Sources: Economic growth rates are calculated from China's real GDP. China's real GDP (in constant 2011 international dollars) from 2000 to 2013 is from the World Bank (2014). China's non-agricultural water use from 2000 to 2012 is from the National Bureau of Statistics of China (2013 and earlier years), updated to 2013 using data from China's "2013 Statistical Communique of National Economic and Social Development" (National Bureau of Statistics of China 2014b). Linear regression results in the following trend relationship over the period 2001–2013: Non-Agricultural Water Use Growth Rate = −0.068 + 0.915 * Economic Growth Rate (regression R-square = 0.370).

indicates that there is an "autonomous" tendency for China's non-agricultural water use to fall by 6.8 percent annually if economic growth rate is zero. However, excluding the autonomous reduction of water use, non-agricultural water use remains significantly correlated with economic growth. Beyond zero economic growth, for each increase in economic growth rate by one percentage point, non-agricultural water use tended to increase by 0.9 percent.

Figure 7.13 shows China's historical and projected total water use from 2000 to 2050. The projections assume that the historical relationship between China's economic growth and non-agricultural water use will hold in the coming decades and assume that China's agricultural water use will stabilize at 390 cubic kilometers (an assumption that may be too optimistic as China's future growth of food production may require an increase in agricultural water use).

Three scenarios with three different economic growth rates are projected. The first scenario assumes that the Chinese economy will grow by 5.5 percent a year from 2014 to 2050, corresponding to an annual decline rate of non-agricultural water use of 1.8 percent. The second scenario assumes that the Chinese economy will grow by 3 percent a year from 2014 to 2050, corresponding to an annual decline rate of non-agricultural water use of 4.1 percent. The third scenario assumes that the Chinese

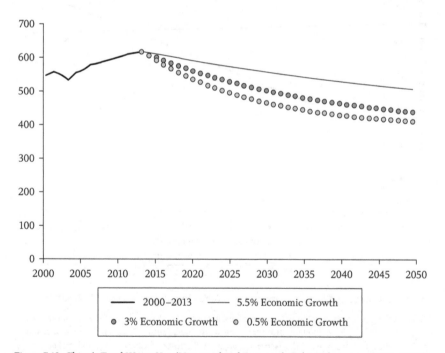

Figure 7.13 China's Total Water Use (Historical and Projected, Cubic Kilometers, 2000–2050)

Sources: China's historical water use from 2000 to 2012 is from the National Bureau of Statistics of China (2013 and earlier years), updated to 2013 using data from China's "2013 Statistical Communique of National Economic and Social Development" (National Bureau of Statistics of China 2014b).

economy will grow by 0.5 percent a year from 2014 to 2050, corresponding to an annual decline rate of non-agricultural water use of 6.3 percent.

China's available annual fresh water resources are about 1,100 cubic kilometers. The annual water demand for pollution dilution is at least 600 cubic kilometers (this is based on the current population, without taking into account future population growth). Thus, China's ecologically sustainable maximum amount of fresh water runoff that is available for human withdrawal is about 500 cubic kilometers. China's current total water use is about 620 cubic kilometers. In terms of fresh water supply, China has already overshot the ecological systems' regenerative capacity by a significant margin.

To prevent the collapse of ecological systems and to reduce the massive damage to the Chinese population's health, China needs to bring its water use back to within the ecological limit as soon as possible. However, if the Chinese economy were to grow by 5.5 percent a year and even if China achieves massive advances in water efficiency, China's total water use will not fall below the ecological limit before 2050.

If the Chinese economy grows by 3 percent a year between now and 2050, China's total water use may fall below 500 cubic kilometers by 2030. If the Chinese economy grows by 0.5 percent a year between now and 2050, China's total water use may fall below 500 cubic kilometers by 2025. However, as the Chinese capitalist economy needs economic growth rates more than 5 percent to sustain profit rates required for economic stability, both the 3 percent economic growth scenario and the 0.5 percent economic growth scenario are incompatible with the normal operation of Chinese capitalism.

Air Pollution

In January 2013, heavy smog broke out in China and it affected 600 million people living in 17 provinces, autonomous regions, and directly administered municipalities. The areas affected covered one-fourth of China's territory. The smog greatly reduced visibility and caused major disruption to transportation and daily activities.

In Beijing, measurements of PM 2.5 (particulate matters smaller than 2.5 micrometers in size) exceeded 800 micrograms per cubic meter on certain days, more than 30 times higher than the standard recommended by the World Health Organization (World Health Organization recommends that a daily average level of PM 2.5 does not exceed 25 micrograms per cubic meter, see World Health Organization 2005).

In response to the massive smog incident, the Chinese government published an "Air Pollution Prevention Plan" in September 2013. But two other massive smog incidents broke out in Northeast China in October 2013 and in Eastern China in December 2013.

Air pollution has emerged as one of the greatest threats to the Chinese population's health. It was estimated that in the early 2000s, only 1 percent of Chinese urban residents breathed air that was considered safe by the European Union (Kahn and

Yardley 2007). In 2010, outdoor air pollution led to 1.2 million premature deaths in China. It was estimated that 40 percent of global total premature deaths caused by air pollution happened in China (Wong 2013).

China's heavy dependence on coal consumption is the primary cause of air pollution. According to a report sponsored by Greenpeace, coal combustion contributes to 25 percent of the primary PM 2.5 emissions, 82 percent of the sulfur dioxide emissions, and 47 percent of the nitrogen oxide emissions in Beijing and the neighboring areas. Oil consumption also makes a significant contribution to air pollution (Guan and Liu 2013).

Among the various air pollutants, sulfur dioxide can be removed at a relatively low cost and without much technical difficulty. Desulfurization technologies are well established. China's investment cost of coal-fired electric power plants is about 4,000 Yuan per kilowatt of generating capacity (Zhongguo Gongyebao 2010). Investment cost of desulfurization equipment is about 100 Yuan per kilowatt, or about 2–3 percent of the coal-fired power investment. Desulfurization equipment can be installed not only in new coal-fired power plants, but also in old coal-fired power plants. Its application is not limited by the pace of infrastructure replacement. By the end of 2012, 680 gigawatts of coal-fired power plants or 90 percent of China's coal-fired electric power generating capacity were already equipped with desulfurization facilities (Xu 2013).

Figure 7.14 shows the relationship between China's coal consumption growth and sulfur dioxide emissions from 2001 to 2013. The trend from 2001 to 2013 indicates that there is an "autonomous" tendency for China's sulfur dioxide emissions to fall by 7.4 percent annually if coal consumption growth rate is zero. However, excluding the autonomous reduction of emissions, sulfur dioxide emissions growth has been significantly correlated with coal consumption growth. Beyond zero coal consumption growth, for each increase in coal consumption growth rate by one percentage point, the sulfur dioxide emissions growth rate tended to increase by 0.9 percentage point.

Sulfur dioxide has a significant impact on human health by causing respiratory diseases and premature deaths. Sulfur dioxide results in acid rain, which causes damage to buildings, human health, and ecological systems. Sulfur dioxide also contributes to the formation of atmospheric particulates that generate smog.

Using acid rain prevention as the threshold, China's environmental absorptive capacity of sulfur dioxide emissions is estimated to be about 16 million tonnes. Using China's national air quality standard as the threshold, China's environmental absorptive capacity of sulfur dioxide emissions is estimated to be about 12 million tonnes (Wang, J. 2005). China's sulfur dioxide emissions peaked in 2006 at 25.9 million tonnes. By 2013, China's sulfur dioxide emissions fell to 20.4 million tonnes. However, the current emissions are still higher than China's environmental absorptive capacity (based on the national air quality standard) by about 70 percent.

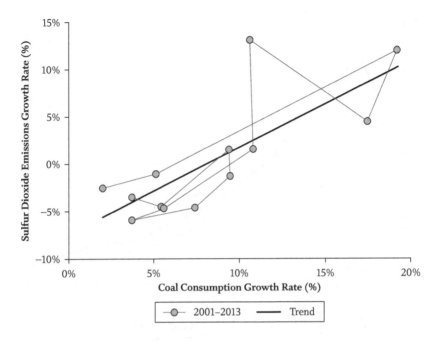

Figure 7.14 China's Coal Consumption Growth and Sulfur Dioxide Emissions (2001–2013)

Sources: China's coal consumption from 2000 to 2013 is from BP (2014). China's sulfur dioxide emissions from 2000 to 2012 are from the National Bureau of Statistics of China (2013 and earlier years), updated to 2013 using data from Zhongguo Xinwen Wang (2014). Linear regression results in the following trend relationship over the period 2001–2013: Sulfur Dioxide Emissions Growth Rate = –0.074 + 0.917 * Coal Consumption Growth Rate (regression R-square = 0.596).

Figure 7.15 shows China's historical and projected sulfur dioxide emissions. The projections assume that the historical relationship between China's coal consumption growth and sulfur dioxide emissions growth will hold in the coming decades. Three scenarios with three different coal consumption growth rates are projected. All three scenarios assume that China's coal consumption will fall by 5 percent in 2015. The first scenario assumes that China's coal consumption will grow by 3 percent a year from 2015 to 2050, corresponding to an annual decline rate of sulfur dioxide emissions of 4.6 percent. The second scenario assumes that China's coal consumption will grow by 1 percent a year from 2015 to 2050, corresponding to an annual decline rate of sulfur dioxide emissions of 6.5 percent. The third scenario assumes that China's coal consumption will decline by 1 percent a year from 2015 to 2050, corresponding to an annual decline rate of sulfur dioxide emissions of 8.3 percent.

If the current trend continues, China's sulfur dioxide emissions are projected to fall rapidly under all three scenarios. Total emissions will fall below 12 million tonnes after 2020–2025. Before then, sulfur dioxide emissions will still be higher than the environmental absorptive capacity. In addition, emissions of other air pollutants (such

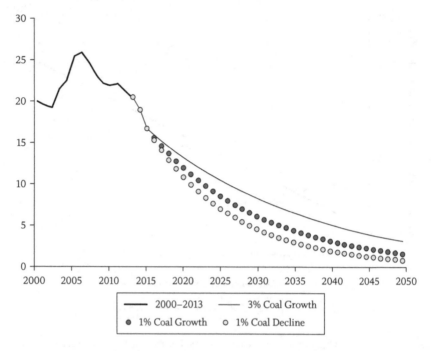

Figure 7.15 China's Sulfur Dioxide Emissions (Historical and Projected, Million Tonnes, 2000–2050)

Sources: China's sulfur dioxide emissions from 2000 to 2012 are from the National Bureau of Statistics of China (2013 and earlier years), updated to 2013 using data from Zhongguo Xinwen Wang (2014).

as nitrogen oxides, ammonia, volatile organic compounds, and primary particulate matters) may not decline as rapidly.

China's Carbon Dioxide Emissions Budget

According to the Fifth Assessment Report of the United Nations Intergovernmental Panel on Climate Change, global cumulative carbon dioxide emissions from burning fossil fuels from 2012 to 2100 need to stay below about 1 trillion tonnes if the world is committed to no more than 1.6°C (degrees Celsius) global warming by the end of the twenty-first century compared to the pre-industrial era. This scenario is summarized as RCP 2.6 (representative concentration pathways corresponding to an average radiative forcing of 2.6 watts per square meter).

Global cumulative carbon dioxide emissions from fossil fuels burning from 2012 to 2100 need to stay below about 3 trillion tonnes, 4 trillion tonnes, or 6 trillion tonnes respectively if the world is committed to no more than 2.4°C, 2.8°C, or 4.3°C global warming by the end of the twenty-first century respectively. These scenarios are summarized as RCP 4.5, RCP 6.0, and RCP 8.5 respectively (see Chapter 6 and IPCC 2013).

To prevent dangerous climate change, humanity needs to stay within RCP 2.6, which will ensure that global warming beyond the twenty-first century will stay below 2°C compared to the pre-industrial era. However, for all practical purposes, it is no longer possible to achieve RCP 2.6. Because the world's existing economic infrastructure is mostly dependent on fossil fuels, even if the world immediately implements zero economic growth and undertakes drastic emissions reduction (for example, by reducing the emission intensity of new capital by 50 percent compared to the old capital), the pace of emissions reduction would still fall short of what is needed to achieve RCP 2.6.

Under RCP 4.5, 6.0, and 8.5, runaway global warming will eventually happen, leading to climate catastrophes that may destroy the material foundation of human civilization. But if the world manages to stay below RCP 4.5 (by keeping unconventional oil, natural gas, and coal resources underground), humanity may be able to avoid the worst climate catastrophes.

If the world is committed to staying below RCP 4.5 over the rest of the twenty-first century, then the global emissions budget from 2012 to 2100 needs to be less than 3 trillion tonnes of carbon dioxide. How should the 3 trillion tonnes of global emissions budget be distributed between nation-states? There are three conceivable criteria: in proportion with a country's current emissions; in proportion with a country's current economic output; or in proportion with a country's population.

Under the first criterion, China's share of the global emissions budget from 2012 to 2100 would be the same as its share in the current global carbon dioxide emissions. Using year 2011 as the reference year, in 2011, China accounted for 26 percent of global carbon dioxide emissions. Using 26 percent as the share, China would be entitled to 840 billion tonnes of cumulative carbon dioxide emissions from 2012 to 2100.

The current emissions criterion favors the core capitalist countries and the emissions-intensive semi-peripheral countries, but is highly unfair for the low-emissions peripheral countries. Under this criterion, India, with 18 percent of the world population, would be entitled to only 5 percent of the world's future emissions. The United States, with only 4 percent of the world population, would have the right to take advantage of 18 percent of the world's future emissions. It deprives most peripheral countries of the right to use some fossil fuels to achieve a decent level of economic and social development even though they are not responsible for most of the historical greenhouse gas emissions that have set humanity onto the current path towards climate catastrophes.

In 2011, China accounted for 15 percent of gross world product. Under the GDP criterion, China would be entitled to 450 billion tonnes of cumulative carbon dioxide emissions from 2012 to 2100. Like the current emissions criterion, the GDP criterion favors the core capitalist countries and is highly unfair to the peripheral countries.

By comparison, the population criterion would seem to be the most reasonable. In 2011, China accounted for 19 percent of the world population. By this criterion,

China would be entitled to 570 billion tonnes of cumulative carbon dioxide emissions. The population criterion would require the core capitalist countries undertake drastic reduction of carbon dioxide emissions, but would allow most peripheral countries to increase their per capita fossil fuels consumption. This would help to partially correct the historically inequitable pattern of carbon dioxide emissions.

In this section, I assume that China will be entitled to 19 percent of the global emissions budget from 2012 to 2100. Thus, to achieve RCP 2.6, China's cumulative emissions of carbon dioxide from 2012 to 2100 need to stay below 190 billion tonnes. To achieve RCP 4.5, China's cumulative emissions of carbon dioxide from 2012 to 2100 need to stay below 570 billion tonnes.

Figure 7.16 compares China's historical carbon dioxide emissions from 2000 to 2014 and the projected carbon dioxide emission from 2012 to 2100 based on the requirements of RCP 2.6 and RCP 4.5.

China's carbon dioxide emissions grew from 3.5 billion tonnes in 2000 to 8.5 billion tonnes in 2010, and to 9.8 billion tonnes in 2014. Between 2000 and 2010, China's carbon dioxide emissions grew at an average annual rate of 9.2 percent. Between 2010 and 2014, China's carbon dioxide emissions grew at an average annual rate of 3.6 percent.

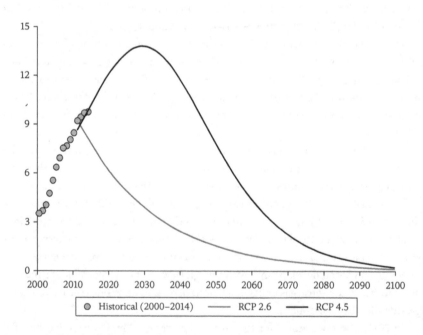

Figure 7.16 China's Carbon Dioxide Emissions (Historical and Projected, Billion Tonnes, 2000–2100)

Sources: China's historical carbon dioxide emissions from 2000 to 2014 are from BP (2015). Under RCP 2.6, China's cumulative carbon dioxide emissions from 2012 to 2100 will be about 190 billion tonnes. Under RCP 4.5, China's cumulative carbon dioxide emissions from 2012 to 2100 will be about 570 billion tonnes.

By comparison, for China to stay within the emissions budget that is compatible with RCP 2.6, China would need to have started reducing emissions in 2012. From 2012 to 2100, China will have to reduce carbon dioxide emissions by 4.5 percent each and every year. If the Chinese economy grows by 5 percent a year, a 4.5 percent reduction of emissions would require a reduction of the emission intensity of GDP by 9.5 percent each year! This would clearly be impossible.

For China to stay within the emissions budget that is compatible with RCP 4.5, the average annual growth rate of China's carbon dioxide emissions growth rate will need to slow down to 3.7 percent from 2011 to 2020 and to 1.3 percent from 2021 to 2030. China's carbon dioxide emissions need to peak in 2029 at 13.8 billion tonnes. From 2031 to 2040, China's carbon dioxide emissions need to decline at an average annual rate of 1.6 percent. From 2041 to 2050, the average annual decline rate will need to accelerate to 4.0 percent.

Figure 7.17 shows the historical relationship between China's economic growth and carbon dioxide emissions growth from 1991 to 2014. Over the period 1991–2014,

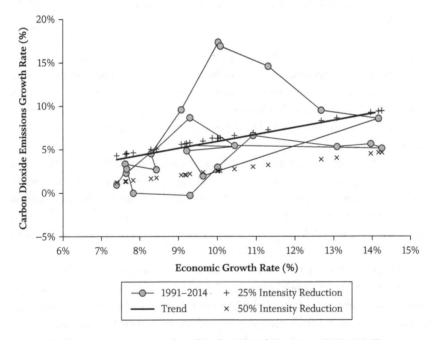

Figure 7.17 China's Economic Growth and Carbon Dioxide Emissions (1991–2013)

Sources: China's gross domestic product in constant 2011 international dollars from 1990 to 2013 is from the World Bank (2014), updated to 2014 using data from the IMF (2015). China's carbon dioxide emissions from burning fossil fuels from 1990 to 2014 are from BP (2015). Linear regression results in the following trend relationship over the period 1991–2014: Emissions Growth Rate = –0.019 + 0.785 * Economic Growth Rate (regression R-square = 0.123). The "25% Intensity Reduction" scenario assumes that the new capital's emissions intensity falls by 25 percent relative to the old capital and the "50% Intensity Reduction" scenario assumes that the new capital's emissions intensity falls by 50 percent relative to the old capital.

there was an "autonomous" tendency for China's carbon dioxide emissions to fall by 1.9 percent a year. Excluding the autonomous tendency, for each increase in the economic growth rate by one percentage point, the carbon dioxide emissions growth rate tended to increase by 0.79 percent. As China's carbon dioxide emissions growth rates experienced wide fluctuations, the linear trend between the economic growth rate and the carbon dioxide emissions growth rate has low R-square (that is, the linear trend explains only a small proportion of the observed variations of carbon dioxide emissions growth).

The observed linear trend from 1991 to 2014 almost exactly overlaps the "25% Intensity Reduction" scenario, which assumes that the new capital reduces emission intensity of economic output by 25 percent compared to the old capital. Assuming a depreciation rate of 5 percent, the "25% Intensity Reduction" scenario implies the following relationship between the economic growth rate and the carbon dioxide emissions growth rate:

Economic Growth Rate = (Carbon Dioxide Emissions Growth Rate + 1.25%) / 0.75

Figure 7.18 compares China's historical economic growth rates from 1991 to 2014 and the projected economic growth rates from 2012 to 2050 under the assumption that China's future carbon dioxide emissions will stay within the budget required by RCP 4.5 and the relationship between the economic growth rate and the carbon dioxide emissions growth rate will be determined by the "25% Intensity Reduction" scenario.

To meet the requirements of RCP 4.5 and assuming that China is entitled to 19 percent of the global carbon dioxide emissions budget, China's economic growth rate will have to fall below 5 percent after 2020. To the extent that the Chinese capitalist economy will probably need to have a more than 5 percent economic growth rate to maintain economic stability, climate stabilization requirement is incompatible with the normal operation of Chinese capitalism.

After 2030, to meet the climate stabilization requirement, China's economic growth rate will need to fall below 2 percent. After 2035, the Chinese capitalist economy will have to contract in absolute terms to stay on the emissions reduction path required by RCP 4.5. No capitalist economy can operate with negative economic growth rates for a prolonged period of time.

The above analysis makes it clear that neither Chinese capitalism nor global capitalism can be made compatible with the basic requirements of climate stabilization under conditions that will promote the long-term sustainability of human civilization. If the global capitalist system continues to operate under its own laws of motion through the rest of the twenty-first century, there is the real possibility that the material foundation of human civilization will be irremediably damaged.

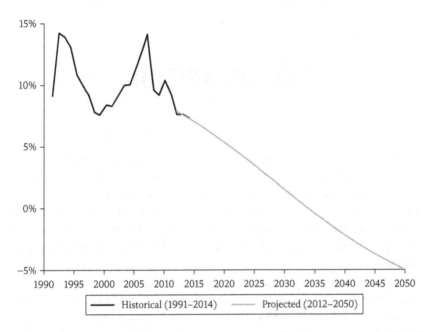

Figure 7.18 China's Economic Growth Rate (Projection Based on Requirements of RCP 4.5, 1991–2030)

Sources: China's historical economic growth rates from 1991 to 2014 are calculated from China's real GDP using data from the World Bank (2014) and the IMF (2015). Projected economic growth rates from 2012 to 2050 assume that China's carbon dioxide emissiions will follow the path required by RCP 4.5 and the relationship between the economic growth rate and the emissions growth rate is as follows: economic growth rate = (emissions growth rate + 1.25%) / 0.75.

Alternatively, the global class struggle in the coming years will lead to the demise of the global capitalist system and replace it with a new social system that is organized on the principles of social equity and ecological sustainability. China will be the key battleground of the coming global class struggle.

8

THE TRANSITION

From the mid-nineteenth century to the mid-twentieth century, China was reduced from the world's largest economy to one of the poorest peripheral nations in the capitalist world system. Neither the traditional ruling class nor the indigenous capitalist class was able to reverse China's national decline. It took a general social revolution that mobilized the peasants and the urban workers to create the basic political conditions required to rebuild China as a viable nation-state in the capitalist world system.

By eliminating foreign imperialist influences and the rural landlord class, economic surplus was concentrated in the hands of the post-revolutionary state, which was committed to capital accumulation and industrialization. The post-revolutionary state entered into an implicit "socialist social contract" with the great majority of the population, promising to meet the people's basic needs in the short run and to reduce economic and social inequality in the long run.

By the 1980s, as China became more dependent on western capitalist economies for the supply of advanced technology and luxury consumer goods, the Communist Party elites realized that the Chinese economy had to become "competitive" in the global capitalist market. Export competitiveness required the dismantling of the historical "socialist social contract" and the establishment of a new social regime based on cheap labor exploitation.

Intense political struggles broke out within the Communist Party elites and between the ruling elites and other social classes, culminating in the massive political turmoil of 1989. By the 1990s, the Communist Party elites had reached consensus on the transition to capitalism. A pro-capitalist alliance between the Communist Party elites and the urban middle class was formed. The state sector working class was isolated and politically disoriented. The defeat of the working class paved the way for massive privatization in the 1990s. By the early twenty-first century, China emerged as the center of global manufacturing exports.

The boom of the Chinese capitalist economy has been based on the rapid growth of exports to western capitalist economies, the intense exploitation of a large cheap labor force, and ruthless environmental degradation. The global capitalist crisis of 2008–2009 brought the double-digit growth of the Chinese economy to an end. Since then, all three conditions of China's capitalist accumulation have been undermined.

As Chinese exports slow down, China has become more dependent on investment to drive economic growth. High investment–GDP ratios have led to rapid declines of

China's economy-wide profit rate. Under the current trend, by the 2020s, China's profit rate will fall to a level that is likely to precipitate the Chinese economy into a major crisis (see Chapter 5).

Capitalist accumulation has fundamentally transformed China's social structure. As a growing proportion of China's labor force becomes proletarianized wage workers, a new generation of the Chinese working class begins to get organized. Squeezed between rising living costs and declining income expectations, many Chinese urban youth have seen their "middle class dream" smashed. A new anti-capitalist alliance that includes the working class and the progressive sections of the urban middle class begins to take shape. As China's non-agricultural employment rises above 70 percent of the total labor force, it will be increasingly difficult for Chinese capitalism to accommodate the urban population's rising demands. By the 2020s, China is likely to be confronted by both an accumulation crisis and a political crisis (see Chapter 2).

To maintain economic and political stability, it is necessary for the Chinese capitalist economy to grow rapidly. But if the Chinese economy continues to grow rapidly, China's rising demand for oil, natural gas, and coal is likely to impose an unbearable burden on world energy markets by the 2020s or the 2030s. China's ecological systems will continue to deteriorate in the coming decades. Beyond the 2030s, climate stabilization consistent with the long-term sustainability of human civilization may require negative growth of the Chinese economy (see Chapter 7).

The previous chapters of this book have argued that by the 2020s, economic, social, and ecological contradictions are likely to converge in China, leading to a major crisis of the Chinese capitalist system.

China has been at the center of global capital accumulation in the early twenty-first century. As economic, social, and ecological contradictions begin to overwhelm Chinese capitalism, the global capitalist system is entering into a structural crisis that can no longer be resolved within its own institutional framework. The age of transition has arrived (on the concept of the "age of transition," see Hopkins and Wallerstein 1996).

The Rise and Fall of Global Capitalism

The modern capitalist world system emerged in Western Europe in the sixteenth century. Competition between multiple states created favorable political conditions that encouraged accumulation of capital.

Before the sixteenth century, the expansion of the European economy was constrained by the locally available resources and ecological space. The constraints were overcome through the conquest of the Americas that provided the early capitalist world system with an enormous geographical space with abundant natural resources.

Large-scale consumption of coal began in the second half of the eighteenth century. Fossil fuels allowed the capitalist world system to overcome the limits imposed by traditional renewable energies, providing the material foundation for the spectacular growth of the global capitalist economy in the nineteenth and the twentieth century.

By the late nineteenth century, capitalism became the first truly global system in human history. Global capitalist dominance transformed social conditions in both the core and the periphery. By the early twentieth century, the western industrial working classes and non-western national liberation movements challenged the capitalist world system. The non-western communist movement, as a radical variant of the national liberation movement, created the necessary political conditions that allowed several large geographical areas (Russia and China) to participate in effective capital accumulation.

By the mid-twentieth century, the global capitalist system was forced to make concessions to the increasingly more powerful "anti-systemic movements." The global "New Deal" established after 1945 created a new set of global social compromises, laying down the foundation for the unprecedented global capitalist boom in the 1950s and the 1960s. However, the post-1945 global "New Deal" strengthened the economic bargaining power of the working classes in the core and the semi-periphery. By the second half of the 1960s, rising popular expectations led to major revolutionary upsurges in every geographical region in the world. Profit rates declined everywhere. The global capitalist system was in a major economic and political crisis.

In response to the crisis, the global capitalist classes undertook a massive counter-offensive that became known as "neoliberalism." China's counter-revolution and the transition to capitalism turned the global balance of power decisively in favor of the system's ruling elites. This allowed global capitalism to overcome the system-wide crisis from 1968 to 1989 through the strategy of "spatial fix." Much of the world's industrial production was relocated from the core and some high-cost semi-peripheral countries to Asian peripheral countries. China was the main beneficiary of global capital relocation in the late twentieth century.

The "spatial fix" in the late twentieth century helped the capitalist system to win the global class war by partially dismantling the post-1945 global "New Deal." However, the victory of global neoliberalism was purchased at a very high price, at the expense of the long-term sustainability of the global capitalist system.

The relocation of industrial production to the peripheral areas with a large cheap labor force helped to increase the production of global surplus value and revive the worldwide profit rate. However, the de-industrialization of the core countries and especially the financialization of the United States—the incumbent hegemonic power—led to new economic and social contradictions. Rising inequality undermined the political legitimacy of the core capitalist states. Financial liberalization greatly increased the instability of the global capitalist system. In the short term, financial expansion helped to revive American imperialism. In the long term, the deepening economic and social contradictions have accelerated the decline of the American hegemonic power, depriving the global capitalist system of effective leadership exactly when the system enters into its structural crisis (on the decline of the American hegemonic power, see Arrighi 2007).

On the other hand, the rapid industrialization of China and other Asian peripheral countries has created several new industrial working classes. In particular, the Chinese industrial working class has become the world's largest and begins to demand a growing range of economic and political rights. In the twentieth century, global capitalism already struggled to accommodate the economic and political demands of the core and the semi-peripheral working classes that together accounted for less than one-third of the global labor force. The rise of the Chinese working class expands the potential size of the labor force that demands high material living standards and democratic governance to about one-half of the global labor force. Could the global capitalist system in the twenty-first century manage to accommodate not only the demands from the working classes in the historical core and semi-periphery, but also the demands from the entire Chinese population (about one-fifth of the world total)? If yes, will the economic cost of accommodation be so high that it eventually leads to a global accumulation crisis? If not, will the political cost of lack of accommodation be so high that it eventually leads to a global political crisis?

The global capitalist system is based on the pursuit of endless accumulation of capital, which needs to be motivated by sufficiently high and stable profit rates. According to neoclassical economics, economic growth is driven by population growth (the growth of labor input), accumulation of physical capital (the growth of capital input), and technological progress. In the long run, the growth rate of capital stock will converge with the growth rate of economic output. Thus, long-term economic growth can only be sustained if there is positive population growth or positive growth of "total factor productivity." As birth rates decline in most parts of the world, world population is likely to peak after the mid-twenty-first century (for world population projections, see United Nations 2012). Some leading neoclassical economists (such as Robert Gordon) begin to realize that technological progress may not last forever (see Chapter 3). If the recent deceleration of "total factor productivity" is not reversed, economic growth will eventually come to an end. If economic growth comes to an end, the profit rate will eventually approach zero and capitalism will cease to exist as a viable economic and social system.

From the ecological perspective, the historical growth of the global capitalist economy has been made possible by the massive consumption of fossil fuels. Much of the world's high-quality, low-cost fossil fuels have already been exploited. World production of oil, natural gas, and coal is likely to peak before the mid-twenty-first century. Nuclear and renewable energies are constrained by technological and ecological limits. The growth of nuclear and renewable energies will be unable to offset the decline of fossil fuels. With the decline of fossil fuels production, world economic growth rate will eventually approach zero. Nevertheless, the remaining recoverable amount of fossil fuels may be sufficiently large to lead to major climate catastrophes beyond the twenty-first century (see Chapter 6).

China's rapid industrialization has led to the re-acceleration of global carbon dioxide emissions growth. Under the current trend, cumulative carbon dioxide emissions over the twenty-first century will lead to long-term global warming of more than three degrees Celsius that will threaten to destroy the material foundation of human civilization.

Figure 8.1 compares alternative paths of global economic growth that are compatible with different scenarios of global carbon dioxide emissions. It is assumed that each year, new capital's emission intensity falls by 25 percent relative to the old capital. Therefore the relationship between the economic growth rate and the emissions growth rate is defined as follows: economic growth rate = (emissions growth rate + 1.25%) / 0.75 (see Chapter 7).

To avoid dangerous climate change, it is necessary for humanity to follow the emissions pathway of RCP 2.6 (see Chapter 6 for the RCP scenarios). If the world had started emissions reduction in 2012, it would have required annual reduction of carbon dioxide emissions by 3 percent each year between 2012 and 2100. Assuming reasonable paces of technological progress, this implies absolute reduction of the global economy by 2.3 percent each year between 2012 and 2100.

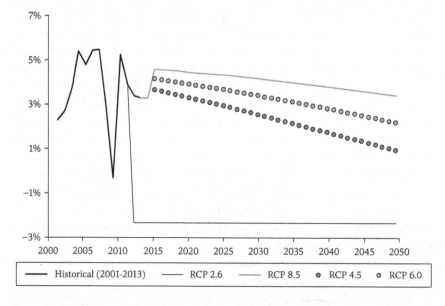

Figure 8.1 World Econmic Growth Rate (Climate Stabilization Scenarios, 2001–2050)

Sources: Historical world economic growth rates from 2001 to 2012 are from the World Bank (2014). World economic growth rates in 2013 and 2014 are from the IMF (2014). RCP 2.6, RCP 4.5, RCP 6.0, and RCP 8.5 refer to global carbon dioxide emissions pathways (see IPCC 2013 and Chapter 6). New capital is assumed to have emission intensity 25 percent lower than the old capital so that economic growth rate = (emissions growth rate + 1.25%) / 0.75 (see Chapter 7).

Thus, even if the world immediately commits to zero economic growth, for all practical purposes, it is already too late to avoid dangerous climate change. The question is whether the world can prevent the worst climate catastrophes that may undermine the material foundation of human civilization. Under the scenario of RCP 6.0 and RCP 8.5, the global economy is allowed to grow by 4–4.5 percent a year in the coming decade. Under the two scenarios, world economic growth rate will gradually decline to 2.5–3.5 percent a year by the 2040s. However, both scenarios will almost guarantee runaway global warming and major climate catastrophes beyond the twenty-first century.

Under RCP 4.5, there will still be a significant chance of runaway global warming and major climate catastrophes. Thus, to achieve long-term global sustainability and to protect the future of the human civilization, it is absolutely necessary for the world to stay below the emissions pathway defined by RCP 4.5. This would require the world economic growth rate to fall below 2 percent by the 2030s and to fall below zero after 2060. Historically, global capitalism tended to suffer from major economic and political instabilities when the world economic growth rate fell below 2 percent and the global capitalist system certainly cannot function with negative economic growth.

Thus, the normal operation of the global capitalist system cannot be made compatible with the basic requirements of climate stabilization. Whether the material foundation of human civilization can be preserved depends on whether humanity can replace the existing global capitalist system with a new social system based on social equity and ecological sustainability.

"Spatial Fix" of the Twenty-first Century?

In the past, the global capitalist system managed to resolve several major crises through the strategy of geographical expansion or "spatial fix" (Harvey 2001). In the twenty-first century, could the global capitalist system again overcome its current structural crisis through "spatial fix"?

In the twentieth century, the periphery of the capitalist world system had consistently accounted for about two-thirds of the world population. The core and the semi-periphery each accounted for about one-sixth. Through unequal exchange, economic surplus was transferred from the periphery to the core. The concentration of economic wealth in the core allowed the core countries to lead global capital accumulation and buy off domestic working classes. In the twentieth century, the core countries accounted for 50–60 percent of gross world economic product and the periphery's share of gross world economic product was 20–30 percent (see Chapter 4).

In the late twentieth century, to contain rising labor and resources costs, it became necessary for the capitalist world system to mobilize new geographical areas for active participation in world industrial production. China became the center of global industrial production. China's economic rise has begun to fundamentally transform the structure of the capitalist world system. For the first time in capitalist history, the gap between the core and the periphery began to narrow. By 2013, the share of the core countries in gross world economic product was reduced to about 40 percent and the share of the peripheral countries increased to about 40 percent (see Table 4.9).

In the coming years, China is likely to advance into the semi-periphery (when China's per capita GDP rises above the world average and China's gains from unequal exchange begin to exceed the losses). The peripheral share of the world population will decline to about 50 percent. This raises the question whether the remaining labor force in the periphery can generate sufficiently large economic surplus to be transferred to the core. If world wealth is no longer concentrated in the core, could the core capitalist countries still manage to maintain economic and social stability?

In the late twentieth century, China's participation in the global capitalist division of labor helped to lower the global labor cost and revive the global profit rate. In the future, when Chinese workers demand more economic and social rights, could another large geographical area be mobilized to contain the rising labor cost in China and the rest of world?

For a new geographical area to replace China as the new center of global industrial production, the new area needs to meet several requirements. The new geographical area needs to provide a sufficiently large cheap labor force that is at least comparable to China's in size. The labor force needs to be equipped with adequate infrastructure and the necessary qualities and skills required for capitalist industrial production. The geographical area needs to be ruled by an effective capitalist state that can provide various political and social conditions required for capitalist accumulation. Finally, capitalist accumulation in this newly developed geographical area will not be constrained by resources depletion and ecological crisis.

Excluding China, the periphery of the capitalist world system now includes mainly Southeast Asia, South Asia, and Sub-Saharan Africa. Many countries in these geographical areas currently suffer from political instability and do not have the adequate physical infrastructure required for capitalist industrialization. India is probably the only country that can potentially supply an industrial labor force that is comparable to China's in size.

Figure 8.2 compares the industrial sector employment of China, India, and the OECD countries (the Organization for Economic Co-Operation and Development, an economic association of "developed" capitalist countries).

In the early 1990s, when China began to accelerate the transition to capitalism, China already had an industrial labor force that was comparable to the industrial labor force of all the OECD countries combined. From 1998 to 2002, China's industrial sector employment declined from 158 million to 151 million as massive privatization laid off tens of millions of state sector workers. From 2002 to 2011, China's industrial

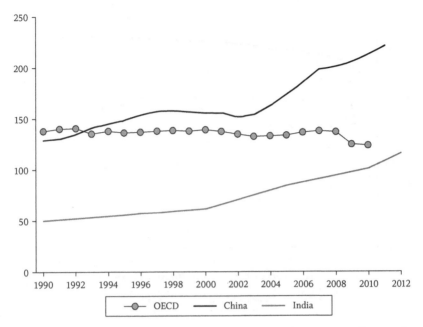

Figure 8.2 Industrial Sector Employment (China, India, and the OECD, Million Workers, 1990–2012)

Source: World Bank (2014).

sector employment grew from 151 million to 221 million, with an average annual growth of 7.7 million.

India's industrial sector employment grew from 62 million in 2000 to 101 million in 2010, with an average annual growth of 3.9 million. India's industrial sector employment grew by 7.4 million in 2011 and 7.3 million in 2012. By 2012, India's industrial sector employment reached 116 million, about a half of China's current industrial sector employment. If India's industrial sector employment keeps growing by 7 million a year and China's industrial sector employment peaks at 250 million, it would still take about 20 years for India to catch up with China's industrial sector employment.

Capitalist industrialization requires not only a large number of low-wage workers but also workers who have the adequate skills and physical qualities that can perform intense physical labor and operate high-tech industrial equipment. Figure 8.3 compares the relationship between per capita real GDP and the population's life expectancy in China and India.

Both China and India began the pursuit of modern industrialization in the 1950s. Unlike China, the modern Indian state was not the historical product of a popular revolution. India did not eliminate the influences of the traditional landlord class in its rural areas. The rural class conflicts have contributed to the Maoist insurgency that currently affects 40 percent of India's territory (Ismi 2013).

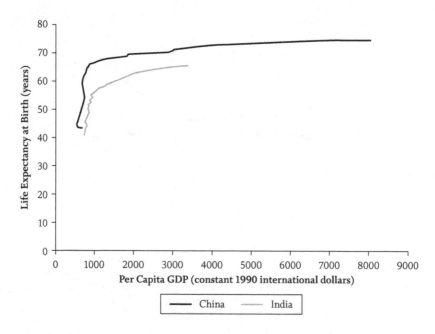

Figure 8.3 Per Capita GDP and Life Expectancy (China and India, 1960–2010)

Sources: Life expectancy at birth for the total population from 1960 to 2010 is from the World Bank (2014). Per capita real GDP in constant 1990 international dollars from 1960 to 2010 is from Bolt and Zanden (2013).

China has been much more successful than India in meeting its population's basic needs. In the 1960s, although China's per capita real GDP stagnated, the Chinese population's life expectancy improved dramatically from 43 years in 1960 to 63 years in 1970. By 1970, China's life expectancy was fully 14 years higher than India's. By 2010, India's life expectancy reached 66 years and India's per capita real GDP reached near 3,400 dollars (in constant 1990 international dollars). India's life expectancy in 2010 is comparable to China's life expectancy in 1975 when China's per capita real GDP was only 870 dollars. By this measure, India lagged behind China by about 35 years in term of meeting the population's basic health demands.

Figure 8.4 compares the relationship between the per capita real GDP and the adult literacy rate for China and India. In the early 1980s, China and India had similar levels of per capita real GDP. China's adult literacy rate was 66 percent in 1982 and India's adult literacy rate was only 41 percent in 1981. By 2006, India's adult literacy rate rose to 63 percent, still lower than China's adult literacy rate in 1982. Moreover, after 2001, India's adult literacy improvement appears to have leveled off. From 2001 to 2006, India's adult literacy rate improved only by 1.8 percentage points. At this rate, it will take India about 90 years to reach China's current adult literacy rate (about 95 percent).

Thus, at best, it will take India another 20 years to supply an industrial labor force that is as large as China's. However, in terms of physical health and basic literacy, the

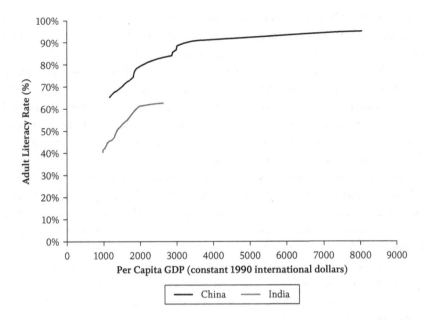

Figure 8.4 Per Capita GDP and Adult Literacy Rate (China, 1982–2010 and India, 1981–2006)

Sources: Adult literacy rate is from the World Bank (2014). Per capita real GDP in constant 1990 international dollars is from Bolt and Zanden (2013).

quality of India's labor force is likely to fall behind China's in the foreseeable future. The insufficient quality of labor force will be a serious constraint on India's future industrialization.

To function as the center of global industrial production, a country needs not only a large cheap labor force with adequate skills and physical health, but also massive investment in capital infrastructure and abundant energy supply. In this respect, Indian capitalism faces insurmountable obstacles.

China's rapid industrialization has been based on the massive consumption of coal. China is largely self-sufficient in coal. In 2013, China's coal production to consumption ratio (the ratio of coal production to coal consumption) was 96 percent. Like China, India relied upon coal as its largest source of energy. In 2013, coal accounted for 55 percent of India's primary energy consumption. But unlike China, India has struggled to increase its domestic coal production. In terms of physical volume, India is the world's third largest coal producer (after China and the United States). But because of the low quality of India's domestically produced coal, in terms of energy content, India is ranked the world's fifth largest coal producer (after China, the United States, Australia, and Indonesia). India depends on imports to meet 29 percent of its coal demand.

China is the world's fourth largest oil producer and fifth largest natural gas producer. India's oil production is less than one-fifth of China's and depends on imports to meet 76 percent of its oil demand. India's natural gas production is less than one-third of China's and depends on imports to meet 35 percent of its natural gas demand (India's and China's energy statistics are from BP 2014).

India's per capita energy consumption in 2013 was 475 kilograms of oil equivalent, less than a quarter of China's (2.1 tonnes of oil equivalent). India's population in 2013 was 1.25 billion. If India's per capita energy consumption were to rise to China's level in 2013, the world would have to find an additional energy supply of 2 billion tonnes of oil equivalent. This is almost equivalent to the US primary energy consumption in 2013 (2.3 billion tonnes of oil equivalent).

India's per capita carbon dioxide emissions from burning fossil fuels in 2013 were 1.5 tonnes, about one-fifth of China's (7 tonnes). If India's per capita carbon dioxide emissions were to rise to China's level in 2013, the world's annual carbon dioxide emissions would have to increase by 6.8 billion tonnes. This would be significantly higher than US carbon dioxide emissions in 2013 (5.9 billion tonnes).

The world's available fossil fuels resources and environmental space are already struggling to sustain the rise of industrialized China. They certainly cannot sustain industrialized India in addition to industrialized China, at least within the current framework of global capitalism.

The recognition of this material reality by no means denies the right of the Indian people to live decent lives and to have full access to opportunities of human development. Historical experience from China's Maoist socialism and the progressive social experiments in India's Kerala state demonstrate that rapid improvements in various human development indicators can be achieved with comparatively low levels of material consumption (for the achievements of India's Kerala state in meeting people's basic needs, see Navarro 1993).

Reform, Revolution, or Collapse

Within the current capitalist world system, Chinese capitalism specializes in manufacturing exports based on the exploitation of a large cheap labor force and the massive consumption of natural resources. As labor and resources costs rise, Chinese capitalism begins to be squeezed between rising costs and the relatively low value-added commodities it sells in the global capitalist market. This is a fundamental contradiction that Chinese capitalism cannot overcome (in addition to the on-going global capitalist structural crisis).

In the mid-twentieth century, western core capitalist states met the challenges from the industrial working classes by undertaking internal reforms, which accommodated the demands of the working classes through economic and social concessions (Keynesian macroeconomic policy, a welfare state, and legitimate roles for labor unions). The reform was made possible by the economic surplus transferred from the periphery and the abundant supply of cheap oil. By contrast, Chinese capitalism in the twenty-first century is confronted by the peak of fossil fuels production and the rapidly escalating ecological contradictions. Although China is going to advance into the semi-periphery of the capitalist world system, there is no evidence suggesting that China will soon become a large net gainer in the global system of unequal exchange. If China does become such a large net gainer, the interesting question will be – at whose expense? If Chinese capitalism somehow manages to rise further in the global capitalist hierarchy at the expense of the existing core capitalist countries (a development that this author considers to be unlikely), it will certainly destabilize the entire global capitalist system. Such a destabilization by itself could be sufficient to destroy both Chinese capitalism and global capitalism.

In the late twentieth century, in response to the profit rate crisis in the 1970s and the 1980s, global capitalism pursued the strategy of "spatial fix." A new geographical area with a large cheap labor force was mobilized to contain global labor and resources costs. However, as is argued in the previous section, currently there is not another large geographical area that can replace China to become the new center of global industrial production.

In the 1980s, several semi-peripheral countries (South Korea, Brazil, and Poland) suffered from both accumulation crisis and political crisis. Eventually, these crises were resolved within the basic framework of capitalism by restoring favorable conditions of capital accumulation (see Chapter 2). After the 1997 economic crisis, South Korean capitalism relocated low value-added industrial activities to China and focused on higher value-added segments of global commodity chains. Unlike South Korean capitalism, Chinese capitalism cannot relocate its low value-added activities on a large scale. Chinese capitalism continues to depend on the core capitalist economies for the supply of advanced technologies.

Unlike Brazilian capitalism or Russian capitalism, Chinese capitalism does not have access to abundant high-value natural resources that could allow Chinese capitalism to achieve at least temporary social stability by sharing with the population a portion of the monopolistic rent generated from natural resources exports.

In the case of Poland, the 1980s crisis was eventually "resolved" through the neoliberal "shock therapy" which dismantled the socialist social contract that provided the Polish working class with basic social welfare and security. The Polish working class was "persuaded" to give up their historical socialist economic and social rights in exchange for political democracy and the promise that in the long run, Poland would become a part of the "west." In reality, Polish capitalism was absorbed into the European capitalist system of division of labor in which Poland supplied relatively cheap labor. Polish capitalism's peripheral position is partly legitimized by the long-term, uncertain prospect that Polish workers' wage rates might eventually converge with the wage rates of the Western European workers.

In the Chinese case, the capitalist transition was completed under the Communist Party dictatorship. Any political change that delegitimizes the Communist Party dictatorship will also delegitimize the capitalist transition. A general popular anger against China's current inequality in wealth distribution could lead to popular demands to investigate and reverse the entire process of massive privatization in the 1990s.

Unlike the Polish workers who were protected by a comprehensive package of social welfare in the 1980s, Chinese workers and urban middle class professionals now demand the re-establishment of decent social welfare and what they consider to be a fair share of the national income. These demands focus on material interests (wages, pensions, housing, education, health care, and the environment) that can only be met through redistribution of national income and wealth. Rather than having the effect of persuading the workers and the urban professionals to give up their economic and social demands, a system of political democracy is likely to raise the popular expectation and further strengthen their demands.

Finally, Chinese capitalism is already integrated into the global capitalist system as a supplier of cheap labor force. However, unlike Poland, the Chinese labor market cannot be incorporated into the labor market of a core capitalist economy and Chinese workers will not have even the long-term, uncertain expectation that eventually their wage rates may converge with wage rates in the core capitalist countries.

As China's economic, social, and ecological contradictions converge, the Chinese Communist Party elites will be confronted with a major political dilemma. The Party has counted on rapid economic growth to provide legitimacy to its political dictatorship. The general population has been persuaded to accept the Party's political rule based on the expectation of rising material living standards despite increasing inequality and insecurity, environmental degradation, and political oppression. But, as the capitalist contradictions deepen and China's economic growth slows down, there is already a rising gap between people's expectations and the ability of the Chinese capitalist system to deliver.

The so-called "mass incidents" (a term used by the Chinese government to refer to a wide range of social protests including strikes, sit-ins, marches, rallies, and riots) increased from about 8,700 in 1993, 60,000 in 2003, to 120,000 in 2008. It is estimated that in recent years, the annual occurrence of massive incidents has stayed above 100,000. According to the data collected by the Chinese Ministry of Public Security, the cases of various forms of "social order" violation increased from 3.2 million in 1995, 11.7 million in 2009, to 13.9 million in 2012 (Tanner 2014). In some large-scale mass incidents, tens of thousands of people participated in riots and occupied local governments for days (Tong and Lei 2013). Assuming that a mass incident on average involves about 100 people, there would be about 10 million Chinese people who are involved in various social protests each year.

When China's economic, social, and ecological contradictions converge to produce a general accumulation crisis, popular frustration could easily be translated into a surge of "mass incidents" in scale and intensity. Within a short period of time, the "mass incidents" could multiply to levels that overwhelm the capacity of the Chinese state to deal with them.

The Chinese state could choose to use its available resources to appease the growing popular discontents. But concessions by the state will increase the cost of capitalist accumulation and raise popular expectations, leading to more costly demands in the future. The state could attempt to repress the popular protests. But repression will seriously undermine the state's legitimacy, greatly increasing the risk of a nation-wide popular rebellion.

After the political turmoil in 1989, the Chinese ruling class eventually managed to restore political legitimacy as the economic restructuring in the 1990s created favorable conditions for capitalist accumulation. In the future, Chinese capitalism will struggle with rising labor and resources costs and falling profit rates. Without a major defeat of the working class, the labor cost cannot be effectively contained. In the absence of a large geographical area where Chinese capitalism can relocate its industrial capital, it will be very difficult for the Chinese capitalist class to win a decisive victory against the working class. In addition, Chinese capitalism has to confront insurmountable ecological contradictions. If Chinese capitalism fails to restore favorable conditions for capital accumulation, political repression is unlikely to have more than a temporary effect.

Overall, it is unlikely that the coming major crisis can be resolved within the existing framework of Chinese capitalism. China's political future may follow one of the following three scenarios.

Under the first scenario, pressured by the growing popular protests, the Communist Party leadership may begin to undertake serious economic and social reforms to accommodate the interests of the working class and the urban middle class. The Communist Party leadership may decide to abandon the neoliberal policy of "reform and openness," implement some form of wealth redistribution, and tax the capitalists to pay for the social and environmental costs. However, with rising wage, taxation, and resources costs, the capitalists will reduce investment, leading to growing unemployment and economic crisis. At this stage, to sustain the progressive economic and social policies, the Communist Party leadership may be persuaded to pursue a more socialist-oriented model of development. To offset the decline of capitalist investment, the Communist Party leadership may decide to revive state-owned enterprises. As public investment gradually replaces private investment, the economic foundation for a new socialist economy may be established. Under such a scenario, China will be able to revive the socialist model of development with comparatively less political turbulence.

However, back to the 1990s, the Communist Party ruling elites were already committed to the transition to capitalism. Since then, the political and economic interests of the Communist Party leadership have converged with the interests of the transnational and domestic capitalist classes. After the Bo Xilai incident, the Communist Party leadership purged from its own ranks the last significant faction that was in opposition to neoliberal capitalism. Given these developments, it is highly unlikely that the Communist Partly ruling elites will give up their power and wealth without a major fight.

Under the second scenario, the coming crisis of Chinese capitalism will lead to the disintegration of the Communist Party dictatorship. Throughout the country, "mass incidents" will explode, leading to a popular revolution overwhelming the Party state. At the national level, formal liberal democracy may be established. But the capitalist class may retain substantial influence through their control over the army, the police, and the tax revenue. Because there is not a nationally recognized, unified leftist political party, the revolutionary socialist left may initially have difficulty in taking over national political power.

However, China is a big country. There will be many places where the working class has a relative advantage over the capitalist class. In many cities and provinces, the political rule of the capitalist class may be sufficiently weakened so that local political power falls into the hands of the workers and revolutionary socialists. By taking advantage of the weakness of the newly established "liberal democratic" national government, leftist local governments may survive and become consolidated. By undertaking preliminary progressive policies that meet the local population's immediate needs, such as housing, health care, education, improvement of working conditions, pollution cleaning, and the elimination of local mafias, local leftist governments will begin to gain popular support.

On the other hand, the capitalist economic, social, and ecological crisis will continue to deepen. Unable to solve these crises, the national capitalist government and the various local governments under the control of local capitalists will be further weakened. The working class and the urban middle class will continue to make economic and political demands that the national and local capitalist governments are unable to accommodate. As the legitimacy of capitalist national and local governments declines and the popular support for local leftist governments grows, the nation-wide balance of power will be gradually turned in favor of revolutionary socialist forces, laying down the foundation for nation-wide socialist transformation.

Under the third scenario, the coming crisis of Chinese capitalism may lead to a general political and social collapse. Effective central government may not be restored for a prolonged period of time. In the worst case, China may fall into a civil war. Certain areas where ethnic minorities are concentrated, such as Southern Xinjiang and Tibet, may begin to split away from China. Under such a scenario, there will still be certain geographical areas where the conditions are relatively favorable for the working class. In some cities and provinces, workers may be able to take over local political power and the revolutionary socialist left may be able to provide political leadership. Whether the local workers' governments can survive depends on whether they can defend themselves with an effective armed force (such as workers' militia), whether they can establish a secured base of economic revenue, and whether they can skillfully take advantage of the internal contradictions of the capitalist class.

If local workers' governments can survive the initial phase of collapse and gain popular support, their political influence is likely to consolidate and expand. As the political powers under capitalist control fail to resolve the on-going economic, political, and ecological crises, revolutionary socialist forces will have the opportunity to gradually gain the upper hand in the struggle for national political supremacy.

Socialist Economics: The Twentieth Century

Having learned from the historical experience of twentieth-century socialism, revolutionary socialists in the twenty-first century will understand that the taking over of the state power will only be the first step in a ten-thousand-mile "long march" towards a new society based on social equity and ecological sustainability. All future socialist governments will be confronted with the question: how should a socialist economy be organized in the twenty-first century?

According to classical Marxism, capitalism is characterized by the basic contradiction between the objective tendency towards socialization of material production and the capitalistic system of private appropriation. The contradiction would lead to growing class conflicts and increasingly devastating economic crises. The contradiction could only be resolved by replacing capitalism with a new economic system based on social ownership of the means of production and society-wide economic planning that would allocate social resources rationally to meet social needs (Engels 1978[1880]).

Twentieth-century socialist states were the historical products of social revolutions in the periphery and the semi-periphery of the capitalist world system. The basic means of production were nationalized or collectivized. Industrial and agricultural production was organized by state-wide economic planning. Despite their historical limitations, twentieth-century socialist states were characterized by internal class relations that were more favorable for ordinary working people than those typically found in the peripheral and semi-peripheral capitalist states.

Twentieth-century socialist states remained a part of the capitalist world system and had to compete against the capitalist states economically and militarily. Political and economic power was concentrated in the hands of privileged bureaucrats and technocrats, who over time evolved into a new exploitative ruling class.

Initially, socialist states were generally successful in achieving both effective capital accumulation and improvement of people's living standards. By eliminating the traditional ruling classes, socialist states were able to mobilize economic surplus to achieve rapid industrialization. However, by the 1970s and the 1980s, socialist states were squeezed between rising labor and resources costs and their inability to compete with the core capitalist countries on the technology frontier. The Communist Party's ruling elites took advantage of the economic crisis to dismantle the socialist social contract and complete the capitalist transition. The former socialist economies were restructured to become suppliers of cheap labor force or raw materials in the capitalist world system.

After 1989, a consensus was established among the mainstream economists and many leftist intellectuals believed that socialism as an economic system was fundamentally flawed. According to this consensus, an economic system based on social ownership of the means of production and society-wide planning inevitably suffers from several fatal problems.

According to the mainstream consensus, a modern economy with millions of different inputs and outputs is too complicated for centralized economic planning to operate effectively and rationally. It is not possible for the central planning authority to collect, process, and efficiently utilize the massive amount of economic information required for the rational allocation of resources. Moreover, without private property, people are not rewarded properly and adequately for their work effort and risk-taking. As a result, the overall levels of effort and risk-taking tend to be far below the economically optimal levels.

By comparison, in a capitalist market economy, all individuals are rewarded for their pursuit of self-interest. All individuals are motivated to collect and utilize potentially useful economic information that is dispersed throughout the economy. Through market prices, the economic information collected by many different individuals is efficiently transmitted and shared across the whole economy. The individuals, intending to maximize their self-interest, are guided by the market prices to pursue actions that turn out to lead to socially optimal outcomes. A market economy thus efficiently solves both the information problem and the motivation problem. Market prices act as a wonderful "invisible hand," guiding selfish individuals towards the enhancement of social welfare (for a classical critique of socialism with central planning, see Hayek (1996[1948]); for a modern summary of the flaws of the socialist economic system, see Stiglitz (1994)).

However, the reality of the global capitalist system provides ample evidence that the capitalist market not only fails to meet the basic needs of the great majority of the population on earth, but also threatens to undermine the foundation of human civilization. In fact, a careful reading of the latest development of mainstream economics would reveal that if one takes the current theoretical understanding of various "market failures" to its logical conclusion, a reasonable person would have to conclude that there is no theoretical reason to believe that the capitalist market can solve the information problem and the motivation problem any better than socialist planning. On the contrary, in a capitalist market economy, individuals are strongly motivated to pursue socially adverse outcomes, with potentially devastating consequences for human civilization.

Capitalist Economics: Invisible Hand vs. Market Failures

Since 1989, faith in the efficiency and rationality of the capitalist market has been the basis of economic policy in virtually every country. It continues to guide the economic thinking of the Chinese ruling class today. However, since 1989, the world has witnessed not only massive increases in economic and social inequality, but also growing instability of the global capitalist economy. During 2008–2009, the global capitalist economy had its deepest recession after World War II. It is currently heading towards a possibly more devastating economic crisis.

On the other hand, the global capitalist system has completely failed to address the global ecological crisis. Despite many promises by governments, corporations, and environmental groups, global carbon dioxide emissions continue to rise relentlessly, threatening to bring about worse climate catastrophes that will destroy the foundation of human civilization.

Apparently, global economic reality works very differently from the beliefs of mainstream neoclassical economics. Moreover, the gap between reality and mainstream economic beliefs is probably much larger than many people have realized.

No serious modern economist would deny that in the real world, there are many forms of market failures. In economics, when there are market failures, it means that prices are "wrong" or prices do not correctly reflect social costs or social benefits. For example, current fossil fuel prices typically do not capture the long-term social and environmental costs of fossil fuels consumption. As a result, it can be argued that the observed market prices of fossil fuels are lower than what they should be, encouraging excessively high levels of fossil fuels consumption.

Despite the recognition of market failures, mainstream economists and even some relatively enlightened non-neoclassical economists continue to maintain that the positive side of capitalism greatly outweighs the negative side and capitalism remains the best among all possible economic systems.

The belief that capitalism is the best among all possible economic systems could be valid if wrong prices are limited to exceptional cases, if wrong prices do not deviate from the correct prices by large margins, or if wrong prices can be corrected quickly.

However, a careful consideration of the actual performance of global capitalism suggests that there are at least two types of major "market failures" that have led to capitalist market prices that are pervasively wrong, persistently wrong, and wrong by large margins.

First, there are the market failures in the labor market and the capital market. It is well known to economists that both markets normally suffer from asymmetric information and moral hazards. In economics, the term "asymmetric information" refers to situations where the two sides of a market transaction have access to different sets of information. When the two sides of a transaction have access to different sets of information and the two sides have conflicts of interest (as is the case between capitalists and workers or between capital lenders and borrowers), one side of the transaction will have the incentive to engage in "moral hazards," that is, to pursue actions that would harm the interests of the other side. When there are moral hazards, market competition would lead to perverse outcomes such as "non-clearing" market equilibrium. That is, at "equilibrium," market supply would not be balanced by market demand (this would help to explain the persistent existence of unemployment in the capitalist labor market and the *de facto* rationing by capital lenders in the financial market; for a classical academic paper on non-clearing labor market equilibrium, see Shapiro and Stiglitz (1984)).

Asymmetric information and moral hazards affect not only the markets for the "factors of production" (the labor market and the capital market) but also many important services markets (such as the markets for health care, education, insurance, consultancies, and law services). This means that the prices of the factors of production and many important services prices normally are likely to be wrong. Since the prices of all goods and services are based on the prices of the factors of production, it follows that the prices of all goods and services normally tend to be wrong. For this reason, it can be concluded that in a capitalist market economy, wrong prices must be pervasive.

Because of the lack of complete future markets, uncertainty about the future could result in sudden and wide fluctuations of capital asset prices that bear no relation to the actual economic performance. In capitalist financial markets, capital asset bubbles could result in capital asset prices that deviate from "fundamental values" (the underlying values of capital assets determined by their long-term economic returns) by very large margins and wrong capital asset prices may fail to correct themselves for prolonged periods. Thus, capital asset prices could be persistently wrong and wrong by large margins (on the instability of the capitalist financial market, see Keynes (1964[1936]: 147–164) and Minsky (2008[1986]: 191–245)).

To the extent that capital asset prices help to determine the future production of goods and services, the prices of all goods and services could also be wrong by large margins and for prolonged periods.

Second, consider the environmental externalities. All economic activities directly or indirectly involve material exchanges with the natural environment. In this sense, all economic activities have environmental impact. The global ecological system is currently deteriorating in almost every important dimension. In many aspects, the deteriorating trends have continued since the publication of *The Limits to Growth* in 1972, which warned that exponential economic growth would eventually deplete the earth's natural resources and cause runaway ecological damage (Meadows et al. 1972).

In a study published in 2008, Turner (2008) studied the historical data for world population, industrial production, services production, remaining nonrenewable resources, and pollution from 1970 to 2000. Turner found that the observed data agreed well with the original "standard run" scenario presented in *The Limits to Growth*, a scenario which predicted global collapse by the mid-twenty-first century. In June 2012, *Nature* magazine, one of the world's leading science journals, published a paper co-authored by 22 scientists. The scientists argue that due to over-consumption, population growth, and environmental destruction, the earth is rapidly approaching a global tipping point beyond which the biosphere could experience swift and irreversible change, with catastrophic consequences for humanity and other species (Barnosky et al. 2012).

When environmental externalities are concerned, it is safe to conclude that the observed prices of goods and services in capitalist markets are persistently and pervasively wrong. Moreover, the global ecological crisis has by now developed to the point that the various global ecological systems are on the verge of collapse and the very survival of human civilization is at stake. Thus, one has to conclude that the observed prices of goods and services are likely to be wrong by very large margins compared to what are required to achieve global ecological sustainability.

Why do wrong prices matter? The entire invisible hand argument rests upon the belief that capitalist market prices are "correct," or at least roughly and generally tend to be correct. It is because of the "correct" prices that the individual's pursuit of self-interests could happily end with socially optimal outcomes or at least the best among all possible outcomes.

Both advocates and critics of capitalism agree that in a capitalist society, individuals are strongly motivated or heavily pressured to pursue the maximization of their self-interests. But if the individuals' actions are not guided by at least roughly correct prices but by prices that are pervasively and persistently wrong, it would have to mean that under capitalism, individuals are motivated to pursue far from socially optimal objectives. Nobel Prize winner Joseph E. Stiglitz recognized that the recognition of pervasive market failures amounted to a refutation of Adam Smith's "invisible hand" argument: "individuals and firms, in the pursuit of their self-interest, are not necessarily, or in general, led as if by an invisible hand, to economic efficiency" (Stiglitz 2007). In fact, not only does the capitalist market generally fail to produce "efficient" outcomes, to the extent that the pervasively and persistently wrong prices are wrong by large margins, individuals under capitalism are strongly motivated to pursue socially adverse outcomes.

No wonder the world is rapidly approaching economic, social, and ecological catastrophe!

The Twenty-first Century: Is There An Alternative to Socialism?

A society's surplus product is the part of a society's total product that is above what is needed to replace the material production inputs and to provide the population's basic consumption. In the early years of human historical development, there was no significant surplus product and class conflicts did not exist.

With the rise of agriculture, a significant amount of surplus product began to be produced. It became possible for a small minority of the population to be freed from directly productive labor to specialize in religion, arts, and social management. An exploitative ruling class emerged that lived on the surplus labor of the great majority of the population.

In pre-capitalist societies, the elites used most of the surplus product for luxury consumption or other non-productive activities (such as war expenses and the building of grand palaces). As a result, material production and consumption grew slowly.

Under capitalism, market relations become the dominant economic relations. Under the pressure of market competition, every capitalist and every state is under constant and intense pressure to use a large portion of its surplus product to pursue capital accumulation. Those who fail in the competition will be eliminated as an effective player in the capitalist market. Because of this basic law of motion, there is an inherent tendency for the capitalist economy to pursue material production and consumption on an increasingly larger scale. No economic or social reform can change this tendency without changing the basic institutional framework of capitalism.

The previous chapters of this book have argued that with an economic growth rate that would be required for capitalist economic stability, the world will almost certainly head towards the worst climate catastrophes. In the long run, global ecological sustainability will probably require zero economic growth.

To achieve zero economic growth or a sufficiently low economic growth rate compatible with ecological sustainability, the socially necessary condition is that society as a whole has control over the surplus product so that society can democratically decide how to use the surplus product and to limit the pace of capital accumulation to a level that is consistent with ecological sustainability. For example, society can collectively decide to use most of the surplus product for public consumption and environmental cleaning and to use only a small portion of the surplus product for capital accumulation, or not to use any surplus product for capital accumulation at all.

As the global capitalist system begins to collapse, the immediate concern for future socialist governments will be how to organize the economy to meet people's basic needs without worsening the ecological crisis. To meet the immediate demands of the great majority of the population (for food, housing, health care, education, and other basic needs) and to reduce environmental degradation, socialist governments should pursue economic policies that would help to slow down the pace of capital accumulation as soon as possible. This can be achieved by imposing taxes on capitalists, forcing capitalists to pay for the social and environmental costs of capitalist production, and by effectively enforcing labor and environmental regulations.

Socialist economic policies will inevitably lead to lower profit rates, discouraging capitalist investment. Capitalists may respond by attempting to move capital abroad or by undertaking investment strikes (withdrawal of capital from productive investment). The threat of capital flight can be defeated through strict control over financial capital flows across national borders. To fight back against capitalist investment strikes, socialist governments should increase public investment rapidly. In addition to investing in social infrastructure, socialist governments should build and expand productive state-owned enterprises on a massive scale so that socialist governments can count on the productive state-owned enterprises to provide most of their tax revenue. In countries where much of the capitalist wealth is politically illegitimate (for example, in former socialist countries, much of the current capitalist wealth originated from illegitimate privatization), the socialization of the economy can be accelerated through confiscation of illegitimate capitalist wealth.

With the above policies, socialist governments can achieve socialization of the economy within a reasonably short period of time. However, future socialist governments will have to confront the classical challenge of how to build "socialism in one country" in a capitalist world system. Although the future socialist revolutions will take place in an environment in which the global capitalist system has entered into structural crisis, at least initially, socialist economies will still be partially constrained by the laws of motion of the capitalist world system. Socialist economies will remain a part of the global capitalist division of labor and will be under pressure from global market competition, which may force the socialist economies to pursue "competitiveness" thorough exploitation of cheap labor and resources.

To reduce and temporarily remove such pressure from the global capitalist market, future socialist governments may learn from the experience of twentieth-century socialist economies by pursuing the strategy of "delinking." That is, the socialist economies can try to delink from the global capitalist economy by imposing strong protectionist policies and drastically reducing the size of foreign trade. In countries that heavily depend on imports of fossil fuels (such as China and India), the strategy of "delinking" can be pursued in combination with the de-carbonization of the economy (that is, reducing the total consumption of fossil fuels).

In the short run, the strategy of "delinking" would help socialist governments to establish a state monopoly over domestic markets and greatly reduce the pressure of global market competition. This would provide the maneuvering space for socialist governments to socialize the economy and to implement socially and environmentally progressive policies (which tend to increase labor and resources costs).

The experience of twentieth-century socialism demonstrates that in the long run, if global capitalism manages to survive major crisis (as happened in the twentieth century), socialist economies would have great difficulty in surviving the pressure of global market competition. However, in the twenty-first century, global capitalism most likely will enter into a structural crisis that can no longer be resolved within its own institutional framework. In such a world-historical context, the strategy of "delinking" pursued by individual socialist countries will help to accelerate the breakup of the global capitalist system. For example, if China undergoes a socialist revolution, given China's central position in the current global capitalist division of labor, the entire global capitalist commodity chain will begin to fall apart. The disintegration of the global capitalist division of labor will further destabilize the rest of the global capitalist system, leading to more socialist revolutions.

By 2050, much of the world will begin to live under one or several economic and social systems that are fundamentally different from the current global capitalist system. Future generations will face the urgent world-historical task of cleaning up the global environment and searching for a new socio-economic path that will lead to long-term sustainability.

As capitalism ceases to be a viable economic and social system, humanity will have to ask if there is any economic and social alternative to socialism, however socialism will come to be defined in the twenty-first century.

APPENDICES

Chapter 3: Estimating Profit Share and Profit Rate

England and Wales, 1688–1801

The "social tables" from the seventeenth century to the nineteenth century provided the only available quantitative information on the distribution of national income in Britain before the mid-nineteenth century. The data are summarized in the *British Historical Statistics*, Section on "Labor Force", Table 1 (Mitchell 1988: 102).

The table provides total incomes made by nine social classes: high titles and gentlemen, professions, military and maritime, commerce, industry and building, agriculture, laborers, cottagers and paupers, and vagrants.

I estimate the total labor income by adding up the incomes of professions, military and maritime, laborers, cottagers and paupers, vagrants, and one-half of the incomes of commerce, industry and building, and agriculture. The rest is considered property income (capitalist profit).

Gross national product is estimated as the sum of total incomes from the nine social classes, net public income, and consumption of fixed capital.

Net public income of Great Britain from 1688 to 1801 is from Mitchell (1988: 575–577). It is multiplied by 0.9 to provide a rough estimate of the net public income of England and Wales. For 1801, net public income includes property and income tax. The latter is subtracted from the estimated property income for the year.

Consumption of fixed capital is estimated by multiplying the value of capital stock by 2.5 percent. Net stock of fixed capital of Great Britain in 1688 is from Goldsmith (1985: 232). Great Britain's net stock of fixed capital in 1760 and 1800 is from Mitchell (1988: 864). These are multiplied by 0.9 to derive a rough estimate of the value of capital stock in England and Wales in 1688, 1759, and 1801.

Profit share, wage share, taxation share, and capital cost share are then calculated respectively as the ratio of property income, labor income, net public income, and consumption of fixed capital to the estimated gross national product.

United Kingdom, 1855–1920

British Historical Statistics, Section on "National Accounts," Table 4 provides data on "Gross National Product and Its Component Incomes" from 1855 to 1980 (Mitchell 1988: 828–830).

For the period 1855–1888, income from self-employment, gross trading profits of companies, and gross trading surplus of public enterprises are lumped together into one column. For this period, I estimate total labor income as the sum of income from employment and one-half of the sum of income from self-employment, gross trading profits of companies, and gross trading surplus of public enterprises.

For the period 1889–1913, labor income is estimated to be the sum of income from employment and 70 percent of the income from self-employment.

For the period 1914–1920, income from self-employment and gross trading profits of companies are lumped together. For this period, labor income is estimated as the sum of income from employment and 40 percent of the sum of income from self-employment and gross trading profits of companies.

Capitalist profit is then estimated as the gross national product (at factor cost) less capital consumption less estimated labor income.

Table 5 of the National Accounts Section provides data on gross domestic product and gross national product from the expenditures approach (Mitchell 1988: 831–835). The table includes a column of "factor cost adjustment", which equals taxes on expenditures less subsidies (indirect business taxes less subsidies). For this period, taxation cost includes only taxes on expenditures less subsidies.

Because of the discrepancy between the expenditures approach and the incomes approach, gross national product at market prices reported in Table 5 cannot be used. I estimate the gross national product at market prices (incomes approach) by adding the gross national product at factor cost reported in Table 4 with the "factor cost adjustment" reported in Table 5.

With the above estimates, profit share, wage cost share, taxation cost share, and capital cost share can be calculated.

Profit rate is the ratio of the capitalist profit over the business sector capital stock. Net stock of fixed capital of the United Kingdom from 1855 to 1980 is provided by Table 14 of the National Accounts Section (Mitchell 1988: 864–868). For the period 1855–1920, Table 14 does not provide data for the non-residential capital stock and how the non-residential capital stock is divided between the business sector and the government sector. The total net stock of fixed capital is multiplied by 0.6 to derive a rough estimate of the business sector net stock of fixed capital.

United Kingdom, 1920–1980

For the period 1920–1980, the value of economic output is defined as gross domestic product rather than gross national product. Gross domestic product at market prices (incomes approach) is calculated as the sum of gross domestic product at factor cost and taxes on expenditures less subsidies.

Labor income is the sum of income from employment and 70 percent of the income from self-employment.

Capitalist profit is gross domestic product at factor cost less capital consumption and labor income.

Taxation cost is the sum of taxes on expenditures less subsidies and profits tax. Profits tax began to be collected in 1938. Data for profits tax are from Mitchell (1988: 581–586).

For the period 1920–1980, the net stock of non-residential fixed capital can be calculated as the difference between the total net stock and the net stock of dwellings. Data are from Mitchell (1988: 864–888). The net stock of non-residential fixed capital is multiplied by 0.75 to derive a rough estimate of the business sector net stock of fixed capital.

United Kingdom, 2000–2013

In September 2014, the United Kingdom's Office of National Statistics introduced significant changes to national account statistics to conform to the international standards adopted by the European Union. The revisions were applied to British national economic statistics for years after 2000 (ONS 2014a).

The United Kingdom national accounts statistics from 2000 to 2013 are from the Office of National Statistics, *The Blue Book 2014* (ONS 2014b).

Labor income is the sum of compensation of employees and 70 percent of the "mixed income."

Taxation cost is the sum of taxes on production less subsidies and corporation tax. Corporation tax is from "Public Sector Finances First Release Data Set" (ONS 2014c).

Capitalist profit is gross domestic product at market prices less consumption of fixed capital, labor income, and taxation cost.

For 2000–2007, capital stock is defined as the sum of the net stock of non-residential buildings, other structures, plant and machinery, transport equipment, and intangible fixed assets. The business sector net stock of fixed capital is then calculated as the difference between the total economy capital stock and the general government sector capital stock. Data are from *The National Balance Sheet Dataset* (ONS 2013). For 2008–2013, capital stock is defined as the sum of the net stock of non-residential buildings and structures, machinery and equipment, and intellectual property products. The business sector net stock of fixed capital is then calculated as the difference between the total economy capital stock and the general government sector capital stock. Data are from *The Blue Book 2014* (ONS 2014d).

United States, 1900–1929

For US historical data from 1900 to 1929, I mostly rely on Goldsmith's *A Study of Saving in the United States* (Goldsmith 1956).

Gross national product, net national product, and national income are from Table N-1 (Goldsmith 1956: 427).

Labor income and property income are estimated by multiplying Goldsmith's national income with the labor income share and the property income share estimated by Johnson (1954). Capitalist profit is calculated as the estimated property income less corporate profit tax liability.

Taxation cost is the sum of indirect business tax and corporate profit tax liability. Data are from Table N-5 (Goldsmith 1956: 435).

Capital stock is defined as the net stock of private non-residential fixed assets. It is calculated as the sum of total structures and producer durables less the residential and government structures. Data are from Table W-1 (Goldsmith 1956: 14).

The estimated capital stock is divided by a ratio of 0.84 to make it roughly comparable to the capital stock series after 1929.

United States, 1929–2013

For the period 1929–2013, profit share, wage cost share, taxation cost share, and capital cost share are calculated respectively as the ratio of capitalist profit, labor income, taxation cost, and consumption of fixed capital to gross domestic income (GDI). Gross domestic income is the gross domestic product measured by the incomes approach.

Labor income is the sum of compensation of employees and 70 percent of the proprietors' income.

Taxation cost is the sum of taxes on production and imports less subsidies, taxes on corporate income, and surplus of government enterprises.

Capitalist profit is gross domestic income less consumption of fixed capital less the sum of labor income and taxation cost.

The above data are from the US *National Income and Product Accounts Tables*, Table 1.10, "Gross Domestic Income by Type of Income" (BEA 2014a).

Capital stock is defined as net stock of private non-residential fixed assets. Data are from the US *Fixed Assets Accounts Tables*, Table 1.1, "Current-Cost Net Stock of Fixed Assets and Consumer Durable Goods" (BEA 2014b).

Chapter 4: Appendix A: Defining Core, Semi-Periphery, and Periphery

In world system theory, the structural positions of the capitalist world system are defined by their relative positions in the production and extraction of economic surplus. Economic surplus is the part of total economic product that is above what is necessary to replace the material production inputs and to provide basic consumption for the population. The core regions, because of their strong military power and monopoly over the leading sectors of the capitalist world economy, are able to extract economic surplus from the periphery and the semi-periphery through unequal exchange. Much of the economic surplus produced by the periphery is extracted by the core and the semi-periphery. The semi-peripheral regions extract economic surplus from the periphery but are exploited by the core.

The extraction of economic surplus through unequal exchange cannot be easily measured. But a country's relative position in the capitalist world system (benefiting or suffering from surplus extraction as well as the degree of benefiting or suffering) is usually correlated with the country's rank of per capita GDP in the global economy. In this chapter, I use the national ranking of per capita GDP as the first approximation in deciding the geographical distribution of the three structural positions of the capitalist world system from 1600 to 2013. On the basis of this approximate indicator, I make further adjustments for individual countries, taking into account various specific historical conditions.

For the most recent historical period (from 1990 to the present), available economic data make it possible for the transfer of economic surplus between different countries through unequal exchange to be directly measured. An exercise of this direct measurement is explained in Appendix B of this chapter.

According to Wallerstein (1979: 26), by the sixteenth century, Northwest Europe had advanced to the core, the former core regions (Italy, Spain, and Portugal) had declined into the semi-periphery, and Eastern Europe and Latin America had become the peripheral regions.

According to Angus Maddison's "Statistics of World Population, GDP, and Per Capita GDP, 1-2008 AD" (Maddison 2010), in 1600, the Netherlands was the only country with a per capita GDP that was more than twice the world average (measured in constant 1990 international dollars). In Table 4.1, the Netherlands is listed as the only core capitalist country in 1600.

In Table 4.1, the semi-periphery includes most large Western European countries. Their per capita GDP in 1600 ranged between 120 and 180 percent of the world average. Both the United Kingdom and France are included in the semi-periphery. In 1600, both countries (defined by their modern national boundaries) included both core and peripheral regions and their per capita GDP was within the semi-peripheral range.

The periphery in 1600 included Ireland, Norway, Eastern Europe, and Latin America. Their per capita GDP in 1600 ranged between 70 and 100 percent of the world average.

The vast majority of the world population in 1600 lived outside the capitalist world system. The "external areas" refer to geographical areas with separate systems of division of labor that were independent of the European-centered capitalist "world economy."

During the seventeenth century, the Indonesian archipelago and Ceylon became Dutch colonies. The British, the French, and the Dutch established colonies in North America.

By 1700, Dutch per capita GDP rose to more than three times the world average and British per capita GDP was twice the world average. In Table 4.2, the Netherlands and the United Kingdom are listed as the core capitalist countries in 1700.

The other large Western European countries constituted the semi-periphery of the capitalist world system in 1700. Their per capita GDP in 1700 ranged between 120 and 190 percent of the world average.

The periphery expanded to include Ireland, Norway, Eastern Europe, Indonesia, Latin America, and North America. In 1700, the peripheral regions' per capita GDP ranged between 80 and 120 percent of the world average.

By the early nineteenth century, the Russian Empire, the Ottoman Empire, India, South Africa, Malaya, the Philippines, and Australia were incorporated into the capitalist world system. In 1820, the two core capitalist countries (the Netherlands and the United Kingdom) had an average per capita GDP about two and a half times the world average (Table 4.3).

By 1820, the United States became a semi-peripheral country. Russia entered the capitalist world system as a semi-peripheral country, reflecting its strength of state machinery and degree of early industrialization. The newly independent Latin American countries remained peripheral in their economic and political relations with the rest of the capitalist world system (Wallerstein 1979: 27). The semi-peripheral regions' per capita GDP in 1820 ranged between 100 and 190 percent of the world average.

The periphery was greatly expanded as India became a British colony and the Ottoman Empire was incorporated into the capitalist world system. In 1820, most peripheral regions' per capita GDP ranged between 70 and 100 percent of the world average.

By 1870, almost the entire globe was incorporated into the capitalist world system. Capitalism became the first truly global system in human history. In 1820, there were only two countries (the Netherlands and the United Kingdom) that had per capita GDP greater than 200 percent of the world average. By 1870, the list expanded to 11 countries. Australia, the United States, France, Austria, and Germany advanced into the core. The core regions' per capita GDP ranged between 210 and 380 percent of the world average (see Table 4.4).

The semi-periphery included Canada, Italy, Norway, Sweden, Spain, Czechoslovakia, Hungary, Portugal, and the Russian Empire. Their per capita GDP in 1870 ranged between 110 and 190 percent of the world average.

The periphery included the entire rest of the world (Asia, Africa, Latin America, and most Eastern European countries). With the exception of a few well-to-do Latin American countries (Argentina, Chile, and Uruguay), most peripheral regions' per capita GDP ranged between 60 and 110 percent of the world average.

In Table 4.5, the core regions include all countries that had per capita GDP between 220 and 350 percent of the world average in 1913 (except Argentina, which is listed as semi-peripheral country).

Most semi-peripheral regions' per capita GDP in 1913 ranged between 130 and 220 percent of the world average. Russia and Japan are included in the semi-periphery considering their relatively strong military power, despite their relatively low per capita GDP in 1913.

More peripheral regions' per capita GDP in 1913 ranged between 40 and 110 percent of the world average.

In 1950, the core regions' per capita GDP ranged between 180 and 450 percent of the world average (see Table 4.6).

Most semi-peripheral regions' per capita GDP in 1950 ranged between 100 and 170 percent of the world average. Several high-income Latin American countries (Venezuela, Argentina, and Uruguay), very high-income small West Asian countries (Qatar, Kuwait, and United Arab Emirates), and 14 small Western European countries are included in the Semi-Periphery in 1950. Portugal and Japan are also included in the semi-periphery even though their per capita GDP in 1950 was lower than 100 percent of the world average, considering that Portugal remained a colonial empire and Japan's industrial infrastructure was only temporarily destroyed.

Most peripheral regions' per capita GDP in 1950 ranged between 20 and 100 percent of the world average. A few small countries that had per capita GDP in 1950 higher than 100 percent of the world average but had a population of less than 1 million are also included in the periphery.

In 1975, the core regions' per capita GDP ranged between 260 and 420 percent of the world average (see Table 4.7).

Most semi-peripheral regions' per capita GDP in 1975 ranged between 100 and 200 percent of the world average. Three very high-income small West Asian countries (Qatar, Kuwait, and United Arab Emirates), Saudi Arabia, Venezuela, and Israel are included in the semi-periphery in 1975. Turkey, which had a per capita GDP being 95 percent of the world average but was a significant regional power, is also included in the semi-periphery in 1975.

Most peripheral regions' per capita GDP in 1975 ranged between 20 and 100 percent of the world average. A few small countries that had per capita GDP in 1975 higher than 100 percent of the world average but had a population of less than 2 million are also included in the periphery.

In Table 4.8, the core regions include all countries that had per capita GDP between 220 and 480 percent of the world average in 2000, except 14 small Western European countries and Puerto Rico which are included in the semi-periphery.

Most semi-peripheral regions' per capita GDP in 2000 ranged between 100 and 210 percent of the world average. But Trinidad and Tobago, Mauritius, Equatorial Guinea, Seychelles, Lithuania, and Costa Rica are included in the periphery because of their small size and economic dependency. On the other hand, Brazil and the Russian Federation are included in the semi-periphery taking into account their large geographic size, economic potential, state capacity, and the consideration that their per capita GDP in 2000 was temporarily lowered by neoliberal restructuring.

Most peripheral regions' per capita GDP in 2000 ranged between 20 and 100 percent of the world average.

In 2013, most core regions' per capita GDP ranged between 220 and 380 percent of the world average (see Table 4.9). Singapore and Norway are included in the core. Both had very high per capita GDP in 2013. Saudi Arabia, Oman, Bahrain, and several very small economies with very high per capita GDP are included in the semi-periphery.

Most semi-peripheral regions' per capita GDP in 2013 ranged between 100 and 190 percent of the world average. Several small economies with per capita GDP in 2013 higher than 100 percent of the world average are included in the periphery.

Most peripheral regions' per capita GDP in 2013 ranged between 20 and 100 percent of the world average.

Chapter 4: Appendix B: Measuring Labor Terms of Trade and Unequal Exchange

All data for the calculation of the labor terms of trade and unequal exchange are from the World Bank's *World Development Indicators* (World Bank 2014).

A country's or a region's labor term of trade is defined as follows:

Labor Term of Trade = Labor Embodied in 1 Million Dollars of Goods Imported / Labor Embodied in 1 Million Dollars of Goods Exported

A country's or a region's labor embodied in goods exported is calculated as follows:

Labor Embodied in 1 Million Dollars of Goods Exported = Total Labor Embodied in Goods Exported / Total Value of Goods Exported (measured in million dollars)

The World Bank (2014) provides data for countries' and regions' merchandise exports, which are used as the value of goods exported.

Merchandise exports include exports of agricultural goods and exports of industrial goods:

Total Labor Embodied in Goods Exported = Labor Embodied in Agricultural Goods Exported + Labor Embodied in Industrial Goods Exported

Labor Embodied in Agricultural Goods Exported = Value of Agricultural Goods Exported / Labor Productivity in the Agricultural Sector

Labor Embodied in Industrial Goods Exported = Value of Industrial Goods Exported / Labor Productivity in the Industrial Sector

The World Bank (2014) provides the percentage of agricultural exports in total merchandise exports. Non-agricultural merchandise exports are considered exports of industrial goods.

Labor productivity in the agricultural sector and the industrial sector is calculated as the ratio of total value added in the sector over the total employment in the sector.

The World Bank (2014) provides the agricultural value added, the industrial value added, the total labor force, the unemployment rate, and the percentage of each sector's employment in the total employment. Total employment can be estimated from the total labor force and the unemployment rate. Each sector's employment can then be estimated from the total employment and the percentage of each sector's employment in the total employment.

A country's or a region's labor embodied in goods imported is calculated as follows:

Labor Embodied in 1 Million Dollars of Goods Imported = Total Labor Embodied in Goods Imported / Total Value of Goods Imported (measured in million dollars)

The World Bank (2014) provides data for countries' and regions' merchandise imports, which are used as the value of goods imported.

The World Bank (2014) provides the percentage of different regions in a country's merchandise imports. The regions include high income economies, East Asia and the Pacific, Europe and Central Asia, Latin America and the Caribbean, the Middle East and North Africa, South Asia, and Sub-Saharan Africa. The regions other than "high income economies" refer to "developing economies" only.

For each region listed above, average amount of labor embodied in 1 million dollars of goods exported can be calculated. A country's total labor embodied in goods imported can then be calculated as the sum of the total labor embodied in goods imported from each of the regions. For goods imported from each region, the total labor embodied simply equals the value of goods imported from the region (measured in million dollars) multiplied by the average amount of labor embodied in 1 million dollars of goods exported by the region.

Once a country's labor term of trade are calculated, the country's net gain or loss from unequal exchange can be decided by the following formula:

Net Gain (Loss) from Unequal Exchange = Total Labor Embodied in Goods
Exported * (Labor Term of Trade − 1)

The above formula says that a country gains from unequal exchange if the country's
labor term of trade is greater than one, but suffers from unequal exchange if the
country's labor term of trade is smaller than one. The gain or loss is proportional to
the country's total labor embodied in goods exported.

Note that the above formula about unequal exchange does not take into account
possible transfer of economic surplus through trade surplus or deficit. Nor does it take
into account international flows of capital or capital incomes.

Chapter 5: Estimating China's Total Capitalist Profit and Capital Stock

All data used to estimate China's total capitalist profit and the business sector capital
stock are from The China Statistical Yearbook, various issues (National Bureau of
Statistics of China 2013 and earlier years).

Total capitalist profit is gross domestic product less wage cost, taxation cost, and
capital cost.

Total wage cost (total labor income) is the sum of the economy-wide total wages,
the labor income by self-employed workers, and the social insurance contribution
by employers.

The economy-wide total wages are the sum of total wages of urban non-private units
employees, urban private units employees, urban unregistered workers, and rural
local non-agricultural workers. Labor income by self-employed workers includes
100 percent of the entrepreneurial income of rural households and 70 percent of the
entrepreneurial income of urban households. It is assumed that 80 percent of the
annual receipts of social insurance funds are contributed by employers.

Taxation cost is defined as the total government taxes less the individual
income tax.

Capital cost is defined as depreciation of fixed capital. The China Statistical
Yearbook provides gross domestic product (income approach) by provinces. The
provincial gross domestic product is divided into compensation of laborers, net
operating surplus, net producer taxes, and depreciation of fixed capital. Partly due
to double counting between different provinces, the sum of gross domestic product
of China's provinces is greater than China's national gross domestic product. To
estimate China's total depreciation of fixed capital, I first sum up the depreciation of
fixed capital of all provinces and then calculate its share in the sum of gross domestic
product of all provinces. I then estimate China's total depreciation of fixed capital by
multiplying the national gross domestic product by the share of the depreciation of
fixed capital calculated from the sum of all provinces.

There are no official statistics for China's capital stock. To estimate China's business sector net stock of fixed capital, I first estimate the business sector's real net stock of fixed capital (in constant 1990 prices) using the following formula:

$$K(T) = K_{1990} + \Sigma_{t=1991}^{T}(NI_t)$$

K(T) is the real net stock of fixed capital in year "T". K_{1990} is the real net stock of fixed capital in 1990 (the initial year). NI_t is the real net investment in fixed capital in year "t". For example, real net stock of fixed capital in 2000 is the sum of the initial real capital stock in 1990 and the cumulative real net investment from 1991 to 2000.

Using data from China's Input–Output Tables for 1990, it can be estimated that the business sector's depreciation of fixed capital was 75 percent of China's total depreciation of fixed capital in 1990. Using data for China's industrial enterprises, it can be estimated that the industrial sector depreciation rate was about 7 percent. This is assumed to be the Chinese business sector's depreciation rate in 1990. The initial business sector's real net stock of fixed capital in 1990 is then estimated by dividing business sector depreciation by the depreciation rate.

Net investment in fixed capital is the difference between gross investment in fixed capital (fixed capital formation) and depreciation of fixed capital.

The China Statistical Yearbook provides data for China's total economy's fixed capital formation. Using data from China's Flow of Funds Accounts, one can estimate the share of the business sector's fixed capital formation (including the non-financial business sector and the financial business sector) in the total economy fixed capital formation for every year from 1992 to 2011. For 1990 and 1991, it is assumed that the business sector's fixed capital formation was 73 percent of the total economy's fixed capital formation. For 2012, it is assumed that the business sector fixed capital formation was 64 percent of the total economy's fixed capital formation. The business sector's fixed capital formation is then estimated by multiplying the total economy's fixed capital formation by the business sector share.

Using data from China's Input–Output Tables, one can estimate the share of business sector depreciation of fixed capital in China's total depreciation of fixed capital. The business sector depreciation of fixed capital is then estimated by multiplying China's total depreciation of fixed capital by the business sector share.

The business sector's real net investment in fixed capital for each year from 1991 to 2012 is then calculated by dividing the business sector's net investment in fixed capital by the fixed investment price index.

After the business sector's real net stock of fixed capital is estimated for each year from 1990 to 2012, the business sector's net stock of fixed capital in current prices can be estimated by multiplying the estimated real net stock of fixed capital by the fixed investment price index.

BIBLIOGRAPHY

Aleklett, Kjell (with Michael Lardelli). 2012. *Peeking at Peak Oil*. New York: Springer.

Alva, J. Jorge Kolr de and Gregory S. Wilsey. 1993. "The Impact of the Encounter on the Americas and Europe," in *The Ibero-American Heritage Project: Latinos in the Making of the United States of America, Yesterday, Today, and Tomorrow*, II, pp. 361–370. Albany, New York: The State Education Department.

Anonymous College Graduate. 2008. "*Daxuesheng Guandian: Kuaiyao Huo Bu Xiaqu le, Yuexin 4000 Yuan de Beican Shenghuo* (A College Graduate's Perspective: I Can Barely Survive— The Miserable Life with a Monthly Salary of 4,000 Yuan)," March 23, 2008, http://ido.3mt. com.cn/Article/200803/show932079c31p1.html.

Arrighi, Giovanni. 1994. *The Long Twentieth Century: Money, Power, and the Origin of Our Times*. London: Verso.

———. 2007. *Adam Smith in Beijing: Lineages of the Twenty-First Century*. London: Verso.

Arrighi, Giovanni, Iftikhar Ahmad, and Miin-wen Shih. 1999. "Western Hegemonies in World-Historical Perspective," in Giovanni Arrighi and Beverly J. Silver (eds.), *Chaos and Governance in the Modern World System*, pp. 217–270. Minneapolis and London: University of Minneapolis Press.

Arrighi, Giovanni, Kenneth Barr, and Shuji Hisaeda. 1999. "The Transformation of Business Enterprises," in Giovanni Arrighi and Beverly J. Silver (eds.), *Chaos and Governance in the Modern World System*, pp. 97–150. Minneapolis and London: University of Minneapolis Press.

Arrighi, Giovanni, Po-keung Hui, Krishnendu Ray, and Thomas Ehrlich Reifer. 1999. "Geopolitics and High Finance," in Giovanni Arrighi and Beverly J. Silver (eds.), *Chaos and Governance in the Modern World System*, pp. 37–96. Minneapolis and London: University of Minneapolis Press.

Arrighi, Giovanni and Beverly J. Silver. 1999. "Introduction," in Giovanni Arrighi and Beverly J. Silver (eds.), *Chaos and Governance in the Modern World System*, pp. 1–36. Minneapolis and London: University of Minneapolis Press.

Baidu Baike. 2014. "*Zhongguo Renjun Shui Ziyuan Liang* (China's Per Capita Water Resources)." http://baike.baidu.com/view/11695216.htm.

Barboza, David. 2012. "Billions in Hidden Riches for Family of Chinese Leader," *New York Times*, October 25, 2012. http://www.nytimes.com/2012/10/26/business/global/family-of-wen-jiabao-holds-a-hidden-fortune-in-china.html?pagewanted=all&_r=0.

Barnosky, Anthony D., Elizabeth A. Hadly, Jordi Bascompte, Eric L. Berlow, James H. Brown, Mikael Fortelius et al. 2012. "Approaching A State Shift in Earth's Biosphere," *Nature* 486: 52–58. http://www.nature.com/nature/journal/v486/n7401/full/nature11018.html.

BBC. 2012. "Neil Heywood: Briton Killed in China Had Spy Links," November 6, 2012. http://www.bbc.com/news/world-asia-china-20216757.

BEA. US Bureau of Economic Analysis. 2014a. *National Income and Product Accounts Tables*. http://www.bea.gov/iTable/index_nipa.cfm.

———. 2014b. *Fixed Assets Accounts Tables*. http://www.bea.gov/iTable/index_FA.cfm.

Bolt, Jutta and Jan Luiten van Zanden. 2013. "The First Update of the Maddison Project: Re-estimating Growth before 1820." http://www.ggdc.net/maddison/maddison-project/abstract.htm?id=4.

Bowles, Samuel, Richard Edwards, and Frank Roosevelt. 2005. *Understanding Capitalism: Competition, Command, and Change.* New York and Oxford: Oxford University Press.

BP. 2014. *Statistical Review of World Energy.* http://www.bp.com/en/global/corporate/about-bp/energy-economics/statistical-review-of-world-energy.html.

———. 2015. *Statistical Review of World Energy.* http://www.bp.com/en/global/corporate/about-bp/energy-economics/statistical-review-of-world-energy.html.

Castro, Carlos de, Margarita Mediavilla, Luis Javier Miguel, and Fernando Frechoso. 2011. "Global Wind Power Potential, Physical and Technological Limits," *Energy Policy* 39(10): 6677–6682.

———. 2013. "Global Solar Electric Power Potential: A Review of Their Technical and Sustainable Limits," *Renewable and Sustainable Energy Reviews* 28 (December 2013): 824–835.

Chazan, Guy. 2014. "Ex-BP Chief Warns of Danger Russian Sanctions Will Choke World Oil Supplies," *Financial Times,* September 15, 2014, p.1.

Chazan, Guy, and Jack Farchy. 2014. "Russian Oil Braces for Chill of Sanctions," *Financial Times,* September 2, 2014, p. 14.

Chevron. 2014. "Gas-to-Liquids: Transforming Natural Gas into Super Clean Fuels," updated May 2014. http://www.chevron.com/deliveringenergy/gastoliquids/.

China Coal Industry Association. 2015a. "*Zhong Mei Xie: Jinnian Meitan Chanliang Jiang Tongbi Jianshao 5%* (China Coal Industry Association: This Year's Coal Production Will Fall from Last Year by 5%)," April 13, 2015. http://www.sxcoal.com/coal/4099458/articlenew.html.

———. 2015b. "*Meitan Gongye Fazhan Xingshi ji Shi San Wu Zhanwang* (The Situation of Coal Industry Development and its Prospect during the Thirteenth Five-Year Plan)," *Meitan Yanjiu* (Coal Research), February 10, 2015. http://60.223.238.81:8076/KXDBmeitanzhoukan/page/2661/2015-02-10/C3/25111423792640250.pdf.

China Water Risk. 2010. *China's Water Crisis,* Part I and II. China Water Risk Fact Books, March 2010. http://chinawaterrisk.org/media-room/china-water-risk-downloads/china-water-risk-fact-books/.

Chongqing Ribao. 2012. "*Chongqing Jini Xishu Cong 0.438 Jiangzhi 0.421, Liangji Fenhua Qushi Nizhuan* (Chongqing's Gini Coefficient Declined from 0.438 to 0.421, the Trend towards Polarization Begins to be Reversed)," January 1, 2009. http://www.gov.cn/gzdt/2012-01/09/content_2040153.htm.

Devine, James N. 1987. "An Introduction to Radical Theories of Economic Crisis," in Robert D. Cherry et al. (eds.), *The Imperiled Economy: Book 1, Macroeconomics from A Left Perspective,* pp. 19–31. New York: Union for Radical Political Economics.

Economic Report of the President, United States. 2010. *Economic Report of the President,* Appendix B: Statistical Tables Relating to Income, Employment, and Production. http://www.gpo.gov/fdsys/browse/collection.action?collectionCode=ERP&browsePath=2010&isCollapsed=false&leafLevelBrowse=false&isDocumentResults=true&ycord=1505.

———. 2014. *Economic Report of the President,* Appendix B: Statistical Tables Relating to Income, Employment, and Production. http://www.gpo.gov/fdsys/browse/collection.action?collectionCode=ERP&browsePath=2014&isCollapsed=true&leafLevelBrowse=false&isDocumentResults=true&ycord=0.

Economist. 2013. "Bo Xilai's Trial: Going Down Fighting," *The Economist,* August 31, 2013. http://www.economist.com/news/china/21584367-china-has-been-gripped-extraordinary-courtroom-drama-going-down-fighting.

EIA. The US Energy Information Administration. 2014a. *Annual Energy Outlook 2014.* http://www.eia.gov/forecasts/aeo/.

———. 2014b. "International Energy Statistics." http://www.eia.gov/countries/data.cfm#undefined.

———. 2014c. "U.S. Natural Gas Marketed Production," Natural Gas Data. http://www.eia.gov/dnav/ng/hist/n9050us2a.htm.

———. 2015. *Annual Energy Outlook 2015.* http://www.eia.gov/forecasts/aeo/.

Engels, Friedrich. 1978[1880]. "Socialism: Utopian and Scientific," in Robert C. Tucker (ed.), The Marx-Engels Reader, pp. 683–717. New York: W. W. Norton & Company.

EPI. Earth Policy Institute. 2013a. "Global Carbon Dioxide Emissions from Fossil Fuel Burning, 1751–2012," July 23, 2013. http://www.earth-policy.org/data_center/C23.

———. 2013b. "Global Carbon Dioxide Emissions from Fossil Fuel Burning by Fuel Type, 1900–2012," July 23, 2013. http://www.earth-policy.org/data_center/C23.

———. 2014. "Grain Use for Ethanol, Feed, and Food in the United States, 1960–2013," February 25, 2014. http://www.earth-policy.org/data_center/C24.

Federal Reserve, the United States. 2014. *Financial Accounts of the United States.* http://www.federalreserve.gov/releases/z1/current/data.htm.

Feng Huang Wang. 2012. *"Wen Jiabao 2012 Nian 3 Yue 14 Ri Da Zhongwai Jizhe Wen* (Transcripts of the Press Conference by Wen Jiabao on March 14, 2012), March 14, 2012. http://news.ifeng.com/mainland/special/2012lianghui/detail_2012_03/14/13190724_0.shtml.

Gaines, Linda and Paul Nelsen. 2009. "Lithium-Ion Batteries: Possible Materials Issues." Center for Transportation Research, Argonne National Laboratory, June 2009. http://www.transportation.anl.gov/pdfs/B/583.PDF.

Global Change. 2006. "Human Appropriation of the World's Fresh Water Supply," January 4, 2006. Course on "Global Change: The Sustainability Challenge," University of Michigan. http://www.globalchange.umich.edu/globalchange2/current/lectures/freshwater_supply/freshwater.html.

Goldsmith, Raymond W. 1956. *A Study of Saving in the United States,* Volume III. Princeton, New Jersey: Princeton University Press.

———. 1985. *Comparative National Balance Sheets: A Study of Twenty Countries, 1688–1978.* Chicago and London: The University of Chicago Press.

Gong Ping She. 2014. *"Shui Tuidong le Zuidi Gongzi? Ershisan Nian Lai Zuidi Gongzi Zengzhang Huigu* (Who Pushed up the Minimum Wages? A Review of the Growth of Minimum Wages over the Past Twenty-Three Years)," August 22, 2014. http://blog.sina.com.cn/s/blog_ed2baf420102v113.html.

Gordon, David M., Thomas E. Weisskopf, and Samuel Bowles. 1987. "Power, Accumulation, and Crisis: The Rise and Demise of the Postwar Social Structure of Accumulation," in Victor D. Lippit (ed.), *Radical Political Economy: Explorations in Alternative Economic Analysis,* pp. 226–246. New York: M. E. Sharpe.

Gordon, Robert. 2012. "Is U.S. Economic Growth Over? Faltering Innovation Confronts the Six Headwinds." NBER Working Paper 18315. http://www.nber.org/papers/w18315.

Guan, Dabo and Liu Zhu. 2013. *Tracing Back the Smog: Source Analysis and Control Strategies for PM$_{2.5}$ Pollution in Beijing-Tianjin-Hebei.* Beijing: China Environment Press. http://www.greenpeace.org/eastasia/Global/eastasia/publications/reports/climate-energy/2013/Tracing%20back%20the%20smog%20(English%20full%20report).pdf.

Hambides, Zac. 2010. "China's Growing Army of Unemployed Graduates." *The World Socialist Website,* October 4, 2012. http://www.wsws.org/en/articles/2010/10/chin-o04.html.

Hansen, James. 2009. *Storms of My Grandchildren: The Truth about the Coming Climate Catastrophe and Our Last Chance to Save Humanity.* New York: Bloomsbury.

Hansen, James, Pushker Kharecha, Makiko Sato, Valerie Masson-Delmotte, Frank Ackerman, David J. Beerling et al. 2013. "Assessing 'Dangerous Climate Change': Required Reduction of Carbon Emissions to Protect Young People, Future Generations and Nature." *PLOS One* 8(12): e81648. http://www.plosone.org/article/info%3Adoi%2F10.1371%2Fjournal. pone.0081648.

Hansen, James, Makiko Sato, and Reto Reudy. 2014. "Global Temperature Update through 2013," January 21, 2014. http://www.columbia.edu/~jeh1/mailings/.

Hart-Landsberg, Martin. 2011. "The Chinese Reform Experience: A Critical Assessment," *Review of Radical Political Economics* 43(1): 56–76.

Harvey, David. 2001. "Globalization and the Spatial Fix," *Geographische Revue* 2/2001: 23–30. http://opus.kobv.de/ubp/volltexte/2008/2436/pdf/gr2_01_Ess02.pdf.

Hayek, Friedrich. 1996[1948]. *Individualism and Economic Order*. Chicago: University of Chicago Press.

Heinberg, Richard. 2009. *Blackout: Coal, Climate, and the Last Energy Crisis*. Gabriola Island, BC: New Society Publishers.

Höök, Mikael and Kjell Aleklett. 2009. "A Review on Coal-to-Liquid Fuels and Its Coal Consumption," *International Journal of Energy Research* 34(10): 848–864.

Hopkins, Terence K. and Immanuel Wallerstein. 1996. *The Age of Transition: Trajectory of the World System, 1945–2025*. London: Zed Books.

Hubbert, M. King. 1982. "Techniques of Prediction as Applied to the Production of Oil and Gas in Oil and Gas Supply Modeling," in Saul I. Gass (ed.), *National Bureau of Standards Special Publication 631*, pp. 16–141. Washington, DC: National Bureau of Standards.

Huesemann, Michael H. 2003. "The Limits of Technological Solutions to Sustainable Development," *Clean Technology and Environmental Policy* 5: 21–34.

Hughes, J. David. 2014. *Drilling Deeper: A Reality Check on U.S. Government Forecasts for A Lasting Tight Oil & Shale Gas Boom*, Report prepared for Post Carbon Institute, October 27, 2014. http://www.postcarbon.org/publications/drillingdeeper/.

IEA. International Energy Agency. 2012. *Golden Rules for a Golden Age of Gas: World Energy Outlook Special Report on Unconventional Gas*. http://www.worldenergyoutlook.org/media/ weowebsite/2012/goldenrules/WEO2012_GoldenRulesReport.pdf.

——. 2014. *Key World Energy Statistics*, October 2014. http://www.iea.org/publications/ freepublications/publication/key-world-energy-statistics-2014.html.

IMF. International Monetary Fund. 2009. *World Economic Outlook: Crisis and Recovery*, April 2009. http://www.imf.org/external/pubs/ft/weo/2009/01/pdf/text.pdf.

——. 2014. *World Economic Outlook: Legacies, Clouds, and Uncertainties*, October 2014. http:// www.imf.org/external/pubs/ft/weo/2014/02/.

——. 2015. *World Economic Outlook: Uneven Growth: Short- and Long-Term Factors*, April 2015. http://www.imf.org/external/pubs/ft/weo/2015/01/.

IPCC. United Nations Intergovernmental Panel on Climate Change. 2013. *The Fifth Assessment Report*, "Climate Change 2013: The Physical Science Basis," Summary for Policy Makers. http://www.climatechange2013.org/images/report/WG1AR5_SPM_FINAL.pdf.

Ismi, Asad. 2013. "Maoist Insurgency Spreads to Over 40% of India, Mass Poverty and Delhi's Embrace of Corporate Neoliberalism Fuels Social Uprising." *Global Research*, December 20, 2013. http://www.globalresearch.ca/maoist-insurgency-spreads-to-over-40-of-india-mass-poverty-and-delhis-embrace-of-corporate-neoliberalism-fuels-social-uprising/5362276.

Johnson, D. Gale. 1954. "The Functional Distribution of Income in the United States, 1850–1952." *The Review of Economics and Statistics* 36(2): 175–182.

Kahn, Joseph and Jim Yardley. 2007. "As China Roars, Pollution Reaches Deadly Extremes,"

New York Times, August 26, 2007. http://www.nytimes.com/2007/08/26/world/asia/26china.html?oref=login.

Keynes, John Maynard. 1964[1936]. *The General Theory of Employment, Interest, and Money*. San Diego, New York and London: A Harvest Book, Harcourt Brace & Company.

Lao Tian. 2008. *"Zhuanmen Kongsu Wenge Qijian de Faxisi Pohai* (Focus on the Indictment against the 'Fascist Persecutions' during the Cultural Revolution)." http://washeng.net/HuaShan/RECS/laotian/b5current/158050.shtml.

Li, Minqi. 2009. "Socialization of Risks without Socialization of Investment: The Minsky Paradox and the Structural Contradiction of Big Government Capitalism." The Political Economy Research Institute of University of Massachusetts Amherst, Working Paper 205. http://www.peri.umass.edu/fileadmin/pdf/working_papers/working_papers_201-250/WP205.pdf.

——. 2014. *Peak Oil, Climate Change, and the Limits to China's Economic Growth*. London and New York: Routledge.

Li, Ziyang. 2006. *"Fulideman de Sanci Fanghua* (Milton Friedman's Three Visits to China)," November 28, 2006. http://blog.sina.com.cn/s/blog_4b7f5ebb0100067b.html.

Long, D. Ray. 2014. "In Search of Oil Realism," September 30, 2014. http://raylong.co/blog/2014/9/30/in-search-of-oil-realism.

Maddison, Angus. 2010. "Statistics on World Population, GDP, and Per Capita GDP, 1-2008 AD." http://www.ggdc.net/MADDISON/oriindex.htm.

Marx, Karl. 1967[1867]. *Capital: A Critique of Political Economy*, Volume I (The Process of Capitalist Production). New York: International Publishers.

——. 1967[1894]. *Capital: A Critique of Political Economy*, Volume III (The Process of Capitalist Production as a Whole). New York: International Publishers.

Marx, Karl and Friedrich Engels. 1978[1848]. "Manifesto of the Communist Party," in Robert C. Tucker (ed.), *The Marx-Engels Reader*, pp. 469–500. New York and London: W. W. Norton & Company.

Meadows, Donella H., Dennis L. Meadows, Jorgen Randers, and William W. Behrens III. 1972. *The Limits to Growth*. New York: Universe Books.

Ministry of Human Resources and Social Security, People's Republic of China. 2009–2013. *"Renli Ziyuan he Shehui Baozhang Shiye Fazhan Tongji Gongbao* (The Development of Human Resources and Social Security Statistical Communique)." http://www.mohrss.gov.cn/SYrlzyhshbzb/zwgk/szrs/ndtjsj/tjgb/.

Ministry of Science and Technology, People's Republic of China. 1998–2005. *"Keji Tongji Shuju* (Science and Technology Statistical Data)." http://www.sts.org.cn/sjkl/kjtjdt/index.htm.

Minsky, Hyman P. 2008[1986]. *Stabilizing An Unstable Economy*. New York: McGraw-Hill.

Mitchell, Brian R. 1988. *British Historical Statistics*. Cambridge: Cambridge University Press.

Moore, Jason W. 2002. "The Crisis of Feudalism: An Environmental History." *Organization & Environment* 15(3): 301–322 (September).

NASA. The US National Aeronautics and Space Administration. 2015. "Combined Land-Surface Air and Sea-Surface Water Temperature Anomalies." http://data.giss.nasa.gov/gistemp/.

National Bureau of Statistics of China. 2013 and earlier years. *China Statistical Yearbook*, http://www.stats.gov.cn/tjsj/ndsj/.

——. 2014a. *"2013 Nian Quanguo Nongmingong Jiance Diaocha Baogao* (2013 National Rural Workers Monitoring and Survey Report)," May 12, 2014. http://www.stats.gov.cn/tjsj/zxfb/201405/t20140512_551585.html.

——. 2014b. *"2013 Nian Guomin Jingji he Shehui Fazhan Tongji Gongbao* (2013 Statistical Communique of National Economic and Social Development)," February 24, 2014. http://www.stats.gov.cn/tjsj/zxfb/201402/t20140224_514970.html.

National People's Congress, People's Republic of China. 2002. *The Law of the People's Republic of China on the Contracting of Rural Land*, issued August 29, 2002. http://www.lawinfochina. com/display.aspx?lib=law&id=2433&CGid=#menu4.

Navarro, Vincente. 1993. "Has Socialism Failed? An Analysis of Health Indicators Under Capitalism and Socialism," *Science & Society* 57(1): 6–30.

NOAA. National Oceanic & Atmospheric Administration, the U.S. Department of Commerce. 2014. "Mauna Loa CO_2 Annual Mean Data," Trends in Atmospheric Carbon Dioxide. http://www.esrl.noaa.gov/gmd/ccgg/trends/.

Nuclear Energy Agency. 2012. *Uranium 2011: Resources, Production and Demand* (a joint project by the OECD Nuclear Agency and the International Atomic Energy Agency). Paris: OECD (Organisation for Economic Co-operation and Development).

Oak Ridge National Laboratory, US Department of Energy. 2014. "Car Registrations for Selected Countries, 1950–2012," *Transportation Energy Data Book*, Table 3.2. http://cta. ornl.gov/data/chapter3.shtml.

ONS. The UK Office of National Statistics. 2013. "National Balance Sheet Dataset," August 15, 2013. http://www.ons.gov.uk/ons/rel/cap-stock/the-national-balance-sheet/2013-estimates/ tsd-national-balance-sheet--2013.html.

——. 2014a. "Latest Developments to National Accounts," May 16, 2014. http://www.ons.gov. uk/ons/rel/naa1-rd/national-accounts-articles/changes-to-national-accounts/sty-national- account-changes.html.

——. 2014b. "National Accounts at A Glance," *Blue Book 2014*, Chapter 1. http://www.ons.gov. uk/ons/datasets-and-tables/index.html.

——. 2014c. "Public Sector Finances First Release Dataset," September 2014. http://www.ons. gov.uk/ons/rel/psa/public-sector-finances/september-2014/tsd---public-sector-finances. html.

——. 2014d. "National Balance Sheet," *Blue Book 2014*, Chapter 10. http://www.ons.gov.uk/ ons/datasets-and-tables/index.html.

Patterson, Ron. 2014. "World Oil Production According to the EIA," September 16, 2014. http://peakoilbarrel.com/world-oil-production/#more-4572.

Pollin, Robert and Gary Dymski. 1994. "The Costs and Benefits of Financial Instability: Big Government Capitalism and the Minsky Paradox," in Gary Dymski and Robert Pollin (eds.), *New Perspectives in Monetary Macroeconomics: Explorations in the Tradition of Hyman P. Minsky*, pp. 369–402. Ann Arbor: University of Michigan Press.

Qi, Zhongfeng. 2006. "*Zhuanxingqi Xunzu Guimo de Jingji Gusuan* (An Economic Estimate of the Size of Rent-Seeking during the [Market] Transition)," *Shangye Shidai* (Commercial Times) 2006(21). http://mall.cnki.net/magazine/article/SYJJ200621024.htm.

Reig, Paul, Tianyi Luo, and Jonathan N. Proctor. 2014. *Global Shale Gas Development: Water Availability and Business Risks*, published by World Resources Institute, September 2014. http://www.wri.org/publication/global-shale-gas-development-water-availability-business-risks.

Rutledge, David. 2007. "Hubbert's Peak, the Coal Question, and Climate Change," Excel Workbook. Originally posted at http://rutledge.caltech.edu.

Shapiro, Carl and Joseph E. Stiglitz. 1984. "Equilibrium Unemployment as a Worker Discipline Device," *The American Economic Review* 74(3): 433–444 (June 1984).

Sherwood, Steven C. and Matthew Huber. 2010. "An Adaptability Limit to Climate Change Due to Heat Stress," *Proceedings of the National Academy of Sciences of the United States of America* 107(21): 9552–9555.

Silver, Beverly J. and Eric Slater. 1999. "The Social Origins of World Hegemonies," in Giovanni Arrighi and Beverly J. Silver (eds.), *Chaos and Governance in the Modern World System*, pp. 151–216. Minneapolis and London: University of Minneapolis Press.

Spratt, David, and Philip Sutton. 2008. Climate Code Red: The Case for a Sustainability Emergency. http://www.climatecodered.net.

Stavrianos, Leften Stavros. 1981. *Global Rift: The Third World Comes of Age.* New York: William Morrow and Company.

Stiglitz, Joseph E. 1994. *Whither Socialism?* Cambridge, Massachusetts: The MIT Press.

___. 2007. "The Pact with the Devil," interview by Beppe Grillo's Blog, November 1, 2007. http://www.beppegrillo.it/eng/2007/01/stiglitz.html.

Sun, Liping. 2011. "*Zhongguo Shehui Zhengzai Jiasu Zouxiang Kuibai* (The Chinese Society Is Accelerating towards Decay)," February 16, 2011. http://view.news.qq.com/a/20110215/000054.htm.

Tanner, Murray Scot. 2014. "China's Social Unrest Problem: Testimony before the U.S.-China Economic and Security Review Commission," May 15, 2014. http://www.uscc.gov/sites/default/files/Tanner_Written%20Testimony.pdf.

Tong, Yanqi and Lei Shaohua. 2013. "Large-Scale Mass Incidents in China," *East Asian Policy* 2(2): 23–33. http://www.eai.nus.edu.sg/Vol2No2_TongYanqi&LeiShaohua.pdf.

Turner, Graham. 2008. "A Comparison of *The Limits to Growth* with Thirty Years of Reality." CSIRO Working Paper Series, June 2008. http://www.csiro.au/files/files/plje.pdf.

United Nations. 2012. *World Population Prospects: The 2012 Revision.* United Nations, Department of Economic and Social Affairs. http://esa.un.org/wpp/.

USGS. U.S. Geological Survey. 2014. *Mineral Commodity Summaries 2014*, Lithium. http://minerals.usgs.gov/minerals/pubs/commodity/lithium/mcs-2014-lithi.pdf.

Wallerstein, Immanuel. 1974. *The Modern World-System I: Capitalist Agriculture and the Origins of the European World-Economy, 1600–1750.* New York: Academic Press.

——. 1979. *The Capitalist World Economy: Essays by Immanuel Wallerstein.* Cambridge: Cambridge University Press.

——. 1998. *Utopistics, or Historical Choices of the Twenty-First Century.* New York and London: The New Press.

——. 2000a. "Social Science and the Communist Interlude, or Interpretations of Contemporary History," in Immanuel Wallerstein, *The Essential Wallerstein*, pp. 374–386. New York; London: The New Press.

——. 2000b. "Peace, Stability, and Legitimacy: 1990–2025/2050," in Immanuel Wallerstein, *The Essential Wallerstein*, pp. 435–453. New York and London: The New Press.

——. 2003. "The Twentieth Century: Darkness at Noon?," in Immanuel Wallerstein, *The Decline of American Power*, pp. 31–44. New York and London: The New Press.

Wang, Jinnan. 2005. "*2020 Nian Zhongguo Nengyuan yu Huanjing Mianlin de Tiaozhan he Duice* (Challenges and Options for China's Energy and Environment in 2020)." Xinhua Net, November 5, 2005. http://news.xinhuanet.com/fortune/2005-11/06/content_3738334.htm.

Wang, Xiaolu. 2013. "*Huise Shouru yu Guomin shouru Fenpei: 2013 Nian Baogao Zhaiyao* (Grey Income and National Income Distribution: An Abstract of the 2013 Report), September 26, 2013. http://wang-xl.blog.sohu.com/278627086.html.

Wen, Dale. 2005. *China Copes with Globalization: A Mixed Review.* A Report by the International Forum on Globalization. http://ifg.org/v2/wp-content/uploads/2014/05/FinalChinaReport.pdf.

Wong, Edward. 2013. "Air Pollution Linked to 1.2 Million Premature Deaths in China," *New York Times*, April 1, 2013. http://www.nytimes.com/2013/04/02/world/asia/air-pollution-linked-to-1-2-million-deaths-in-china.html?_r=0.

World Bank. 2014. *World Development Indicators*, http://databank.worldbank.org/.

World Coal Association. 2014. "Uses of Coal: Coal and Steel." http://www.worldcoal.org/coal/uses-of-coal/coal-steel/.

World Health Organization. 2005. *WHO Air Quality Guidelines for Particulate Matter, Ozone, Nitrogen Dioxide, Sulfur Dioxide*, Global Update 2005. http://whqlibdoc.who.int/hq/2006/WHO_SDE_PHE_OEH_06.02_eng.pdf.

World Nuclear Association. 2014. "World Nuclear Power Reactors & Uranium Requirements," October 1, 2014. http://www.world-nuclear.org/info/Facts-and-Figures/World-Nuclear-Power-Reactors-and-Uranium-Requirements/.

Wright, Erik Olin. 1997. *Class Counts: Comparative Studies on Class Analysis*. Cambridge: Cambridge University Press.

Wu, Jingtang. 2010. "*Tonggang Tuixiu Gongren Wu Jingtang Tan Tonggang* (The Tonghua Steel Retired Worker Wu Jingtang Introduces Tonghua Steel)," Speech at the Symposium Commemorating Chairman Mao on the 116th Anniversary of Mao Zedong's Birth organized by the China Worker Research Website, January 2010. http://boxun.com/news/gb/pubvp/2010/01/201001061234.shtml.

———. 2013. "*Tonggang Shijian Huigu jiqi Zhigong Dangqian Zhuangkuang* (A Review of the Tonghua Steel Incident and the Current Conditions of the Workers)," Speech at the Third Symposium on the Chinese Workers, June 2013. http://redyouth.net/?p=251#more-251.

Wuyou Wangkan. 2011. "*Jinian Maozhuxi Danchen 118 Zhounian* (Commemorating the 118th Anniversary of the Birth of Chairman Mao)," December 28, 2011. http://www.wyzxwk.com/s/mao118/index_5.html.

Xin Hua Wang. 2013. "*Zhonggong Zhongyang Guanyu Quanmian Shenhua Gaige Ruogan Zhongda Wenti de Jueding* (The Decision by the Central Committee of the Chinese Communist Party on Some Major Issues Concerning Comprehensively Deepening the Reform)," Adopted by the Third Plenary Session of the Eighteenth Central Committee of the Chinese Communist Party on November 12, 2013. http://news.xinhuanet.com/politics/2013-11/15/c_118164235.htm.

———. 2014 "*Jinnian Yingjie Biyesheng Pingjun Yuexin 2443 Yuan, 3 Cheng Kenlao* (Average Monthly Pay for This Year's College Graduates [Will Be] 2443 Yuan, Three-Tenths Are Dependent on Parents)," August 4, 2014. http://news.xinhuanet.com/edu/2014-08/04/c_126827494.htm.

Xu, Zheng. 2013. "*Huodian Tuoliu Tuoxiao Nanti Ruhe Huajie* (How to Solve the Difficult Problems of Desulfurization and Denitrogenation for Thermal Electric Power)," September 10, 2013. http://www.elechina.com.cn/index.php?c=form&a=show&id=1620&modelid=7&cid=620&page=2.

Xu, Zhun, Ying Chen, and Minqi Li. 2013. "Are Chinese Workers Paid the Correct Wages? Measuring Wage Underpayment in the Chinese Industrial Sector, 2005–2010," *Review of Radical Political Economics*, published before print August 21, 2014. http://rrp.sagepub.com/content/early/2014/08/20/0486613414542780.abstract.

Yang, Congmin and Yang Liyuan. 2010. "*Dangdai Zhongguo Nongmingong Liudong Guimo Diaocha* (A Survey of the Magnitude of the Rural Workers' Migration in Contemporary China)," *Chinese Sociology*. http://www.sociology2010.cass.cn/news/131900.htm.

Zhang, Huajia. 2008. "*Si San Fangan: Xin Zhongguo Di Er Ci Da Guimo Jishu Yinjin* (The Four-Three Proposal: Second Large-Scale Technological Importation under New China)," *Zhuangbei Zhizao* (Equipment Manufacturing), Number 10, 2008. http://wuxizazhi.cnki.net/Article/ZBZA200810027.html.

Zhang, Yaozu. 2010. "*Xin Zhongguo Liushi Nian Gongren Jieji de Yanbian he Fazhan* (Evolution and Development of the Working Class during the Six Decades of New China)," January 2010. http://wen.org.cn/modules/article/view.article.php/2825.

Zhang, Yuzhi and Zhongfu Jiang. 2010. "The Domestic Governance Countermeasure in Order to Enhance Soft Power of China Communist Party," *International Journal of Business and*

Management 5(7): 170–174. http://www.ccsenet.org/journal/index.php/ijbm/article/view/6632.

Zhao, Xin. 2012. "*Gaige Caineng Xiaochu Wenge Yinhuan* (Only Reform Can Eliminate the Latent Danger of the Cultural Revolution)," China Elections and Governance Website, March 17, 2012. http://www.chinaelections.com/article/194/224951.html.

Zhao, Yuezhi. 2012. "The Struggle for Socialism in China: The Bo Xilai Saga and Beyond," *Monthly Review* 64(5): 1–17.

Zhongguo Gongyebao (China Industry Journal). 2010. "*Huodian Zhuangbei Zhizaoye Hequ Hecong* (Whither the Thermal Power Sector Equipment Manufacturing)?," July 29, 2010. http://www.nea.gov.cn/2010-07/29/c_131071210.htm.

Zhongguo Xinwen Wang (China News Network). 2014. "*2013 Nian Zhongguo Zhuyao Wuranwu Paifang Zongliang Quanbu Xiajiang* (Total Emissions of China's Main Pollutants All Declined in 2013)," September 3, 2014. http://dgepb.dg.gov.cn/dgepb/hbxw/201409/792412.htm.

INDEX

Chinese names are entered uninverted, for example, Bo Xilai.

capitalist classes: China's grey income 34–35; China's transition to capitalism 3, 12, 19–21, 22, 23, 170, 181–182, 185; composition of China's labor force 25t, 26, 27; imposing financial austerity 1; New Deal 6; and predicted crisis of Chinese capitalism 182–184; relative strength and economic crisis 43; wealth in peripheral states 66

capitalist world system, structural elements: functions and characteristics 60–62, 73; geographical distribution see geographical distribution, capitalist world system; relationships see spatial fix; unequal exchange

capital-labor accord 6; see also New Deal

capital–output ratio 12, 48

capital stock: and environmental sustainability 111, 141; sources 193a, 194a, 195a, 202a; see also output–capital ratio

carbon dioxide emissions: and climate catastrophe 13–14, 106–107, 134–137, 174, 187; coal 118, 149; and economic growth 14, 110–111, 141–143, 165, 167–168, 174–175; India as twenty-first century spatial fix 180; natural gas 135f, 137, 149; unconventional resources 137; United Nations RCP scenarios 107–110, 136, 137, 164–169, 174–175

cars 118–119

Central Asia: balance of trade 99, 100tf; and China's terms of trade 74f

Chen Yun 20

Chinese Revolution (1949) 17, 30; see also Chinese socialist social contract

Chinese socialist social contract 12, 17–19, 21, 22, 30, 35, 170, 185

Chinese working classes: anti-privatization 31–32, 34, 36; China's changing class structure 23–28; Chinese capitalist sustainability 7, 29–30, 38–40, 171, 182–183, 184; and global economic crisis 12, 41, 173, 181; rise of 28–30, 173; socialist social contract 12, 17–19, 21, 22, 30, 35, 170, 185; transition to capitalism 3, 7, 20–23, 35, 72, 78, 170, 172

Chongqing Model 1, 15, 36–38

class: 1945 New Deal 6, 172; in capitalist world system 24, 59, 60; and China's grey income 34–35; Chinese transformation 20–21, 23, 24–28, 78; global class war 3, 7, 12, 172; Marxist

theory 6; relative strength and economic crisis 43; semi-peripheral working classes and rising wage costs 7, 69; see also Chinese working classes; middle classes; working classes

climate change: and economic growth 14, 110–111, 141–143, 165, 167–168, 174–175; impending climate catastrophe 11, 13–14, 105–107, 134–137, 174, 187; United Nations RCP scenarios 107–110, 136, 137, 164–169, 174–175

coal: air pollution in China 162; and atmospheric aerosols 108; carbon dioxide emissions 135f, 137; and China's economic growth 14, 154–157, 179; and the development of capitalism 8, 171–172; electricity generation 122; formation 7–8; as oil substitute 118; peak production 13, 105, 123–125, 127f; share of total energy consumption 104–105, 131f, 132; twenty-first century spatial fix 179

coking coal 122–123

college graduates (China) 32–34

Colombia 69, 157

Communism: China's socialist legacy 30–32; China's transition to capitalism 3, 12, 17–21, 22, 23, 170, 181–182, 185; growth in semi-/peripheral states 2–3, 67, 172; Nationalist Party-Communist Party alliance (1920s China) 16; Party in China, China's grey income 34–35; and predicted crisis of Chinese capitalism 182–184

core states: class structure 24, 59; early twentieth century social forces 64–65, 66–67, 172, 173; geographical distribution see geographical distribution, capitalist world system; growth rate requirement 104; narrowing disparity with peripheral states 75–78, 176; role in capitalist world system 60–62; structural relationships see spatial fix; unequal exchange

corruption 34–35, 37

costs: Chinese capitalism 7, 11, 13, 28–30, 80, 82–83, 182, 183; estimating 193a, 194a, 195a, 202–203a; and spatial fix see spatial fix; and structural crisis 12, 13, 54; and United Kingdom/Britain's profit share 54, 55, 56, 193a, 194a, 195a; and US profit share 57, 58, 195a

Cuban socialism 1, 36

grain production 118
grey income 34–35
growth accounting 88–91
Guangzhou 20
Gu Kailai 38

Hansen, J. 106, 136
Harvey, D. 13, 58
Haywood, T. 113
hegemonic cycles and long waves 42, 44–48, 52, 65, 90–91
Hisaeda, S. 63
Hughes, D. 10, 113
Hui, P-K. 63
Hungary, semi-peripheral position 65t, 66t, 68t, 70t, 72t, 198a
hydro electricity 104, 105, 127, 131, 132f, 133, 155

illegal trade 101
India: British Empire 63; coal 154f, 155, 156, 179; emissions 165, 180; external (to world capitalist system) status 60t, 61t; and global economic growth 4; natural gas 149, 150, 180; oil 9, 144, 145, 179–180; peripheral status 64t, 65t, 66t, 68t, 70t, 72t, 76t, 198a; spatial fix 63, 176–180
Indonesia: as coal exporter 156, 157; Dutch Empire 63, 198a; peripheral status 61t, 64t, 65t, 66t, 68t, 70t, 72t, 76t, 198a
industrial revolutions 8, 45, 52, 89
intellectual classes see middle classes
investment: affecting output–capital ratio 50, 51, 53; and business cycles 42, 43; China's manufacturing dependence on 13, 81, 98, 138, 170–171; and China's profit rate 5, 13, 86–87, 91, 92, 94, 102, 138–139, 170–171; and Marginal Profit Rate 83; in a new socialist economy 190; and profit rate 91, 92, 93, 94, 102; and ratio of accumulation 83, 98, 138, 139; under big government capitalism 95
IPAT formula 140
IPCC (United Nations Intergovernmental Panel on Climate Change) RCP projections 108–110, 136, 137, 164–169, 174–175
Iran 68t, 69, 70t, 72t, 76t, 151
Ireland 60t, 61t, 197a, 198a
iron rice bowl 19, 22, 30
Italy: core position 70t, 72t, 76t; Marx's theory of tendency for profit rate to

fall 49, 50; semi-peripheral position 60t, 61t, 64t, 65t, 66t, 68t, 197a, 198a

Japan: coal 154f, 155, 156; core status 70t, 72t, 76t; defeat of Russian Empire 69; external (to world capitalist system) status 60t, 61t; Fukushima nuclear accident 99, 150; natural gas 149, 150, 152; oil consumption 144; peripheral status 65t; semi-peripheral status 66t, 68t, 199a; trade balance 99, 100t; wars with China 16
Jiang Jieshi 16
Jiang Qing 19
Jiang Zemin 20

Kerala 180
Keynesian macroeconomic policy 3, 6, 44, 93, 95, 172, 180
Keynes, J.M. 188
Kondriatiev long waves 44

labor: alternative twenty-first century supply 11, 78, 176–179, 181; feudal system 59; peripheral states source 13, 62; see also Chinese working classes; unequal exchange; wage levels/costs; working classes
labor income share see wage levels/costs
labor input, growth accounting 88, 89, 90, 98
labor term of trade 73–75, 76, 200–202a
labor unions 26, 28, 39, 47, 56, 64, 180
Labour Party (UK) 47, 56
Latin America: Argentina 66t, 68t, 69, 70t, 72t, 198a, 199a; and China's labor term of trade 74f, 75; Colombia 69, 157; and the crisis of the semi-periphery 1, 68–69, 71, 78; industrialized working classes 67; Mexico 66t, 68t, 69, 70t, 72t, 76t; peripheral status 60t, 61t, 64t, 65t, 197a, 198a; political instability 1, 69; postwar boom 67, 68, 77; Uruguay 69, 198a, 199a; Venezuela 1, 69, 199a; see also Brazil
liquid fuel 10f, 115, 116, 117, 118, 152
lithium 118–119
Liu Shaoqi 18
local rural workers (China) 21, 26
long waves and hegemonic cycles 42, 44–48, 52

Maddison, A. 17, 197a
manufacturing: emergence of the

Organization for Economic Co-Operation and Development (OECD) countries 176, 177f
output–capital ratio 12, 43, 48–51, 53, 58, 80–83

Pacific Ocean 108
Party and State Bureaucrats in China's labor force 25, 26
peasants: Chinese mobilization 3, 17, 21, 22, 23, 30, 35, 170; role in capitalist system 6, 24; Russian Revolution 67; upward mobility through education 32
peripheral states: China's decline 16, 63, 170; and China's labor term of trade 74–75; emissions targets 165–166; geographical distribution *see* geographical distribution, capitalist world system; growth rate 104; labor 24, 38, 59, 173, 181; narrowing disparity with core states 75–78, 176; role in the capitalist world system 13, 61, 62, 73; socialism and communism 2–3, 185; spatial fix 63, 75–78, 79, 172, 175, 176, 180; unequal exchange 6, 62, 66, 73, 75, 175, 176, 197a
petrodollars 70
Po-keung Hui 63
Poland 38, 39–40, 41, 69, 71f, 76t, 181
Pollution 14, 108, 139–140, 149, 158–159, 161–164, 184, 188
population: capitalist world system distribution 62, 65–66, 175, 176; *see also* geographical distribution, capitalist world system and climate 140, 188; emissions budget 165–166; feudal society 59; GDP and life expectancy 177, 178f; and global water resources 158; total factor productivity 90, 98, 173
Portugal: core status 59, 72t, 197a; peripheral status 66t; semi-peripheral status 59, 60t, 61t, 64t, 65t, 68t, 70t, 76t, 197a, 198a, 199a; urbanization 69, 71f
precious metal 59, 62, 63, 130, 133
pricing/prices: depletion of material resources 141; inflation in China 20; invisible hand 186; as market failure 187, 188, 189; oil 9–10, 99, 112, 117, 132, 147; public protest in Eastern Europe 39, 69
professional and technical workers 23, 25–26
Profit Growth Rate 83, 84, 85–87
profit rate: China's debt–GDP ratio 97, 98; China's investment levels 5, 13, 86–87,

91, 92, 94, 102, 138–139, 170–171; and China's rising production costs 7, 13, 80, 90; equilibrium profit rate 84, 85, 87–88, 90, 94, 138, 141; estimating 193–196a; and growth accounting 87–91; hegemonic cycles 44, 45, 46, 47, 48, 65, 90–91; levels for economic crisis 13, 42, 53, 89–95, 98, 102, 138, 173, 175; Marginal Profit Rate 83, 85–87; and output–capital ratio 43, 48, 50, 53, 58, 80, 83–84; and socialist economic policy 190; spatial fix 11, 45, 46, 62; and technological progress 12; tendency to fall, Marx's theory 48–51, 54, 58, 85; total factor productivity 88, 89–90, 94; US/China 79
profit share 48, 54–58, 81–82, 84, 85, 88, 193–196a
profit squeeze: in China 13, 82–83; leading to signal crisis 43; spatial fix 58, 62; and the structural crisis of capitalism 54; US and Britain 56, 57–58
proletarianization: and China's social structure 7, 26, 27f, 28, 29, 39, 171; Chinese New Left 33; and rising costs of production 11, 54; and the semi-peripheral state crisis 3, 24, 38, 39, 69; threatening capitalism 6
proletarianized urban formal wage workers, China 23–24, 25, 26–27, 28, 38
protectionist policies 191

ratio of accumulation 83, 85–87, 94, 98, 138–139
Ray, K. 63
RCPs *see* representative concentration pathways
Refer, T.E. 63
renewable resources: biofuels 115, 116f, 118, 131, 132f, 146, 147; biomass 118, 127, 131, 132f, 133; defining sustainability 139–140; fossil fuel offset 13, 131–132, 173; geothermal 127, 131, 132f, 133; hydro 104, 105, 127, 131, 132f, 133, 155; intermittency problem (of renewable energy sources) 130, 133, 150, 153; pre-capitalist society 7, 171; share of world energy consumption 104, 105; solar and wind 119, 128–131, 132f, 133, 150; water supply 14, 121, 157–161
representative concentration pathways (RCPs), United Nations IPCC projections 108–110, 136, 137, 164–169, 174–175

Westernization Movement 16
wet bulb temperature 106
wind electricity 119, 128–131, 132f, 133, 150
working classes: accommodation through
  spatial fix 65, 66–67, 69–70, 77–78,
  176; British industrial revolution 45;
  as a capitalist prerequisite 2, 11, 54;
  classes of 23–24; Eastern Europe 39,
  40, 69, 71, 181; global class war 3, 7,
  12, 172; Marx's predictions for the fall
  of capitalism 6; New Deal concessions
  to 6, 172; organization/unionization 6,
  11, 64, 66–67; *see also* trade unions;
  semi-peripheral states 67, 69–70, 71, 72,
  77–78; *see also* Chinese working classes;
  wage levels/costs

World War I 46, 67
World War II 47, 52, 56, 57, 69, 86
Wu Jingtang 31

Yalta Agreement 67

zero economic growth: Chinese
  oil imports 148; Chinese water
  efficiency 160; climate catastrophe 173,
  175; ecological constraints 52, 85,
  190; emissions reduction 111, 141–142,
  165; impact on profit rate 53, 58,
  85, 88, 138, 173; and technical
  progress 51
Zhao Ziyang 20
Zhuhai 20